War of Ideas

Also of Interest

Arms Control and Defense Postures in the 1980s, edited by Richard Burt

The Myth of Victory: What Is Victory in War? Richard Hobbs

Southeast Asia and China: The End of Containment, Edwin W. Martin

The Communist Road to Power in Vietnam, William J. Duiker

Vietnamese Communism in Comparative Perspective, edited by William S. Turley

Big Story: How the American Press and Television Reported and Interpreted the Crisis of Tet 1968 in Vietnam and Washington, Peter Braestrup

A Westview Special Study

War of Ideas:
The U.S. Propaganda Campaign in Vietnam
Robert W. Chandler

Though often overlooked in the study of military strategy and foreign policy, propaganda plays an important role in international conflict. This book tells the story of the most massive leaflet blitz in the history of warfare--the U.S. propaganda effort in Vietnam. In a seemingly unending rain of paper, 50 billion leaflets bombarded the North and South Vietnamese people for nearly a decade, backed up by millions of posters and handbills and thousands of hours of loud-speaker broadcasts, all promoting the cause of South Vietnam and at-tempting to counter support for the North. Analyzing propaganda lit-erature and official military directives, Dr. Chandler considers the effectiveness of U.S. psychological operations within the context of overall military strategy and illustrates the function of propaganda as an instrument of foreign policy. He presents a critical analysis of psychological warfare in Vietnam, compares U.S. and Soviet methods, and suggests measures for increasing propaganda effectiveness. Ninety-five carefully selected illustrations of leaflets and other printed materials offer the reader a sense and appreciation of the intensive psychological campaign. A host of revealing quotations and anecdotes makes this an absorbing account of U.S. participation in the Vietnam-ese "war of ideas."

Lt. Colonel Robert W. Chandler is an international politico-military affairs officer in the Strategy Division, Headquarters, U.S. Air Force. A Vietnam veteran and former intelligence officer, he is a political scientist specializing in national security affairs and international political communications.

War of Ideas:
The U.S. Propaganda
Campaign in Vietnam

Robert W. Chandler

Westview Press / Boulder, Colorado

The study and research which have resulted in this book were an independent effort of the author and were not undertaken in connection with or as a result of his position as an officer of the United States Air Force. He has not had special access to official information or ideas and has employed in his study only cpen-source material available to any student of the subject. The views and conclusions expressed in the book are those of the author. They are not intended and should not be thought to represent official ideas, attitudes or policies of the United States Air Force, the Department of Defense or the United States Government.

A Westview Special Study

Published in 1981 in the United States of America by
Westview Press, Inc.
5500 Central Avenue
Boulder, Colorado 80301
Frederick A. Praeger, Publisher

Library of Congress Cataloging in Publication Data
Chandler, Robert W
   War of ideas.
   A Westview special study
   Bibliography: p.
   Includes index.
   1. Vietnamese Conflict, 1961-1975--Propaganda.
2. Propaganda, American--Vietnam. I. Title.
II. Series.
DS559.8.P65C45   959.704'38   80-24127
ISBN 0-86531-082-3

Composition for this book was provided by the author.
Printed and bound in the United States of America.

For Espy and Karen

Contents

Tables and Figures

xiv

Preface

This book describes and appraises American use of
propaganda in Vietnam (1965-1972) as an instrument of
foreign policy. In an effort to point out pitfalls to be
avoided and successful techniques worthy of emulation in
future psychological operations, the case study shows how
some proven and time-honored prescriptions for effective
propaganda were observed in Vietnam and how many others
were ignored. Accordingly, strengths and weaknesses and
successes and failures are highlighted.

Ninety-five illustrations and numerous quotations of
American leaflets and posters are included. These were
selected to provide the reader a "feeling" or "flavor" of
the propaganda campaign. The English translations are
taken from work sheets prepared by various government
agencies, and they are fraught with a great many
spelling, grammatical, and typographical errors. Most
have been silently corrected by the author; the customary
interpolation sic has been omitted to avoid strewing a
hundred or so through the book. Nonetheless, several
obvious mistakes remain in the selected translations.
These were left untouched to preclude unintentional
alteration of the meaning and emphasis ascribed to the
messages by their originators. The author apologizes for
rankling the reader's grammatical sensibilities.

The U.S. propaganda messages examined as the basis
of this study totaled 1,088 printed communications
(leaflets, banners, posters, handbills, and the like) and
161 loudspeaker tape transcripts prepared by military and
civilian agencies for South Vietnamese target audiences
(1965-1972). Fifty leaflets each were sampled for the
psychological offensives against North Vietnam during the
1965-1968 and 1972-1973 bombing campaigns and from those
strewn along the Ho Chi Minh Trail in Laos and Cambodia
(1965-1973).

Publishing requirements dictated the shortening or
omission of many footnotes referring to obscure
government documents, but a comprehensive list of sources

is presented in the Selected Bibliography. The interested scholar is urged to see specific references in the author's doctoral dissertation, "U.S. Psychological Operations in Vietnam, 1965-72," submitted to The George Washington University (February 1974). It is available at the Library of Congress in microfilm and may be ordered from University Microfilms, Ann Arbor, Michigan.

I owe sincere appreciation to numerous persons who shared their time and ideas with me during the research and writing phases of this book. I am especially and deeply grateful to Dr. Anita M. Mallinckrodt for her advice and assistance in re-writing the original manuscript into its present form, as well as her exacting intellectual standards over the years.

I am also especially thankful to Monta L. Osborne of the U.S. Information Agency and the Joint Chiefs of Staff for his assistance in securing pertinent official documents and for the personal insight he offered during many hours of conversation concerning the communications campaign. Sincere appreciation also is extended to Major George Jurkowich of the U.S. Army Psychological Operations Division at the Pentagon, and Lieutenant Colonel David G. Underhill of the U.S. Army 7th Psychological Operations Group at Okinawa. Both officers shared their time, ideas, and personal experiences, as well as helped to gather research materials relating to the propaganda effort.

Others also rendered invaluable assistance during the writing of this book. Special thanks and sincere appreciation are offered to Professors Ralph K. White and Harold C. Hinton of The George Washington University; Otis Hayes, Everett Bumgardner, Harris Peel of the U.S. Information Agency; Fred Koether of the Advanced Research Projects Agency (Department of Defense); Helen LaRoche of the now defunct Vietnam Training Center of the Foreign Service Institute; Jeanette Koch of the Rand Corporation; Dr. Ernest Bairdain of Human Sciences Research, Inc.; Barry Zorthian, architect and director of the propaganda campaign (1965-1968); Colonel Harry D. Latimer, U.S. Army (retired) of Brown University; Lieutenant Colonel Robert Reimers of the U.S. Air Force Special Operations School; and the staffs of the Battelle Memorial Institute at Columbus, Ohio, and the U.S. Army Psychological Operations School at Fort Bragg, N.C. All were very helpful during my visits to their institutions or through the mail; many others graciously consented to personal interviews.

Most gratitude is reserved for my wife and daughter who gave up many weekends, family night hours, and vacation time for the completion of this book.

Robert W. Chandler

Abbreviations

ARPA	Advanced Research Projects Agency
ARVN	Army of the Republic of Vietnam
CORDS	Civil Operations Revolutionary (also "Rural") Development Support
DRV	Democratic Republic of Vietnam (North Vietnam)
FWMAF	Free World Military Assistance Forces
GVN	Government of Vietnam (South Vietnam)
JUSPAO	Joint U.S. Public Affairs Office
MACV	Military Assistance Command, Vietnam (U.S.)
MEDCAP	Medical Civil Assistance Program
NLF	National Liberation Front (Viet Cong)
NVN	North Vietnam
NVA	North Vietnamese Army
PAVN	People's Army of Vietnam (North Vietnam)
PSYOP	Psychological Operations
PSYWAR	Psychological Warfare
RVN	Republic of Vietnam (South Vietnam)
RVNAF	Republic of Vietnam Armed Forces
USAID	U.S. Agency for International Development
USIA	U.S. Information Agency
USIS	U.S. Information Service
VC	Viet Cong
VIS	Vietnamese Information Service (South Vietnam)
VNAF	Vietnamese Air Force (South Vietnam)
VOA	Voice of America

Part 1
Prologue to Propaganda

1
Introduction

> There are but two powers in the world, the
> sword and the mind. In the long run the
> sword is always beaten by the mind.
>
> -- Napoleon

Americans intervened in South Vietnam in 1965 with
the aim of preventing "Communist domination" and creating
in that country a "viable and increasingly democratic
society." The first political objective was to be
achieved through military action against the Viet Cong
and the North's armed forces; the second by political and
economic action among the South Vietnamese people.[1]
These endeavors were dubbed a "dual war," reflecting both
coercive and noncoercive aspects. Americans also
participated directly in the psychological battle for
Vietnamese "hearts and minds" by unleashing an intensive
propaganda campaign on behalf of the Saigon government.
This effort cut across initiatives in both the military
and political-economic arenas, transforming the "dual
war" into a single war of psychological operations.
During its seven years in Vietnam, the United States
Information Agency (USIA), supported by the armed forces,
littered the countryside of the North, South, and the Ho
Chi Minh Trail in Laos and Cambodia with nearly 50
billion leaflets -- more than 1,500 for every person in
both parts of the country -- trying to create a solid
anti-Communist nationalism among the population.
Political posters, banners, newspapers, magazines,
brochures, and cartoon books, bumper stickers, matchbook
covers, and other kinds of printed matter inundated the
South.
Television was introduced as a propaganda medium.
Studios and broadcasting stations were constructed,
receivers donated, and programs produced for country-wide
telecasting. A network of radio transmitters was

3

organized through which political messages were sent to
Northern and Southern audiences. When it was found that
few persons had receivers, small transistor sets were
parachuted to prospective listeners. Film studios were
built, projectors donated, and thousands of films
produced for viewing throughout South Vietnam.

Aircraft flew over Communist jungle hiding places at
night, broadcasting music, nostalgic pleas by female
voices, and children's wails for "Daddy to come home."
American-paid minstrel and drama teams traveled about the
country with patriotic appeals to the rural populace.
The young were not ignored; kites, puppets, and similar
items imprinted with pro-government themes were
distributed among children in the South; toys accompanied
by leaflets with anti-Communist messages were parachuted
to youngsters in the North.

Since the dawn of history, attempts such as these to
influence, control, or change men's minds have been
undertaken by politicians, generals, advertising
executives, and others with an idea or product to sell.
At varying times these endeavors have been labeled
"propaganda," "psychological warfare," "political
warfare," and "international political communications."
In Vietnam the traditional concept was broadened:
Americans wielded a double-edged psychological sword
designed to cope with the coercive and noncoercive nature
of the "dual war." "Psychological operations" combined
psychological warfare (attacks against the fighting
morale of the Communists) with political-economic
propaganda aimed at convincing the South Vietnamese to
support their government.[2]

The primary goals of this campaign were to divert
popular support away from Hanoi and the Viet Cong and to
create militant anti-Communism among the Southern
population. The targets of these appeals fell into three
broad audiences.

To the first target group, the Communists and their
supporters in the South, the message was: "Give up the
fight and return to the folds of the government of
Vietnam!" Viet Cong and North Vietnamese troops were
threatened with death, while poetry, music, and sketches
of family life played on their homesickness. A
loudspeaker broadcast implored the enemy soldier to
return to loved ones who feared for his life:

(First 20 second: Sounds of women and children
crying)
Announcer 1. "Oh! Why is there such mournful
crying?"
Announcer 2. "These are the sounds of sorrow
coming from the homes you have left. The
heart-broken cry of a young wife who has lost
her husband -- the sad cry of a mother whose

son will not return -- the pitiful cry of a
little child whose father has been killed --
cruelly robbed of life in the so-called 'War of
Liberation' -- the very war in which you now
participate."
Announcer 1. "It is also the sad, sad cry of
families whose sons have died so senselessly
for communism."
Announcer 2. . . .
Announcer 1. "Why don't you return at once to
rejoin your family? They are waiting for
you. Oh, the child's laugh is such a dear
sweet sound. But the child's cry is such a sad
and mournful sound. Isn't it?"
(Last 20 seconds: Crying sounds)[3]

A somewhat different appeal was aimed at the second
audience, the masses and elite of North Vietnam. "Stop
your aggression in the South and throw off the yoke of
Chinese Communist imperialism!" they were told. The Lao
Dong Party, the ruling Communist party, was accused of
betraying the people through its Chinese-inspired assault
against the Republic; bombing was rationalized as
necessary to impede Hanoi's war effort. One of the first
American leaflets airdropped over the North (purporting
to be of South Vietnamese origin) described the reasons
for the aerial attacks:

Compatriots of North Viet Nam: Recently the
Armed Forces of the Republic of Viet Nam bombed
the main roads and bridges of North Viet Nam.
This is a self-defense action to stop the
aggression of the Ho Chi Minh clique, lackeys
of the Red Chinese. The Government . . . of
the Republic . . . only destroys the military
bases and network of the Communists. . . .
Please keep away from the Communists' military
installations and oppose the Communists' plot
to send your sons and husbands to die in South
Viet Nam.[4]

The third audience -- the non-Communist South
Vietnamese -- was told: "Support your government in its
struggle against the North!" Here the appeal ranged from
describing the evils of Communism to encouraging
patriotic support for the Republic. An American-produced
song, for example, was used to promote national unity and
to build a spirit of resistance:

PEOPLE AND SOLDIERS RISE UP!
The people and soldiers share the same
determination to destroy the bloodthirsty
National Liberation Front. Everywhere they

participate with enthusiasm. The people of
South Vietnam believe in the future and brave
people will lift high their flag. . . . With
great sacrifices and determination by the
people and soldiers, the aggressive National
Liberation Front and the Communist invaders
will be destroyed.[5]

But in the end this propaganda effort was
unsuccessful in achieving its psychological goals among
the three target groups, although it scored some
impressive results. It fell short of the mark at least
partly because of the shortcomings of U.S. personnel and
South Vietnamese officials. The primary cause of the
failure, however, was the Americans could not make up for
the weaknesses of the Saigon government nor could they
cope with the "foreign invader" stigma attached to them
by the other side.

"FOREIGN INVADER"

In Hanoi's eyes, the final victory over Saigon and
its American patrons climaxed a thirty year struggle for
independence from a colonial rule that had controlled the
country since the late nineteenth century. The greatest
strength of the Communists lay in the people's continued
determination to free themselves from foreign influence
-- the same inspiration that led their ancestors to
withstand Chinese and Mongol invasions in the past. As
forecast by Ho Chi Minh in 1962, historical nationalism
was a key to Communist triumph:

I think the Americans greatly underestimate the
determination of the Vietnamese people. The
Vietnamese people have always shown great
determination when faced with an invader.[6]

Indeed, the history of Vietnam is rich with examples
of strong popular resistance against foreign intruders.
More than a dozen major revolts highlighted the country's
thousand years of Chinese domination. The first occurred
in 39 A.D. when the Trung sisters, two noble ladies who
proclaimed themselves queens, inspired and led a
successful insurrection. Their fledgling kingdom lasted
only two years; the Chinese soon quelled the uprising and
reimposed their authority. Rather than consent to life
under alien tutelage the Trung sisters drowned
themselves, to be forever revered as national heroines.
From this early beginning a cohesive ethnic and national
Vietnamese identity emerged that finally resulted in a
series of bloody clashes and the ouster of the hated
Chinese in 939.
No less than fifteen times during the next 900 years

the people responded to the call to arms, frustrating
invasion attempts by superior Chinese and Mongol
forces. Each time a trespasser presented itself at their
doorstep, the peasants threw themselves into the
conflict, routing the invaders and preserving
independence. The Mongols, for instance, twice were
thwarted during the thirteenth century. But the
resistance effort most remembered by the Vietnamese was
the successful overthrow of the fifty-year Chinese
interregnum in 1428. Le Loi, an aristocratic landowner
called the "Prince of Pacification," encouraged and led
the people in a decade of incessant guerrilla warfare
that evicted the intruders. Like the Trung sisters, his
leadership became legendary over the following centuries;
his heroic exploits against the "foreign invader" were
repeated by word-of-mouth from one generation to the
next.

European intervention in Vietnam evolved from the
usual pattern: trading posts, an influx of missionaries,
and, finally, total foreign dominance. The Portuguese
were the first, establishing trade in 1535, followed by
the French and the Dutch a hundred years later. But
events during the nineteenth century pushed France into
subjugation of the country to protect its favorable
commercial rights and safeguard the lives and activities
of its missionaries.

Actual conquest was a piecemeal affair. Colonial
rule first was imposed on the south in 1859 and then in
1883 on the north. While the native Emperor's court at
Hue acquiesced to French authority, primitively armed
partisan bands conducted a fierce but disorganized
rebellion. By 1900 this guerrilla action had largely
spent itself; no apparent threat confronted the European
conquerer. But humiliation and deep resentment of
foreign domination boiled beneath the surface. Inspired
by both profound love of country and the legendary
sacrifices of the Trung sisters and Le Loi in combating
"foreign invaders," several underground nationalist
groups kept the hope of independence alive. Most were
convinced that force of arms was the only way to expel
the French but realized too the time for action was not
yet ripe.

By the 1930s excesses of colonial administration and
economic exploitation had undermined the village
society. In imposing an alien capitalist system on the
indigenous populace, the French virtually had destroyed
their traditional Confucian social order. Large
agricultural estates with a few wealthy landowners
reduced most farmers to tenant status. At the same time,
the introduction of rubber plantations, mining
operations, and small-scale industries created needs for
local labor. Reluctant to leave their homes and the
graves of their ancestors, many peasants chose to stay in

their villages and starve rather than work in the foreign-dominated enterprises. Faced with a severe shortage of workers, the Europeans resorted to forced labor at the mines and plantations, further alienating large segments of the population.

Latent nationalism, combined with the harsh realities of colonial society, persuaded many peasants to support any group that showed promise of easing their plight. The first to act was the Vietnamese Nationalist Party, but its attempted military coup in 1930 was a total failure. The French quickly quelled the rebellious native soldiers and hunted down their youthful leaders. Other nationalist groups shared a similar fate; all apparent opposition was subdued.

In the background, a tightly organized Vietnamese Communist Party awaited a propitious time to act. Several members had been trained in Moscow during the 1920s, and their historical and Marxist-Leninist studies had made them sure that expulsion of the French could only be fashioned from mass participation. Just as the peasants had been the ultimate source of power in past resistance to "foreign invaders," these same peasants would be the fountainhead of insurgent power in the coming struggle. To enlist a wide popular base, the Communists adroitly avoided reference to "socialist revolution" in their rallying program. Rather, they fashioned a "negative nationalism" by fusing anticolonialism and anticapitalism with the people's natural love of Vietnam. Throughout the 1930s and during the Japanese occupation in World War II, the Communists laid the root cause of every political, social, and economic problem of the colonial community to the French. Emotionally laden classical nationalism also was promoted, despite the fact that such affections are an anathema to Marxists, who condemn these feelings as bourgeois -- an outgrowth of the system of private ownership.

In the meantime, the various non-Communist nationalist groups vied for power among themselves, diluting their common front against Ho Chi Minh's party. By 1945 there were nine such groups, most in disarray and lacking effective leadership. None could come up with either a sufficiently cohesive ideology or a plan of action that could compete with the Communists. When Ho Chi Minh declared Vietnam's independence and launched the liberation struggle, many non-Communists rallied to his side. This popular revolution, carried out in the spirit of the Trung sisters and Le Loi, released the pent up hatred of the French harbored by Vietnamese of all political persuasions. The true essence of this anticolonial war was nationalist, but its leadership was Communist -- their goal was a complete remaking of the disordered society.

The revolution spanned nearly thirty years and took many turns before final victory was achieved. Expulsion of the French in 1954 led to a divided Vietnam. When subsequent diplomatic efforts failed to reunify the country, the National Liberation Front ("Viet Cong") was formed in 1959 to hasten collapse of the southern Republic and lay the groundwork for reunification. This attempt also failed (partly due to American assistance to the Saigon government), prompting Hanoi to dispatch increased numbers of its soldiers to the South in 1964.

Direct U.S. intervention and participation in the war in 1965 robbed the Communists of victory and precipitated infiltration of major North Vietnamese Army units. This new phase of the revolution was touted as a "national salvation struggle." Portraying the U.S. as a new "foreign invader" and "colonial oppressor," appeals in both parts of the country called on the population to "Save Vietnam from American Imperialism."

The importance of this "foreign invader" theme should not be underestimated; it provided a key to Hanoi's resurrection of the popular platform used so effectively in the past. Coupling the people's anticolonial "negative nationalism" with the "heroic devotion of their forefathers" in driving out alien intruders, the Communists fashioned a mass appeal that would rally widespread support. Thus, the 1965-1975 "War of National Liberation" became a sequel to the successful 1945-1954 nationalist-Communist struggle for independence; "socialist revolution" again was pushed into the background. The Viet Cong instructed its propaganda elite how to emphasize this new "anticolonial" battle: "Every day, a Cadre of the Party in charge of propagandizing the masses must unveil the barbarous and cruel face of the enemy to the population so they can be aware of the pitiless plot and plundering activities, warfare and eager preparation to turn South Vietnam into a U.S. colony."[7]

To reinforce this line, Saigon's officials were described as "puppets" and its soldiers as "paid mercenaries" of the new colonizers. As evidence of U.S. designs and the government's complicity, the Communists constantly said that Saigon's supplies, weapons, and even the clothes of its troops had been provided by the Americans. This appeal gained greater credibility in both parts of the country as U.S. soldiers poured into the South and its aircraft hammered the North.

From the outset of the conflict, these propaganda efforts put Saigon on the ideological defensive. The Communists realized that their potential power base in the South was among the rural population, who showed a great residual respect and admiration for the ouster of the French. Thus Hanoi's psychological campaign was aimed at weakening the will of the Republic's supporters,

while imbuing its own followers with a conviction they
were riding the wave of the future.

Feeling exposed and vulnerable to isolation from the
peasantry, Saigon's response was largely reactive. A
host of "pacification" programs were initiated to win
mass allegiance to counter the threats of political
paralysis posed by Viet Cong activity. But while they
trumpeted the benefits to be derived from liberal
democratic government, no Southern leader developed a
dynamic revolutionary ideology that genuinely shared
power with their countrymen.

The result was a long, drawn out Hanoi-Saigon duel
for the people's "hearts and minds." Paralleling the
death and destruction was a struggle between rival
nationalisms -- a struggle whose weapons were politics
and psychology. To be sure, the side that won the last
military battles prevailed. But, while the armed
conflict continued, the crucial factor was which side
would convince the Vietnamese that its cause was just, it
was the legitimate successor to the nation's precolonial
legacy, and it could best fulfill their needs. The
people ultimately determined the victor; mass support
brought with it the power needed to win the military war.

American bombing sharpened national consciousness
and strengthened support in the North for the Communist
regime and their goal of reunifying Vietnam. In the
South a minority (the Viet Cong and their supporters)
embraced Hanoi's ideals, and a U.S. sponsored anti-
Communist minority opposed them. The majority of South
Vietnamese were, of course, in the middle. Their
Confucian upbringing preconditioned a neutrality and
pragmatism when caught between strong opposing forces;
most assumed a "wait-and-see" outlook and remained
uncommitted to either side throughout the war. The final
accounting finds a novel and informal democratic process
resolving the conflict: some of the population
(including both Northerners and the Viet Cong) supported
a Communist-style unified Vietnam; a minority in the
South was opposed; and a large group of Southerners
abstained. Saigon lost the "hearts and minds" battle --
most people chose or acquiesced to Communist victory.

Where the country was wracked by civil conflict,
U.S. military assistance could have done little more than
buy time -- time to allow South Vietnamese leaders to
initiate meaningful reforms that might have won them
popular support. The primary task was political and
psychological: Communism is an idea. To counter its
appeal, a better idea was needed -- one rooted in the
reality of the people's lives, meeting their social and
economic needs, and holding out the prospect of
fulfilling their future aspirations. While Americans
paid a price of blood and treasury to provide Saigon an
opportunity to rally popular allegiance, its leaders

squandered this breathing spell, failing to take actions necessary to win the people's "hearts and minds."

As foreigners, Americans could not produce national unity for the Vietnamese. Yet it was precisely such an anti-Communist nationalism that the Americans tried to create when they interjected themselves into the Vietnamese civil war. Foreign participation in the Vietnamese war of ideas was doomed from the start.

NOTES

1.   Ho Chi Minh, On Revolution, Bernard B. Fall, ed. (New York: Praeger, 1967), p. 367.
2.   Quoted by U.S., Department of State, Foreign Service Institute, "The Viet Cong: Five Steps in Running a Revolution," M-362-66 (July 28, 1966), p. 4. (mimeographed.)
3.   National Security Memorandum 52 (May 11, 1961) in The Pentagon Papers, Neil Sheehan et al. (New York: Bantam Books, 1971), p. 126.
4.   Note that psychological warfare is aimed at enemy or hostile groups only. Psychological operations, on the other hand, encompasses both the communications toward neutral or friendly foreign audiences on the political-economic side of the war and those toward the enemy to supplement military actions. See U.S., Department of Defense, Joint Chiefs of Staff, Dictionary of Military and Associated Terms, JCS Pubn. 1 (Washington, D.C.: Government Printing Office, September 3, 1974), p. 264.
5.   U.S., JUSPAO, Catalogue of Psyops Tapes (Saigon: n.d.), loudspeaker tape number 6.
6.   U.S., JUSPAO, leaflet number 1. Dropped by the U.S. Air Force at four locations in North Vietnam during the first leaflet raid on April 14, 1965.
7.   Ibid., songsheet number 3019.

2
Cross-Cultural Communication

> The physical, psychological, cultural, and
> racial factors involved are so complex, the
> propagandist's knowledge so limited, access to
> the target audience so uncertain, and changes
> so unpredictable, that wartime psychological
> operations partake of the nature of art rather
> than science.
>
>   -- Carl Berger[1]

Although propaganda had been used to further
American foreign policies during both peace and war, it
had never before been employed in an environment as broad
and complex as Vietnam. The military, political,
economic, and psychological aspects of the conflict were
hopelessly entangled and interdependent. Each also had
an impact on the battle for men's minds. Since no clear
front lines existed in the military war, the political-
economic war could not be waged separately from it. In
the psychological arena the enemy and non-enemy were
often indistinguishable. Moreover, Vietnamese cultural
predispositions presented formidable barriers that had to
be overcome for effective communication.

Nonetheless, the U.S. was in many ways better
prepared to conduct persuasive efforts in the Indochinese
war than in any previous conflict. Psychological warfare
experiences in three military conflicts during this
century, plus propaganda practice during the Cold War,
had evolved a substantial doctrine for psychological
operations for use in Vietnam.

DOCTRINE

Strictly speaking, the roots of American propaganda
go back to the earliest days of the Republic. Thomas
Paine's pamphleteering and the Declaration of
Independence were powerful propaganda. During the
American Revolution campaigns of persuasion were utilized

13

abroad and at home. A primitive technique practiced by
George Washington's soldiers "was to tie to a rock and
throw . . . to the redcoats" strips of paper with this
message:

	Prospect Hill			Bunker Hill
I	Seven Dollars a Month		I	Three pence a day
II	Fresh provisions and in plenty		II	Rotten salt pork
III	Health		III	The Scurvey
IV	Freedom, ease, affluence and a good farm		IV	Slavery, beggary and want[2]

Not until the present century was psychological
strategy systematically organized as an implement of
war. During both World Wars, carefully devised American
propaganda sought to sap the morale and induce surrender
of enemy soldiers as well as to undermine the enemy's
support at home. The successes credited to these
campaigns reinforced confidence in the usefulness of
propaganda as an auxiliary weapon of war and led to a
loose code of prescriptions for such programs. In the
late 1940s the Cold War forced the recognition of the
need to counter Soviet opposition to U.S. foreign
policies. A reluctant Congress passed the Smith-Mundt
Act in 1948, establishing America's first peacetime
international political communications operations.
Charged with launching a "Campaign of Truth" to rebut
Soviet distortions, the program was carried out within
the State Department until the U.S. Information Agency
was formed in 1953. The USIA used a host of
informational and cultural channels aimed at winning
overseas support for American policies. Political
communications was added to the tradition of
psychological warfare.
    The USIA had a profound impact on psychological
operations in Vietnam. The Agency drew upon a
substantial reserve of experienced personnel, provided
extensive machinery to direct and control the propaganda
campaign, and served as a memory bank of lessons learned
in Europe, Japan, and Korea. Moreover, since the USIA
had conducted propaganda operations in Vietnam since
1954, it had a reservoir of knowledge about the country,
its culture, and its people, knowledge that was
indispensable for effective communications. During the
early 1960s a growing U.S. involvement in the Indochinese
conflict gave the Agency the opportunity to prepare plans
for large-scale efforts should the need for them arise.
    The U.S. also derived some of its doctrine from
British counterinsurgency efforts in Malaya (1951-1956)
and the Philippine government's quelling of the
Hukbalahap insurrection (1946-1954). The key to success

in both instances had been a physical and psychological separation of the native guerrillas from the people. Thus, psychological operations had two primary tasks -- convincing the populace that its interests would best be served by supporting the legitimate government and persuading the guerrillas to accept amnesty or surrender offers to avoid certain death. Field Marshal Sir Gerald Templer, who orchestrated the British success in Malaya, pointed out that the main task was winning the "hearts and minds" of the people: "If this can be done, the insurgency is automatically suppressed because the insurgents cannot survive without the support of the civilian population from whom they get their intelligence, food, supplies, and recruits."[3]

The importance of matching propaganda words with military and political actions is emphasized in Alvin H. Scaff's study of the Huk insurrection:

> This indirect approach to communism, by winning the people away from their Communist leaders and leaving the hard core isolated and hard pressed, has been the genius of the Philippine program. Moreover, the appeal carries greatest force when it is rooted in the experience of the people with representative government in democratic communities and is not limited to lectures and leaflets.[4]

Many American-inspired military and psychological tactics employed in Vietnam (such as Saigon's amnesty program, payment of rewards to defectors, and emphasis on winning "hearts and minds") had their origin in these two counterinsurgency efforts.

Clearly a large amount of propaganda information and expertise were available to the United States by 1965, but a doctrine of abstract principles based on past experience does not necessarily make for effective psychological operations. Although USIA propagandists had the necessary technical expertise for persuasive efforts abroad, most were ill-prepared to deal with the cultural predispositions of the Vietnamese people. Barry Zorthian, architect of the propaganda campaign and its director (1965-1968) summed up the problem:

> Our basic experience in conflict usually involved only civilian populations of ethnic and cultural background that had some mutuality and relevance to our own experience. Primarily, this meant Europe with a similar Christian-Judeo tradition, and, thus, with roughly the same ethics and values. Remember we never fought the war with Japanese in Japan or really made much appeal to the Japanese

16

people during World War II. The Korean War was
closer to the population but even that was
limited since the sustained fighting took place
largely in the underpopulated areas. We really
had no experience relevant to Vietnam from the
viewpoint of psychological operations, let
alone military tactics.[5]

THE PSYCHOLOGICAL TERRAIN

Many Westerners experienced "culture shock" when
they first visited Indochina. Vietnamese and American
societies were vastly different in almost every important
aspect -- race, language, outlook on life, and ways of
doing things. Indeed, the cultural gap separating the
two peoples was probably as great as that between any two
societies in the world. This chasm had to be bridged in
order for the Americans to communicate effectively with
the Vietnamese. The success of U.S. psychological
operations largely depended on it.

For example, Americans had to cope with Confucian
passivity, persisting in the South Vietnamese
countryside. Inherited from a thousand years of Chinese
domination, this passivity is deeply imbedded in the
nation's social and political fabric. It prescribes the
rules of conduct and defines the attitudes people are to
hold.

Confucianism requires above all that each man find
his place in the natural order by promoting harmony with
his environment; i.e., passively adapting to present
conditions. "Harmony is the source of good. When
physical, spiritual, and cosmic forces are harmoniously
balanced, all is well. Evil, bad health, natural,
economic, or political disorders all result from lack of
harmony. In human conduct, therefore, the peasant seeks
the 'middle path' of Confucius, a harmonious middle way
between all extremes of conduct."[6] In addition, the
Vietnamese is supposed to promote social harmony by
"bending like the bamboo." The bamboo bends with the
wind; when the wind decreases, the bamboo returns to its
original upright position.

Furthermore, the desires and aspirations of the
peasant reside in his village. He trusts few people
beside his family and a handful of friends; he is
suspicious of strangers. According to a USIA report
prepared in 1965:

> The peasant has little consciousness of Viet-
> Nam as a nation, though he is aware he is a
> Vietnamese. . . . The peasant's loyalties go
> first to his family, then to his village and,
> to a lesser degree, to his region and his
> race. He has virtually no patriotism or

nationalism in the Western sense. For over a
century, no government has given him much
reason to commit himself. Yet, it is this
commitment the Viet Cong and Government are now
asking.[7]

The South Vietnamese peasant views the world outside
his village as being beyond his control; he finds little
reason to concern himself with or take part in national
affairs. He has been taught to accept the authority of
others, first his father and later village elders,
teachers, and government officials.

The world of the peasant revolves primarily around
rice. Growing it gives him a reason for being; its
cultivation dictates his habits, holidays, and worship.
Thus, land ownership, which provides sustenance and
security for himself and his family, is also a major
concern.

Religion is another significant factor in the
peasant's life, for he lives both in the world of reality
and in a world of spirits. His religion is a mixture of
spiritualism and superstition. He is most likely a
Buddhist or a member of one of its sects, though some
Vietnamese (generally former refugees from the North) are
Christians.

The family plays a central role in the peasant's
life and in the social order. People are not independent
individuals but are members of an extended family group,
the living, the departed, and those yet unborn. In this
family system a key concept is filial piety -- a child's
indebtedness to his parents for all the sacrifices they
made in rearing him. No matter what his age, a child
subordinates himself to his parents.

Another manifestation of filial piety is the "Cult
of the Ancestors." Originating in Confucian doctrine,
this belief holds that forebears protect the family
line. Prayers are addressed to them, imploring them to
save those who are sick or in danger. Ancestors are
further venerated because of the belief that a person's
becoming a demon or a good spirit after death depends not
only on his life in the physical world but also on
whether his ancestors look upon him with favor. Rites
and practices of veneration are performed at the family
altar, a symbol of family solidarity around which
relatives gather to celebrate feasts and make major
decisions.

In view of these values, it is not surprising that
so many Vietnamese over the years failed to side firmly
with either Hanoi or Saigon. Confucian principles of
passivity and harmony conditioned them to neutrality and
acceptance of the strongest force at any given time.
Undoubtedly, as Ralph K. White pointed out, a desire to
be on the winning side, general indifference to national

politics, and the numbness and confusion created by the
long war also contributed to their general position of
neutrality in the struggle. On the other hand, many
persons supported either the Viet Cong or the Republic on
the basis of family ties. If an individual committed
himself to one faction, his relatives tended to support
that side too. Moreover, the death or injury of a
relative at the hands of either side was a powerful
determinant of family antipathy toward the injuring
party.[8]

Profound differences between American and South
Vietnamese values were highlighted in a 1968 study by
Human Sciences Research Incorporated. Its interviewers
administered questionnaires to 360 Vietnamese and 300
Americans, with the following results:

> 1. The responses of a majority of the
> Vietnamese respondents indicated a pragmatic
> view of human nature. Americans were more
> inclined to be moralistic.
> 2. The Vietnamese were largely oriented to
> accept things as they are. Americans were
> almost exclusively concerned with control of
> their environment.
> 3. Vietnamese seemed to live in the present,
> adapting to situations on a day-to-day basis
> and showing very little interest in thinking
> about or planning for the future. Americans
> were more future oriented, interested in
> planning and more willing to sacrifice present
> concerns for future goals.
> 4. Vietnamese saw economic activity almost
> exclusively in terms of economic gain.
> Americans viewed economic activity more as a
> means of self-development.
> 5. Vietnamese were strongly oriented toward
> decision by authority and toward the approval
> or disapproval of elders and superiors.
> Americans believed strongly in self-
> determination and in individual conscience as a
> basic guide to behavior.[9]

Such diversities posed major hazards to effective
persuasive communications. They should have been warning
signals for areas where American goals and Vietnamese
values might conflict. The Vietnamese saw American
action-orientation as destroying tradition and disrupting
harmony. Direct actions, or frontal assaults on a
problem were regarded as reckless, wasteful, and
unsophisticated. On the other hand, Americans perceived
Vietnamese middle-of-the-road and indirect actions as
deceitful and dishonest.
Knowledge of these differences should have led U.S.

propagandists to abandon their moralistic, direct-action, future-oriented approach to psychological operations and to take up the pragmatic, present-day, harmony-orientation of the targeted people. Specifically, to prepare optimally persuasive propaganda, Americans should have had sufficient expertise in the native language, history, and culture. As John W. Riley, Jr., and Leonard S. Cottrell, Jr., put it, "The closer a psychological warfare message comes to meeting an existing predisposition or need in the target audience, the more effective the message."[10] Awareness of a people's values provides guidance in devising appropriate themes and appeals and for selecting credible communications media. Without such an awareness, the psychological warrior runs the risk of inadvertently insulting or antagonizing his intended audience.

Two American gaffes illustrate the point. One, the heralded "Grocery Bag Campaign," was launched in 1968. In this campaign, small paper sacks -- overprinted with persuasive themes -- were given to village merchants who had agreed to distribute them to their customers. The goal of these scheme was to transmit political messages into Viet Cong-controlled and contested areas, for it was assumed that many of the grocery bags would eventually end up there. One sack, for example, depicted a family scene of a sorrowful mother, a young wife, and a daughter and had the accompanying message:

> We miss you at the evening meal!
> We miss you at every evening meal; your Mother,
> Your child and I are waiting for you.
> Return to the Just Cause and be reunited
> with Your family.

As the campaign got under way, the foreigners were surprised to find that shopkeepers were methodically disassembling the sacks and using them as wrapping paper.

Unlike Americans, who value the utility of grocery bags, rural Vietnamese regard them as useless. In fact, many peasants feel bags pose certain hazards: contents may easily spill out, or if the bags are dropped, the contents may be scattered to the ground. To avoid these dangers the peasant typically takes a square of cloth or plastic netting to the marketplace and carefully wraps it around his purchases for the trip home. Normally, rural merchants wrap their wares in whatever paper is available, including newspaper and pages from magazines -- and sometimes useless grocery bags provided by foreigners.

A second propaganda effort that went awry was the use of "sex appeal" leaflets. The USIA's Saigon-based agency advised that sex-appeal propaganda be used sparingly and limited to pictures of young girls in traditional dress, such as in Figure 2.1. "Cheesecake" photographs, the bureau warned, might be acceptable to Western standards but would likely offend native canons of good taste.[11] Nevertheless, Americans prepared "cheesecake" leaflets based on their notions of what constitutes sex appeal (see bikini-clad girl depicted in Figure 2.2). As one writer pointed out:

> The Americans often distributed their propaganda messages with pictures of voluptuous, scantily clad women. The Americans assumed the pictures would turn the thoughts of enemy troops toward home. But to most Vietnamese there's nothing captivating about overendowed women. "Pinups just don't have the same appeal here," says an American psywarrior, a little sadly.[12]

While neither of these gaffes in themselves had devastating effects on the psychological operations campaign, they illustrate the point that without immersing themselves in Vietnamese culture and values, Americans were engaging in dangerous and possibly counterproductive activities by participating directly in the Vietnamese battle for Vietnamese minds.

Figure 2.1
Sex Appeal: Girl Wearing <u>Ao Dai</u>

SAO CÁC BẠN LẠI
CHỐI BỎ THÚ VỊ Ở ĐỜI?

WHY DO YOU DENY YOURSELF THE SATISFACTIONS OF LIFE?

Life is full of joy. Yet what good is your life when you turn
your back on it? The animal existence the powerful Army of the
Republic of Vietnam soldiers force you to lead brings no happiness
-- only denial, without hope, love or offspring. You have nothing
to look forward to. Change this hopeless situation. Rally now to
the open arms of the Government of Vietnam.

Source: U.S., MACV, 4th Psychological Operations Group, leaflet
number 4-132-68.

Figure 2.2
Sex Appeal: Bikini-Clad Girl

SAO CÁC BẠN LẠI CHỐI
BỎ THÚ VỊ Ở ĐỜI ?

DON'T DENY YOURSELF THE RIGHT TO BE A MAN

Right now your only satisfaction is that you hope you are able to stay alive through the terrifying Army of the Republic of Vietnam attacks. Don't deny yourself the right to be a man. Return to a life of happiness and personal freedom. Rally to the open arms of the Government of Vietnam.
Why do you deny yourself the satisfactions of life?

Source: U.S., MACV, 4th Psychological Operations Group, leaflet number 4-133-68.

NOTES

1. Carl Berger, An Introduction to Wartime Leaflets (Washington, D.C.: American University, Special Operations Research Office, 1959), p. 130.

2. Quoted by Douglas Southall Freeman and requoted by William E. Daugherty, ed., A Psychological Warfare Casebook (Baltimore: Johns Hopkins Press, 1958), p. 60.

3. Quoted by U.S., Department of the Army, Report of the Internal Defense/Development Psychological Operations Instructor's Conference (Fort Bragg, N.C.: U.S. Army Special Warfare School, October 31-November 4, 1966), p. 71. See also Edgar O'Ballance, Malaya: The Communist Insurgent War, 1948-60 (Hamden, Conn.: Archon Books, 1966), pp. 168-70.

4. Alvin H. Scaff, The Philippine Answer to Communism (Stanford, Calif.: Stanford University Press, 1955), p. 139.

5. Barry Zorthian, "The Use of Psychological Operations in Combatting 'Wars of National Liberation,'" a paper presented at the National Strategy Information Center Conference (March 11-14, 1971), pp. 3-4.

6. U.S., USIA, The Vietnamese Peasant: His Value System. R-138-65 (Washington, D.C.: October 1965), p. 3.

7. Ibid., p. 2. See also John T. McAlister, Jr., and Paul Mus, The Vietnamese and Their Revolution (New York: Harper & Row, 1970), p. 67.

8. Ralph K. White, Nobody Wanted War, rev. ed. (Garden City, N.Y.: Doubleday, 1970), pp. 67,68.

9. John S. Parsons, Dale K. Brown, and Nancy R. Kingsbury, Americans and Vietnamese: A Comparison of Values in Two Cultures, ARPA-TIO-72-6 (Arlington, Va.: Department of Defense, Advanced Research Projects Agency, 1972). Research compiled by Human Sciences Research, Inc., McLean, Va., November 1968, HSR-RR-68/10-Ct, p. 6.

10. John W. Riley, Jr., and Leonard S. Cottrell, Jr., "Research for Psychological Warfare," Public Opinion Quarterly, Vol. 21, No. 1 (Spring 1957), p. 157.

11. U.S., JUSPAO, Use of Sex Appeal on Propaganda Programs and Materials, Policy Number 70 (October 29, 1968), p. 1.

12. "The War of Words," Wall Street Journal (December 5, 1969), p. 9.

3
The Bureaucracy

> There has to be effective communication but it
> cannot be effective through surrogate channels;
> the host government must be the communicator
> with its own tools through its own techniques
> in its own image.
>
>   -- Barry Zorthian[1]

American psychological operations began in the
summer of 1954, during the transition from French rule,
when covert anti-Communist rumor campaigns were conducted
in both parts of the country. Overt persuasive
activities were continued in the South on a limited scale
through the 1950s and were intensified in the early 1960s
as the tempo of insurgency quickened. Substantial help
to Saigon's propaganda and political warfare programs was
provided by the USIA's overseas arm -- the U.S.
Information Service (USIS), by the State Department's
Agency for International Development (USAID), and by the
Joint Chiefs of Staff's Military Assistance Command,
Vietnam (MACV). Although these groups supposedly
coordinated their actions, duplication and inefficiency
often marked their efforts. For example, projectors and
recorders furnished by USAID were sometimes incompatible
with the films and tapes supplied by USIS. By 1964, the
combined effects of this lack of coordination among U.S.
agencies and the general incompetence of the Saigon
government in psychological operations had led many
Americans to suspect that the "hearts and minds" war was
falling short of its goals. In March, 1965, General H.
K. Johnson, representing the Joint Chiefs of Staff, and
Carl Rowan, then director of USIA, visited South Vietnam
and endorsed a single manager to direct and control all
aspects of U.S. propaganda as the national decision for
massive intervention was being made in Washington.

CENTRALIZED AUTHORITY

On July 1, 1965, the Joint U.S. Public Affairs Office (JUSPAO) was delegated authority for all propaganda activities. Barry Zorthian was made its director. Under the supervision of USIA, but operationally subordinate to the ambassador, JUSPAO integrated the USIS, USAID, MACV, and U.S. Embassy psychological operations. As newsman Malcolm Browne put it, "The idea was to avoid the wasteful over-lap that had resulted for years from disputes and lack of coordination not only between Americans and Vietnamese but between American military and civilian agencies."[2]

JUSPAO had five departments: an Office of the Director, plus Information, Cultural Affairs, North Vietnamese Affairs, and Field Development Divisions. The Director's office formulated policy directives to guide field propagandists, planned persuasive campaigns for all target audiences, and maintained liaison with Saigon's Ministry of Information. From this basic structure, it centralized control over all psychological operations in North and South Vietnam and along the Ho Chi Minh Trail in Laos and Cambodia, including both the military and political-economic dimensions of the war. Zorthian explained this inclusive concept:

> If the message must be unified, then so too should the organization. The concept requires the unification in one organization of elements dealing with military and civilian support, press relations and psychological warfare, domestic and foreign audiences, staff and operational functions. All must be part of and contribute to the whole.[3]

To carry out these tasks, JUSPAO and the Military Assistance Command had an extensive array of production and communications facilities. The output of propaganda materials from these agencies combined with material support from USIA and military units located outside Vietnam was immense. Consider, for example, the production figures for 1969, the peak year (Table 3.1).

JUSPAO broke new ground, too, organizationally; it was permitted to be an active participant in the U.S. Mission Council -- the Ambassador's highest policy-making body. This was a breakthrough, because for years propagandists have lobbied for a greater voice in the decisions that affected their operations. Edward W. Barrett, deputy director of the Office of War Information during World War II, had argued:

> It should be standard government policy to have specialists in foreign opinion participate in

decisions of international policy. Sound
policy should not be changed in order to win
popularity, but it can at least be so
formulated, announced, executed and explained
as to win maximum good will.[4]

JUSPAO's presence on the council reflected the
importance attached to propaganda in the
counterinsurgency effort. Further, it was the first
meaningful American attempt to integrate the
psychological aspect of foreign policy with the
political, economic, and military instruments. While the
weight of JUSPAO's voice varied with different
ambassadors, according to Zorthian, its influence was
substantial. Based on his experiences in Vietnam, Harry
Latimer suggests that, by monitoring the ground rules for
military operations, JUSPAO served as an "honest broker"
in Mission Council deliberations. This exerted strong
pressures to minimize the adverse impact of combat
activities on civilians. He says that psychological

TABLE 3.1
Media Produced or Printed in 1969

Category	JUSPAO	MACV
Leaflets	36,000,000	10.2 billion
Pamphlets	3,500,000	500,000
Newspaper articles	6,000	0
Posters	7,800,000	15,800,000
Magazines	9,900,000	1,900,000
Loudspeaker tapes*	11,819	1,327
Motion picture prints	1,514	0
Radio programs	1,272	208
Television programs	27	0

Source: U.S., Senate, Hearings Before the Committee on
Foreign Relations, Vietnam: Policy and Prospects, 1970,
91 Cong., 2nd Sess., 1970, p. 696.

*These loudspeaker type statistics represent the number
produced and do not reflect the number of listeners.
These tapes were broadcast many times before being
destroyed, increasing potential listenership several
fold. See Chapter 4 for 1969 statistics of the number of
loudspeaker hours broadcast. These figures better
illustrate the emphasis placed on this communication
channel.

operations ". . . considerations patently were not
paramount in determining political, economic, and
military action; counsel by the JUSPAO head could not
budge a policy such as that of free fire zones, but the
psyops perspective helped put a rein on defoliation and
crop destruction."[5]
    The "honest broker" role was also significant
because the military, functioning under the over-all
guidance of JUSPAO, had operational control over
psychological warfare against enemy armed forces and
political-economic propaganda intended for the non-
Communist South Vietnamese (see Appendix A for the
JUSPAO-MACV agreement).

MILITARY PROPAGANDA

    MACV's Psychological Operations Directorate
exercised supervision of U.S. Army, Marine Corps, and
Navy communications programs. It also coordinated Air
Force aircraft supporting the effort, assigned advisors
to each of the South Vietnamese political warfare
battalions, and monitored civic action endeavors by the
American armed forces.
    Initially the Army's campaign was carried out by
four psychological operations companies in the field, one
in each of the major tactical zones. However, rapid
escalation and widespread combat activity soon
outstripped their capabilities. Therefore, a large
propaganda headquarters was established in Saigon, and
four battalions replaced the field companies in late
1967. This large-scale reorganization almost doubled the
number of military psychological warriors. Each field
battalion had its own printing plant, photographic
processing and production equipment, tape recorders,
loudspeaker trucks, and related apparatus. To ensure
maximum responsiveness to tactical needs, commanders in
the combat zones maintained operational control over
these units.
    The Navy's psychological operations, too, evolved as
an adjunct to its tactical mission. Leaflets, South
Vietnamese flags, and miscellaneous items were handed out
by sailors during routine searches of merchant and
fishing vessels along the coast and to people traveling
along internal waterways. River patrol boats were
placarded as reception points for defectors and were
equipped with loudspeaker systems for population control
during the day and propaganda broadcasts at night. In
addition, sailors often put up posters and banners on
piers and trees along the waterways to advertise
government leaflets.
    The Air Force concentrated on dropping leaflets.
Two squadrons deployed at five bases were dedicated

solely to the support of psychological operations. In
all, each of the four combat zones had about ten slow-
moving aircraft. Each was equipped with a loudspeaker
system and a chute for dispensing leaflets. Close
coordination between Army propaganda battalions and Air
Force squadrons ensured rapid response to ground combat
operations.[6]

This was a far cry from World War II, when there
were continual problems of securing aircraft to deliver
leaflets, which were normally placed at airfields and
aircrews expected merely to ". . . take them out and drop
them to the right language-groups at the right time in
the right place."[7] Although there were similarly casual
procedures in Vietnam on a lesser scale, at least
airplanes were readily available, and some specific
targeting was possible.

In addition, two aerial delivery techniques were
developed during the war that permitted both widespread
loudspeaker broadcasts and the scattering of billions of
leaflets over the countryside. One technique, developed
in 1967, used 2,100-watt loudspeakers that could be heard
in a two-mile radius from altitudes of 3,000 to 4,500
feet. This was important because early in the conflict
airborne broadcasts from equipment developed during the
Korean War were generally inaudible on the ground. The
new system permitted thousands of hours of taped messages
to be aired during the remainder of the war. Particular
use was made of them at night against Communist troops in
the jungle to try to wear down morale and persuade them
to give up the fight. The system also let the Air Force
psychological warriors -- known affectionately to other
GIs as the "Bullshit Bombers" -- to "torture" their
American compatriots with blasts of propaganda during 3
A.M. landings. By turning their loudspeakers up to full
volume while in the landing pattern, the returning pilots
disrupted their comrades' sleep and became the targets of
many early morning curses.

The second major dissemination technique developed
was leaflets drops from high flying cargo aircraft. A
simple equation of height, wind velocity, and known rate
of descent allowed reasonably accurate targeting on the
ground from high altitudes. Leaflets were often dumped
over the Gulf of Tonkin in international airspace, with
the breeze taking them into North Vietnam. Research had
revealed that scraps of paper of particular sizes and
weights drift with the air flow at about the same speed
and fall to the ground at a fairly predictable rate.
When several leaflets with the same physical
characteristics are dropped simultaneously, they form a
"teardrop"-shaped cloud, tumbling steadily to the ground
as the breeze carries them along. The cloud spreads in
an elliptical pattern; as the bottom of the "teardrop"
strikes the earth's surface, the remainder of the

leaflets continue to glide, forming an oblong design on
the ground. The area to be covered could easily be
increased by including paper of different sizes and
weights, having different wind-drift and rate-of-descent
characteristics, in a single delivery.[8]
    After inadvertently flying through an immense
downpour of these leaflets, at least one American
fighter-pilot almost radioed in a "UFO Report" before
realizing what they were.

POLITICAL-ECONOMIC PROPAGANDA

    American efforts to create a viable anti-Communist
nationalism among the South Vietnamese and generate
popular support for the Saigon government were
consolidated under MACV's Civil Operations and Rural
Development Support Agency (CORDS) in 1967. The CORDS
head carried the personal rank of ambassador; he was
responsible to the commanding general of MACV.
    There was some good rationale behind fusing the
military, political-economic, and psychological
dimensions of the war under a single chief. As American
Ambassador to Vietnam Ellsworth Bunker explained in May
1967:

>   The U.S. advisory and supporting role in
>   revolutionary development [i.e., winning
>   "hearts and minds"] can be made more effective
>   by unifying its civil and military aspect under
>   a single management concept. Unified
>   management, a single chain of command, and a
>   more closely dovetailed advisory effort will,
>   in my opinion, greatly improve U.S. support of
>   the vital revolutionary development program.[9]

Or perhaps as Newsweek put it: "Fed up with failures in
the pacification program and the squabbling between the
soldiers and civilians, President Johnson himself finally
settled the issue reportedly with the words: 'Damn it, I
want it all under Westy'" (i.e., MACV commander, General
Westmoreland).[10]
    JUSPAO's centralized control was sustained after its
field activities were absorbed by CORDS, maintaining
close liaison and coordination throughout the remainder
of the war. At the lower levels, the CORDS Assistant
Province Advisor for Psychological Operations -- usually
a USIA or military officer -- was responsible for all
propaganda within his area. He maintained a small
printing press, public address systems, projectors and
films, and, in some cases, community television sets.
His duties included conducting psychological operations,
advising and supervising propaganda efforts by American
military units, assisting the South Vietnamese and Allied

nations (Thailand, New Zealand, South Korea, Australia, and the Philippines) in their communications campaigns, contending with the pervasive U.S. military influence in his province, seeing to it that combat units exercised restraint in operations involving civilians, and, most important, advising, assisting, and "energizing" officers serving Saigon's field arm, the Vietnamese Information Service (VIS).

In broad outline, the CORDS propaganda structure paralleled the government's framework, allowing some degree of local cooperation. The CORDS advisor's relationships with his native counterparts varied widely, and this affected his ability to "energize" his hosts. Normally, he worked through the Vietnamese Information Service when competent persons were present. But when he found them to be inept or to lack the support of the military province chief, he dealt directly with district-level and political warfare officers. Latimer estimates that only a third of the VIS province chiefs were competent, another third "not really bad," and the remaining third incompetent.[11]

COORDINATION WITH SAIGON

In spite of some lower-level coordination, the Americans and South Vietnamese conducted their own private communications programs with only minimal and superficial integration and cooperation. This occurred despite a U.S. doctrine calling for the joint efforts with allies during war and behind-the-scenes advisory role in counterinsurgency. British psychological warfare expert R. H. S. Crossman explains the substantial success enjoyed in World War II: "The only way in which we achieved a joint Anglo-American propaganda policy was by having a joint Anglo-American propaganda staff under the Supreme Commander, a man who really did believe in Anglo-American teamwork and made it work."[12]

Moreover, the U.S. Army had outlined the advisory nature of counterinsurgency psychological operations in May 1965 -- two months before the formation of JUSPAO:

> Unlike other forms of warfare the normal
> function of the U.S. Army PSYOP resources is to
> advise and assist the host country armed forces
> PSYOP effort, rather than conduct PSYOP.
> Counterinsurgency PSYOP, if it is to be
> effective, must be conducted by indigenous
> personnel and wholly attributed to the host
> government.[13]   [Emphasis in original]

A consistent and well-orchestrated American-Vietnamese campaign could have resulted from close coordination. But cooperation proved to be difficult, if

not impossible, during most of the war because of
continual large turnovers in both JUSPAO and Saigon's
Ministry of Information. For example, there were twelve
different information ministers between 1964 and 1971.
According to Latimer, "Some . . . were hacks, others
among the most corrupt of Vietnamese officials."[14] The
crux of the problem on the Republic's side was summarized
by an American report in December 1967:

> The latest reshuffle of the Information and
> PSYOP function is the eighth the GVN has
> undertaken in five years. . . . The chronic
> instability of the information department, the
> filling of its higher echelons with short-term
> political appointees, who come and go with
> ministerial changes, is not conducive to
> consistent performance and effective
> planning.[15]

In spite of the important role played by
communications in developing and nurturing nationalism,
the VIS was in dire straits when JUSPAO came on the
scene. Its staff had little training and experience, and
it was plagued by general malaise and ineffective
leadership. At the outset Zorthian recognized that
higher quality, better trained information and public
relations officers were a prerequisite for winning
popular support for the government. In a personal letter
in 1966, he outlined a dynamic training program to
upgrade Vietnamese competence, noting some of their
problems: "Among VIS psywar trainees . . . are numerous
sons and daughters of persons of local influence, most of
whom fill administrative-clerical positions at VIS
province headquarters. VIS personnel sent for training
often enough are sent merely to fill a district quota,
and no use is made of specialized training they
receive."[16]
     Over the years, JUSPAO urged stringent reforms in
recruitment and assignment of VIS cadres, and supported
formal schooling of its staff in the basic skills
necessary for successful persuasion. In the field, CORDS
psychological operations advisors played an important
role in on-the-job training. But withdrawal of draft
exemption from the VIS in 1968 worsened the already
dismal level of expertise. As a result, at least in the
villages and hamlets, local propagandists were mostly old
men and women and those who somehow had managed to escape
the draft. One American psychological warrior estimated
that in 1969 up to twenty-five percent of the lower-level
VIS cadres were illiterate or at best semi-literate.
     In addition to contending with Saigon's lack of
expertise, JUSPAO was confronted by a general
unwillingness to conduct person-to-person propaganda

among the rural population. While important, mass media
could not shoulder the communications burden alone.
Instead, face-to-face oral discussion between government
representatives and the peasants in their villages was
needed more than any other medium to establish and
reinforce Saigon's ties with the countryside. As
Zorthian keenly put it: "In the normal insurgency
situation, i.e., the underdeveloped area where the
aspirations of the mass have not been met and the
government in power is somewhat isolated from the people,
the best and most effective medium is the God-given one
of oral communication."[17]

Americans could not do this job for them. The
closest JUSPAO came to using the face-to-face persuasion
technique came when it sent into the countryside some
2,700 Vietnamese performers and entertainers. Organized
into thirty-six cultural drama teams (called "Van Tac
Vu"), these troups offered entertainment-hungry rural
audiences propaganda laden songs, magic shows, dances,
dramatic shows, storytelling, and skits. These Van Tac
Vu productions attracted large crowds. A 1967 survey
revealed that about half the people in hamlets where the
teams performed had attended the shows, and "some
villagers say they gained a better understanding of
Government policies from them."[18]

The American tendency to substitute for Saigon in
communications to the populace was most pronounced in the
mass media. Initially, JUSPAO strove hard to develop
joint policies with the Information Ministry. These
initiatives failed because the South Vietnamese often did
not fully agree with the persuasive programs advocated by
their foreign sponsors. The Americans became
disillusioned, lost patience, and went out on their own
directly to the native population with millions of
leaflets, posters, banners, newspapers, magazines, radio
and television programs, and a host of other media. As
Zorthian explains:

> Our frustrations led to an inevitable result
> . . . Americans could not communicate and the
> Saigon Government would not, at least
> initially. We resorted to the typical American
> reliance on machine and volume and went
> overboard in the provision of hardware in order
> to make up the existing shortcomings. . . .
> This is not to argue against a comprehensive
> national newspaper or radio or television
> system. Quite reverse. Each of these media
> can be extremely effective if properly utilized
> by the central government as a means of
> communicating with the friendly population and
> even with supporters in areas under insurgency
> control. But these media are complementary to

the vital need for oral communication. It is
at the local level that substitution of
mechanical product for direct contact must be
avoided assiduously.[19] [emphasis added]

Americans poured an enormous amount of money into an
effort to equip the Republic with a viable information
and propaganda apparatus. For example, between 1965 and
1971 $22.1 million was provided for national radio and
television networks, a motion picture center, a printing
plant, and substantial amounts of equipment, trucks,
machines, and production supplies. Also, JUSPAO
furnished materials costing $15.5 million (leaflets,
magazines, newspapers, and the like). JUSPAO and MACV
also turned over much of their communications equipment
as "Vietnamization" or de-Americanization of the war went
into full-swing in late 1970.[20]
     Of the mass media introduced, television was among
the most important. Experiments with airborne TV
broadcasts first proved a successful technique in 1966,
and daily telecasting continued until a fixed-site, four-
station network was completed in 1971 -- with the U.S.
footing $8.2 million of the bill. Not surprisingly, the
novelty of "the tube" alone created a huge viewing
audience throughout the country. Because to many
Vietnamese "pictures do not lie," television became one
of the most credible propaganda mediums. According to
JUSPAO, about half of the programming was produced solely
for enjoyment, including news, interviews, musicals,
dramas, speeches, children's shows, soap operas, and
special events coverage. But Time magazine reported that
many of the programs which were supposedly entertainment
were in fact, "long in doctrine and all too short on
drama. Typical plot: North Vietnamese saboteur
infiltrates the South, discovers that life under Saigon
government is not as bad as Hanoi has made it out to be,
defects."[21]
     To increase the potential audience, CORDS
distributed 3,500 community-viewing sets in rural
areas. Crowds as large as 300 gathered regularly in
front of some receivers to watch the nightly fare.
Sometimes the Viet Cong shot up the sets, but this
backfired because of popular enthusiasm for the new
picture medium. Even among guerrillas it was catching;
some entered rural hamlets at night to watch their
favorite programs and then slipped away when the
evening's entertainment was over.
     By 1971 eighty percent of the native populace were
within reach of the telecasts; the country by then had
nearly half a million private receivers in addition to
the community sets. As Time reported, the "tube had
taken hold" in South Vietnam.
     Despite the importance of mass media such as

television in winning popular support, American provision
of hardware and promotional materials "boomeranged."
Saigon's shortcomings multiplied when JUSPAO
overmechanized its Information Ministry and the VIS. As
a result, the Vietnamese, emulating their foreign
benefactors who could not speak directly to the people,
also placed a greater reliance on the printed and
broadcast word. The vital person-to-person communication
was not emphasized enough, and the "hearts and minds"
battle suffered accordingly.

On June 30, 1972, JUSPAO was dissolved, leaving
history to judge whether its concept of a single,
centralized U.S. information agency with over-all
management of American wartime propaganda efforts had
been validated during its seven-year lifetime. In
Zorthian's opinion, "the integration was never perfect
and did not extend to either the Vietnamese or to
Washington and there were flaws in performance, but
nevertheless the concept was tested and proven valid."[22]

History is also left the task of evaluating the
American attempt to substitute for the Saigon government
in creating a viable democratic nationalism. The
following chapters look at that American enterprise in
the Vietnamese war of ideas.

NOTES

1. Zorthian, "Psychological Operations," pp. 9-10.
2. Malcolm W. Browne, "U.S. Trims Psychological
Warfare Effort in Vietnam," New York Times (July 13,
1972), p. 3.
3. Zorthian, "Psychological Operations," p. 15. The
Director wore a second hat a Minister-Counselor for
Information. In this role he was responsible for press
relations and operation of the U.S. Mission Press
Center. See U.S., JUSPAO, JUSPAO Vietnam: General
Briefing Book, rev. ed. (Saigon: June 1968), pp. 14-40.
4. Quoted in Daugherty, Psychological Warfare
Casebook, pp. 298-99.
5. Harry D. Latimer, U.S. Psychological Operations
in Vietnam (Providence, R.I.: Brown University,
September 1973), p. 13.
6. U.S., MACV, Guide for Psychological Operations
(Saigon: April 27, 1968).
7. Paul M. A. Linebarger, Psychological Warfare,
2nd rev. ed. (Washington, D.C.: Combat Forces Press,
1954), p. 192.
8. U.S., Department of the Army, 7th Psychological
Operations Group, Low, Medium and High Altitude Leaflet
Dissemination Guide (APO San Francisco 96248: n.d.), pp.
4-8.
9. Quoted in U.S., Department of State, Department
of State Bulletin, Vol. LVI, No. 1458 (June 5, 1967).

36

See also U.S., MACV, Organization and Functions for Civil
Operations and Revolutionary Development Support, MACV
Directive 10-12 (Saigon: May 28, 1968).

10. "The Heart of the Matter," Newsweek (May 22,
1967), p. 51.

11. Latimer, Psychological Operations, pp. 30-34,
and U.S., MACV, Organizations and Functions--
Psychological Operations, MACV Directive 10-7 (Saigon:
December 11, 1967).

12. R. H. S. Crossman, "Psychological Warfare,"
Journal of the Royal United Services Institution, Vol.
98, No. 591 (August 1953), p. 354, and No. 592 (November
1953), p. 529.

13. U.S., Department of the Army, Psychological
Operations--U.S. Army Doctrine, Field Manual 33-1
(Washington, D.C.: Government Printing Office, May 18,
1965), p. 25.

14. Latimer, Psychological Operations, p. 11.

15. U.S., JUSPAO, "1967 Highlights--JUSPAO,"
attached to "JUSPAO Monthly Report for December, 1967,"
FM 33 (January 16, 1968).

16. "Professionalization of the Vietnamese
Information Service: Concept for Short and Long-Term
Training Programs," letter by Barry Zorthian, Director,
JUSPAO (Saigon: April 25, 1966): with permission of Mr.
Zorthian.

17. Zorthian, "Psychological Operations," p. 20.

18. U.S., JUSPAO, Nationwide Hamlet Survey (An
Interpretive Analysis), Research Report (Saigon: January
23, 1968), p. 7 and "Organization and Operation of U.S.-
Supported Culture-Drama Teams," Consolidation of JUSPAO
Field Memoranda 42 thru 58, Vol. III (Saigon: n.d.).

19. Zorthian, "Psychological Operations," pp. 21-
22.

20. U.S., Senate, Hearings Before the Committee on
Foreign Relations, Vietnam: Policy and Prospects, 1970,
92 Cong., 2nd sess., 1970, pp. 677-97.

21. "South Viet Nam: The Tube Takes Hold," Time
(November 30, 1970), p. 26.

22. Zorthian, "Psychological Operations," p. 15.

Part 2
U.S. Psychological Operations

4
The Chieu Hoi
and Surrender Programs

SECRET (Viet Cong classification)
The impact of increased enemy military
operations and 'Chieu Hoi' programs has, on the
whole, resulted in lowering the morale of some
ideologically backward men, who often listen to
enemy radio broadcasts, keep in their pockets
enemy leaflets, and wait to be issued weapons
(in order to go over the enemy side). This
attitude on their part has generated an
atmosphere of doubt and mistrust among our
military ranks.

-- South Vietnam Liberation
Army, December 20, 1966[1]

The Viet Cong and North Vietnamese armed forces hold
the dubious honor of being targets of the most massive
propaganda campaign in the history of warfare. Billions
upon billions of leaflets were dumped on them from the
air, and thousands of hours of loudspeaker broadcasts
from airplanes, boats, and the ground penetrated their
jungle hiding places in attempts to persuade them to give
up the fight.

The plight of the Communist soldier was a tough
one. He was hounded by fears of dying or of being
abandoned, wounded or dead, on the battlefield. Always
on the move, his jungle hide-outs were often damp and
offered little shelter. Disease was rampant, food
insufficient, and the lack of medical supplies resulted
in many deaths. He endured these fears and hardships
against a background of nostalgia, loneliness, and
concern for the well-being of his family.

As the number of defeats multiplied following
American intervention, he began to lose faith in ultimate
victory. Moreover, as he witnessed the widespread
destruction of his country, he became increasingly
disillusioned with the Communist cause. The more his
leaders' propaganda was intensified to make up for

reverses in battle, the more adept he became at contrasting what he heard with what he knew. Many who had no great love for the Republic were having less and less enthusiasm for the National Liberation Front as well.

Thus, Saigon offered the enemy soldier the opportunity to defect or surrender as a way out of his difficult situation, an action compatible with the Confucian search for a middle path between extremes. The primary focus of this psychological attack was the government's American-inspired and funded amnesty$_2$ invitation, the Chieu Hoi or "Open Arms" Program. Modeled after British and Philippine counterinsurgency operations in the 1950s, the Chieu Hoi policy was adopted in 1963 as a magnanimous offer of forgiveness and exoneration to those who had been temporarily seduced into following the "alien" Communist path -- "Try every way to escape from this bloody war created by the communists," they were told. It set before them an opportunity to wipe the slate clean and return to their families. The term "surrender" was avoided; instead the Viet Cong were implored to atone for their past sins by "rallying" to the "just cause" of the Republic. Saigon was cast in the paternalistic role, forgiving its errant children for their unwitting support of Hanoi and Peking. Psychological communications called on them to "Come back," "Come home to your loved ones," "Come home to your own people and rightful government." And, most important, the promises of amnesty were followed up with a program of positive action to make the invitation credible.

Efforts to persuade Communist surrenders were miniscule in contrast to attempts to induce defections. Because of their strong resistance to the Chieu Hoi call to "Come Home," different appeals were focused on the North Vietnamese soldiers deployed to the South. Most themes were aimed simply at informing Hanoi's troops of the opportunities to surrender. Promises included good treatment, medical attention, and repatriation after war -- "Do not fear detention after your capture or surrender. You will be comfortable and well cared for. Wounded prisoners receive the best medical care." Reminiscent of World War II propaganda were assurances that POW facilities conformed to Geneva Convention standards: "The Government of Vietnam is using human love to wipe out hatred." Surrender was pictured as an honorable way for the North Vietnamese to escape the difficult situation in the South, and as a pathway to earning a living and returning home after the war. "Do not risk death for a useless war -- allow yourselves to be captured," they were advised (Figs 4.1, 4.2).

These urgings often were accompanied by hard-sell approaches tied to combat operations. During a battle in

Figure 4.1
Surrender Appeal

CÙNG CÁC BẠN CÁN-BINH CHÍNH-QUY BẮC-VIỆT : KHI CÁC BẠN VỀ QUY-HÀNG :

1. Bạn sẽ được bảo-đảm tính-mạng.

2. Bạn sẽ được bảo-đảm ăn-uống và thuốc-men đầy đủ.

3. Các bạn sẽ được trở về với gia-đình nếu các bạn muốn khi hòa-bình lập lại.

CÙNG CÁC BẠN CÁN-BINH CHÍNH-QUY BẮC-VIỆT :

Sớm muộn gì các bạn cũng sẽ bị thương nặng hoặc bị tiêu-diệt.
Các bạn có thể thoát khỏi tình-trạng nguy-cấp khi làm-chiến nếu :

1. Bạn không chống cự.

2. Bạn hạ khí-giới.

3. Bạn quy-hàng Quân-Đội Việt-Nam Cộng-Hòa

North Vietnamese Army cadre and troops:
When you surrender:
1. You will be safe.
2. You are guaranteed sufficient food and medicine.
3. You will return home if you want after the fighting stops.
Sooner or later you will be killed or seriously wounded, you can escape your dangerous situation on the battlefield:
1. Do not fire.
2. Put down weapons.
3. Surrender to Government of Vietnam forces.

Source: U.S., JUSPAO, leaflet number 4333.

Figure 4.2
Prisoners-of-War Receive Good Treatment

CÁCH ĐỐI XỬ TỬ TẾ VỚI TÙ BINH NÓI LÊN LÒNG NHÂN ĐẠO
CỦA NHÂN DÂN VÃ CHÍNH PHỦ VIỆT NAM CỘNG HÒA

POWs LEARN NEW SKILLS

Good treatment . . . demonstrates the humane policy of the people and Government of South Vietnam.

Many of the Communist prisoners-of-war enthusiastically learn new jobs so that they can earn a better living when the country returns to peace.

With patience they learn new skills.

Source: U.S., JUSPAO, leaflet number 2921.

1966 near Tuy Hoa, for example, a U.S. unit mauled a previously elusive battalion of the 95th North Vietnamese Army Regiment. After two days of heavy fighting, the remnants of the enemy unit were surrounded by the American forces. The commander stopped his advance and called in a team of psychological warriors to broadcast surrender appeals over mobile loudspeakers:

> "Soldiers of the 95th, do you want to be buried in an unmarked grave? That is the only honor you will have left if you continue your senseless fight. Do you think that right? The soldiers of the U.S. are everywhere. There is no escape. Approach the Americans with your hands above your head. Wave something white. Have your weapon muzzle down and you will not be harmed. This is your last chance and only hope. Life or death . . . the choice is yours."[3]

By late afternoon, thirty-six soldiers had come in; most cited the broadcasts as being a decisive factor in their yielding.

In spite of the importance of the surrender program for the Northern troops, the Chieu Hoi policy, aimed primarily at the home-grown Southern Viet Cong, received the greatest amount of American emphasis and money. Reception centers for defectors, or "ralliers" (hoi chanh), were built at various locations throughout the country for the rank and file, and a national center for high-ranking defectors was established in Saigon. These hoi chanh normally remained in the camps from forty-five to sixty days before being released and resettled. Each could accommodate several hundred ralliers; facilities typically included sleeping, cooking, medical, recreation, and related conveniences. The hoi chanh were given rewards for turning in weapons, money for food and clothing, and basic necessities. Their families were allowed to visit them, and, beginning in 1967, were encouraged to live at or near the centers.

To counteract Communist catechism and to develop strong feelings of allegiance and loyalty to the Republic, political indoctrination was administered to both the ralliers and their families. In addition, vocational training was provided in skills that would help the move back into South Vietnamese society; barbering, brickmaking, carpentry, automobile repair, agricultural techniques, and livestock raising were typical courses. Following their stay at the detention camps, they were given a six-month draft deferment and were released to live wherever they chose in areas controlled by Saigon. Hoi chanh who could not find employment were placed in jobs with government or Allied agencies, and special hamlets were established for those who could not find suitable places to live (Figs 4.3, 4.4).[4]

These Chieu Hoi and surrender campaigns were the cutting edge of American attempts to convince the Communist armed forces to lay down their arms. Analysis of in-depth interviews and interrogations of defectors and prisoners revealed several psychological receptivities shared by many Viet Cong and Northern fighters. To exploit these weaknesses, a concise plan of attack was drawn up by JUSPAO in April 1966. It included general and specific campaigns concentrating on five major appeals designed to take advantage of the gaps found in the mental armor of the beleaguered Communist soldier.[5]

MAJOR PSYCHOLOGICAL APPEALS AND THEMES

The fear appeal was used to convince the individual soldier or civilian that he faced an overwhelming danger of being killed if he remained with the Communists -- "Death lurks everywhere." Propaganda messages told him: "There are just two choices -- more of this hell which can only end in death for you, or Chieu Hoi and life." Hanoi's troops were asked, "Are you haunted by the question, 'Born in the North to die in the South'" Thus is was hoped that they would overcome their fear of mistreatment by the South Vietnamese and rally or surrender. The omnipresent threat of death was reinforced by complementary themes, including the surprise and destructiveness of B-52 bomber raids, the mounting casualty rate, and the possibility of being buried in an unmarked grave, forever forgotten.

The B-52 strikes brought special terror to the hearts of many Communist fighters; the huge aircraft dropped their bombs unseen and unheard from altitudes of over 30,000 feet. The first indication soldiers had of the attack was when the ground around them suddenly erupted. To further reinforce the troops' fear, these raids were followed within hours by leaflet drops or aerial loudspeaker broadcasts (Fig 4.5). Typically, the messages informed the survivors about what they had just experienced, reminded them they would be struck again, and urged them to use a safe conduct pass to rally or surrender; "A B-52 just passed here! Avoid a sad death. Leave this worldly hell! Return to the National Government." A loudspeaker broadcast blared: "Your have just survived death from the rain of bombs of the B-52 flying fortress. No shelters are safe from the bombs of the B-52. Your lives have been threatened, don't be killed by the deceit of the Viet Cong."[6]

But not all such approaches were effective. One major misassumption occurred in 1966 when U.S. soldiers

Figure 4.3
Training Provided Ralliers

Bạn cuñg có thể sống tự do như nhuñg công dân khác theo chánh sách Đại Đoàn Kết của Chánh Phủ Việt Nam Cộng Hòa.

ANH NGUYỄN-ĐỨC-THẮNG,
24 TUỔI, CỰU HỒI CHÁNH
NGƯỜI XÃ TƯ-THUẬN,
QUẬN TƯ-NGHĨA TỈNH
QUẢNG-NGÃI.

YOU CAN BECOME A FREE CITIZEN UNDER THE DAI DOAN KET
POLICY OF THE GOVERNMENT OF VIETNAM

Mr. Nguyen Duc Thang, 24 years old, an ex-rallier, a native of Tu Thuan Village, Tu Nghia District, Quang Ngai Province.

He joined the VC ranks in 1964. After three years of working for the VC as a platoon leader in the 139th Provincial Main Force Battalion, he had seen the cruel face of the VC. Moreover, he had to live miserably in jungles and did not have enough food and medicine. He returned to the government on 12 December 1966. He was housed in the Chieu Hoi Center in Saigon. During the period of time in the center, he was trained on repairing cars, scooters, and bicycles, and then was released to return to Quang Ngai. Now he is a skilled mechanic with a salary of 22 piasters per hour. With the money he earns he can buy things he wants and is not afraid. . . .

Source: U.S., JUSPAO leaflet number 2399.

Figure 4.4
Life in Chieu Hoi Centers

Những anh em
Hồi chánh viên
đang sống thoải
mái cùng gia đình
tại các Trung-tâm
Chiêu-hồi ₃₇₀₄

RETURNEE LIVES PLEASANTLY WITH HIS FAMILY IN A
CHIEU HOI CENTER

To friends still remaining on the other side:
    The life of returnees in Chieu Hoi Villages fully reflects the
National Reconciliation Policy of the Government of Vietnam, which
wipes out hatred and animosity with love and compassion. Since
inception of the Chieu Hoi Program, over 147,000 returnees have
enjoyed a new life with freedom and well being.
    Today, they don't have to hide in jungles and mountains
suffering privations, hardships, and constantly facing the threat of
death. They earnestly wish their friends remaining on the other
side of the frontline to come back soon to the Government, so as to
heal the wounds of the country and reconstruct a free and thriving
South Vietnam.

Source: U.S., JUSPAO, leaflet number 3704.

Figure 4.5
B-52 Bomber Raids

ĐÂY PHÓNG PHÁO CƠ KHỔNG LỒ B.52

THIS IS THE MIGHTY B-52

    Now you have experienced the terrible rain of death and destruction its bombs have caused. These planes come swiftly, strongly speaking as the voice of the Government of Vietnam proclaiming its determination to eliminate the Viet Cong threat to peace. Your area will be struck again and again, but you will not know when or where. The planes fly too high to be heard or seen. They will rain death upon you again without warning. Leave this place to save your lives. Use this leaflet or the GVN National Safe Conduct Pass and rally to the nearest government outpost. The Republic of Vietnam soldiers and the people will happily welcome you.

(Picture of Safe Conduct Pass on Reverse)

Source: U.S., U.S. Mission, Vietnam, leaflet number 146-66-R.

scattered fear-appeal leaflets overprinted with the ace
of spades as an omen of death (Fig 4.6). In some cases
actual playing cards were left along trails in Communist-
controlled territory (American troops wrote to playing
card manufacturers requesting numerous aces of spades to
supplement the campaign). A subsequent review and
evaluation by the USIA revealed, however, that the ace of
spades was not included in the Vietnamese deck of
cards. Thus, except for a few Montagnard hill tribesmen,
they were unfamiliar with its meaning as a death omen.
Despite these findings and a JUSPAO policy directive
prohibiting the ace of spades practice, American soldiers
began using the technique again in 1971. This repeated
error probably was symptomatic of problems in trying to
maintain continuity and high-quality psychological
operations with military persons being shuffled into and
out of the country on one-year tours of duty.[7]
    Another attempt to reinforce the enemy's fear of
death that went awry was the use of brutally macabre
leaflets (Figs 4.7, 4.8). Photographs and sketches of "a
head torn from a body, a mass grave, or a skull roasting
in flames" were used to scare Communist troops into
giving up. Others depicted battlefield dead with flies
crawling over them and grotesque corpses with twisted
limbs showing advanced stages of rigor mortis. As early
as 1967, however, it became evident that these appeals
failed to impress the enemy and had little effect on
their decision to rally. In fact, a reverse or
"boomerang" effect resulted from the use of such
leaflets; many hoi chanh felt that these grisly pictures
reflected unfavorably on the Republic because the
government seemed to be gloating over the deaths of
fellow Vietnamese. Appeals to "brotherly love" and "the
happiness of being with one's family" were much more
potent than "rally or die" themes.[8]
    Despite the "boomerang" phenomenon of gruesome
leaflets, the American propaganda machine continued to
crank them out in large numbers. It appears evident that
MACV and, to a lesser extent, JUSPAO went overboard with
death topics. In some cases, they may well have
unwittingly reinforced Communist allegations testifying
to the callousness of the Saigon government.
Nonetheless, "fear" of being killed was a primary
psychological vulnerability among the Communist armed
forces. Death themes were repeated over and over in
virtually all enemy-oriented communications; they enjoyed
substantial success in motivating many defections and
surrenders, especially when used in combination with
messages exploiting other anxieties of the besieged
soldiers.
    The second major appeal was developed when it came
to light that many quit the enemy ranks because of the
severe hardships they suffered in the jungles.

Figure 4.6
Ace of Spades as a Death Omen

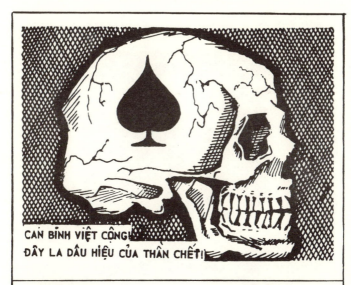

CAN BINH VIỆT CỘNG!
ĐÂY LA DẤU HIỆU CỦA THÂN CHẾT!

CÒN TIẾP TỤC CHIẾN ĐẤU CHỐNG LẠI CHÁNH NGHĨA QUỐC
GIA, CÁC BẠN CHẮC CHẮN SẼ BỊ CHẾT THỀ THẢM NHƯ THỀ
NÀY !!   246-362

VIET CONG! THIS IS A SIGN OF DEATH!
Continue your struggle against the National Cause and you will
surely die a mournful death like this!

Source: U.S., MACV, 246th Psychological Operations Company, <u>Leaflet
Catalogue</u>, leaflet number 362.

Figure 4.7
Macabre Death Scene

TRUNG-TƯỚNG TRẦN-ĐỘ

SỐNG TẠI MIỀN BẮC

CHẾT TẠI MIỀN NAM

The Republic of Vietnam Armed Forces have completely crushed the Viet Cong's general offensive against the cities.

From 30 January 1968 to 15 February 1968, over 34,000 North Vietnamese Regulars and Viet Cong soldiers paid for their crimes. Among them was Major General Tran Do, who was killed in an action at 46th Street in Cholon on the outskirts of the Saigon city.

The death of Tran Do . . . proved that the Communist aggressive policy to take over South Vietnam has severely failed. It was not their inability or incompetence, but the Communist adventurous acts that caused their deaths.

Then why do you still hesitate? Try to find opportunities to return to the National community and rejoin your families, as tens of thousands of other soldiers did.

Source: U.S., JUSPAO, leaflet number 2448.

Figure 4.8
Fear of Being Killed

Các bạn sẽ được giúp đỡ
ĐỂ LÀM LẠI CUỘC ĐỜI

YOU WILL BE HELPED TO REBUILD YOUR LIFE

Your leaders keep telling you that you have killed many
soldiers of the Republic of Vietnam and its Allies. Your leaders
will deceive you, but your own eyes will not. In the battles in
which you have fought, did you not mostly see the bodies of your
dead comrades? Today you have far fewer comrades than before, and
after the next battle you will have even fewer.

You have fought long and hard, but you must know by now that
you have been misled by your leaders. . . . You are fighting for a
dangerous and losing cause and against your own people. You will
lose.

The Government of Vietnam soldiers do not wish to kill you or
imprison you. They want only to give you a chance to live as a
Vietnamese, with your Vietnamese brothers, in a land of peace, the
free South Vietnam. If you will come in voluntarily . . . you will
have the great satisfaction of knowing you are with the Right Cause.

Source: U.S., JUSPAO, leaflet number 2744.

Psychological exploitation of these adversities and of
the soldiers' loneliness often had a significant
impact. American propagandists attempted to profit from
these mental vulnerabilities by informing the Communist
troops that Saigon was aware of their hardships, was
sympathetic, and wished to provide them a means of escape
from the severity of their life through the Chieu Hoi
Program. The enemy fighters were reminded of their
loneliness and homesickness, of night marches and being
constantly on the move, of poor living and sleeping
conditions, insufficient and low-quality food, and
disease, compounded by frequent shortages of medical
supplies and services -- "Are you sick? Have you been
wounded? Are you one of those who might die horribly and
alone?" "We know the hardships you face. . . . Every
day you are closer to a lonely death far from home -- far
from your ancestors. What a shameful way to die.
LISTEN! You can stay alive. Surrender and you will be
well treated," they were told. As a former Viet Cong
explained the effect of such loudspeaker appeals: "One
time it was raining. The broadcast said, 'It is raining
and you must be cold. . . .' I was in the hospital and
the patients . . . said, 'That s.o.b., he even knows were
are cold!'"[9] (Figs 4.9, 4.10, 4.11).

Some leaflets reproduced nostalgic writings found in
the personal effects of dead soldiers, and added an
appropriate punchline. The following lines, for example,
were allegedly recorded in a North Vietnamese platoon
leader's diary in 1971:

I am entering these lines in my diary on the
first day of my 30th spring. Yes, spring is
here, and what is there to enjoy this year?
Nothing. Nothing at all except the feeling of
loneliness and longing for my sweet, young wife
and for my innocent children who are anxiously
waiting at home for my return. Besides this,
there is also my survival after six years of
absence during which I've experienced
everything, and undergone every trial. Oh, yes,
spring is here, and yet, where is the
traditional peach blossom branch, the birds'
songs and the feminine voice? Their absence
makes the bank of this small waterfall all the
more deserted and silent. Meanwhile death is at
any moment waiting at the next corner. . . .
Spring is here, and yet we have not one second
of rest.

Obviously the suffering of the Viet Cong and North
Vietnamese soldier varied in intensity, depending on
location and time. Yet Americans continued the wide use
of preprinted and prerecorded general hardship appeals

Figure 4.9
Loneliness of Viet Cong Soldiers

GIỜ CHƯA PHẢI LÚC TRỞ VỀ VỚI GIA ĐÌNH SAO ?
ANH CHỌN CẢNH NÀO TRÊN NÀY ?

REMEMBER YOU

I sadly remember you day and night,
You are alone with blanket and pillow, because of whom?
In the jungle I lead the gloomy life,
Facing rain, sun and racking hunger.
The more I think of it the more I hate,
Who spread the smoke and fire to interrupt the melody?
When can we meet again,
With you lying on my arm to reward the days of nostalgia?
And we get drunk with the wine of love,
To see happiness come true in our loving arms.

The Viet Cong cadre who wrote these
verses was killed on October 10, 1966
at Chu Lai.

Source: U.S., JUSPAO, leaflet number SP-1517

Figure 4.10
Thinking of Family in the North

While sitting by yourself in the heart of the forest did it ever occur to you to think that:

    -- Your old parents will soon leave this world. Day and night they long for you, praying to God that you may be in good health, and that you may be spared danger so you can return and see them again one more time before they die.

    -- Your young children play around frivolously for lack of their father's care and guidance.

    -- Your wife is feeling sorry for herself and feels resentment each time she looks at her friends who have a happier married life by their husband's and children's side.

    --What has become of your family life? Isn't it on the verge of collapse only because of you - because of the uncertainty about your death or survival? Did it ever occur to you that your life is in great danger and that you will called upon to bear unsurmountable hardships until the day you will be sacrificed to no purpose like so many others? What are you waiting for? Heed this appeal and report to the Government of Vietnam forces, for this is the only way for you to return to your family once the war ends.

Source: U.S. JUSPAO, leaflet number 4385.

Figure 4.11
Leaflets-at-a-Glance

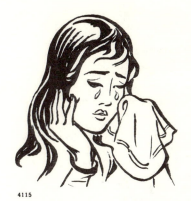

ANH ƠI! NƯỚC MẮT TRÀN TRỀ, BAO GIỜ RỜI CỘNG ANH VỀ CÙNG EM ?

4115

DARLING! MY EYES ARE FLOODED WITH TEARS, WHEN WILL YOU LEAVE
THE COMMUNISTS AND RETURN HOME?

Source: U.S., JUSPAO, leaflet number 4115. This variation of the
standard leaflet was employed in an attempt to counter orders by
enemy cadres forbidding Communist soldiers from picking up leaflets
to read them. The idea behind "Leaflets-at-a-Glance" was to drop
leaflets in enemy-controlled areas with short messages in bold type
large enough to be read while it lay on the ground.

throughout the war, regardless of the actual situation.
It is safe to assume that many of the messages airdropped
or broadcast to Communist troops enduring severe troubles
had the desired effect. It is equally likely that
several of these communications reached well-fed and
sheltered enemy audiences. Whether such mis-targeted
blandishments produced desired or counterproductive
effects is one of the many imponderables of the
propaganda campaign.

A third major appeal dealing with Chieu Hoi and
surrender inducements was the loss of faith in Communist
victory experienced by several among the enemy ranks.
This approach was based on the premise that the
Confucian, harmony-oriented Viet Cong and North
Vietnamese trooper would be more apt to lay down his arms
once he became convinced the Republic would win the
struggle. Supporting themes showed the Communist cause
as doomed. Primary emphasis was given to their losses on
the battlefield -- "How many defeats have you suffered
lately?" Another major technique was the "bandwagon
appeal" -- citing the number who had already rallied and
using the personal testimonials of hoi chanh in leaflets
and loudspeaker broadcasts. As one rallier implored the
Viet Cong in 1966, "You cannot continue to fight in this
immoral war. Follow my example and 90,000 others of your
former comrades and find an honorable escape." Some
leaflets were prepared in letter form; a previous Viet
Cong cadre wrote to four friends serving the National
Liberation Front:

> Dear Bay Sa, Tu Binh, Nam Be, Sau Tu: My name
> is Dao Van Ba. . . . I rallied on May 19th
> 1967. I would like to tell you that I'm very
> well and happy. I'm having a joyful life and
> have seen my relatives here. They're having a
> comfortable life. I feel very safe; not as I
> feared. I mean, I was not sent to jail or
> beaten as I had thought. I am sending this
> letter to you now and hope that I'll see you
> all in this free land of the government of
> Vietnam.

Photographs of massed government and Allied weapons
were used to reinforce the impression of ultimate victory
by the Republic -- "The Government forces are winning.
Their firepower is overwhelming. Their resources are
inexhaustible." Another primary topic was the amount of
aid other nations had given the South Vietnamese, thus
making them even more formidable -- "Having the
wholehearted support of the peace-loving countries of the
world, we will surely win. Communists will surely be
defeated" (Figs 4.12, 4.13). After 1969 the attempt to
improve the image of Saigon's armed forces became more

Figure 4.12
Government Forces Defeat the Communists

Các chiến sĩ Quân-Lực Việt-Nam
Cộng-Hòa bảo vệ đồng bào

Cán binh Việt-Cộng bị cấp chỉ huy phản
bội, đẩy vào chỗ chết hơn 30.000 mạng.
\\\\\\\ —— ///////
Hỡi các cán binh Việt-Cộng !!!
Các anh còn đủ thì giờ trở về với
chính phủ Việt-Nam Cộng-Hòa là một
chính phủ của dân và vì dân để phục
vụ cho hòa bình, nhân đạo và phồn
vinh của Tổ-Quốc và để cứu lấy sinh
mạng của chính các anh.

(Photograph: Dead enemy soldiers)
These Viet Cong soldiers, betrayed by their leaders, were sent to a
senseless death with over 30,000 more of their comrades.

(Photograph: ARVN soldiers in combat)
These soldiers of the Armed Forces of the Republic of Vietnam defend
the people of South Vietnam.
You may still rally to the People's Government of the Republic
of Vietnam to work for a worthy cause and save your own life.

Source: U.S., JUSPAO, leaflet number 2430.

Figure 4.13
Worldwide Support for the Government

TÌNH THƯƠNG KHÔNG BIÊN GIỚI

HOA KỲ, MỘT TRONG SỐ 31
QUỐC GIA ĐÃ VIỆN TRỢ CHO VNCH

Người Cộng Sản có dám khẳng định rằng
đây là một "hình thức xâm lược" của người
nữ y tá Hoa Kỳ này hay chăng?

BA TƯ
MỘT TRONG SỐ 31
QUỐC GIA VIỆN TRỢ CHO VNCH

Ba Tư là một nước ở miền Trung Đông
cũng tích cực giúp đỡ nạn nhân Cộng Sản
ở miền Nam Việt-Nam.
Đoàn giải phẫu Ba Tư đang làm việc
tại một bệnh viện ở Việt Nam Cộng Hòa.

2732

America, one of 31 countries which have provided assistance for
the Republic of Vietnam. Dare the Communists declare that this is a
"kind of aggression" of this American nurse?
Iran is a country in the Middle East which is also actively
helping the victims of Communism in South Vietnam. Iranian surgical
team working in a hospital in the Republic of Vietnam. Iran, one of
31 countries which have provided assistance for the Republic of
Vietnam.

Source: U.S., JUSPAO, leaflet number 2732.

important prior to the American withdrawal. The
intention was to show the "troop replacement" as the
result of the presence of a well-armed, trained, and
disciplined military that had the support of the people
-- "Now, because the Army of Vietnam is mature, fully
experienced and equipped with superior weapons, it is
able to take the struggle against the Viet Cong upon
itself. That is why the U.S. soldiers are returning to
their homes."

To underline the "loss of faith" appeal, the
invasions of Cambodia in April 1970 and Laos in February
1971 were the subjects of special campaigns aimed
primarily at the Northern soldiers in those areas.
Messages dealing with the Cambodian incursion were tied
closely to already existing appeals, but the Communist
situation was said to be even more hopeless than before
because of the loss of their sanctuaries -- "By land, air
and sea the mighty forces of South Vietnam have come to
destroy your caches. Rally now and save your lives." In
the face of the changed circumstances the soldier's only
logical escape from death was depicted as defection or
surrender -- "The fate of an unmarked grave on Cambodian
soil, of preying jungle beasts, await your dying breath"
(Fig 4.14).

Although significantly less successful militarily
than the Cambodian foray, the invasion of Laos provided
many similar messages. Often the attacks were described
as a logical step following the success of the operations
in Cambodia. The situation of the enemy was shown as
greatly worsened because their supply lines and
sanctuaries in Laos had been lost. The chances of
returning home to the North were described as very risky
and bleak because the South Vietnamese Army was blocking
the Ho Chi Minh Trail (Fig 4.15). One leaflet exclaimed:

> Viet Cong and North Vietnamese Troops!
> Sihanoukville port in Cambodia is no longer
> available for bringing supplies to you. The Ho
> Chi Minh Trail has been completely cut off by
> the Republic of Viet-Nam Armed Forces. You are
> isolated and are in a FISH-ON-THE-CHOPPING-
> BLOCK situation. Certainly you know it! . . .
> You have only one road: Report to the Army of
> the Republic of Viet-Nam.

To counter any "loss of faith" in victory, the Viet
Cong conducted vigorous political indoctrination among
their troops. In 1966 a "Top Secret" resolution of the
Saigon Military Region Committee outlined a dynamic
counterpropaganda program: "Our cadre and soldiers were
demoralized. A number of them were influenced by the
Chieu Hoi policy. . . . We must unmask the enemy's
deceitful propaganda, brief cadre on the general

Figure 4.14
Cambodia Incursion

Tình bạn chiến đấu, tình quân dân thắm thiết giữa
hai quốc gia Việt Nam Cộng Hòa và Kampuchia.   4011

CADRE AND SOLDIERS OF THE NORTH VIETNAMESE REGULAR ARMY:
   Comradeship-In-Arms Creates Deep Friendship Between The
   Two Nations of Cambodia and the Republic of Vietnam.
   In order to withstand an invasion by the North Vietnam
Communists, at the request of the Cambodian government, the Army of
the Republic of Vietnam and Cambodian forces fought and are fighting
side by side to annihilate the North Vietnamese Communist invaders
for the defense and freedom and independence of the Cambodian
people.
   This Army-People friendship is solidified by the warm welcome
of the Republic of Vietnam soldiers by the Cambodian people and this
has created the deepest friendship between the two nations. . . .
   Whereas in South Vietnam the Communist Cadre spread the
propaganda that "One must fight for National Salvation." Then in
Cambodia for whom do you fight? Is it not the stupid aggressive act
of Red China and North Vietnam collectively?

Source: U.S., JUSPAO, leaflet number 4011.

Figure 4.15
Invasion of Laos

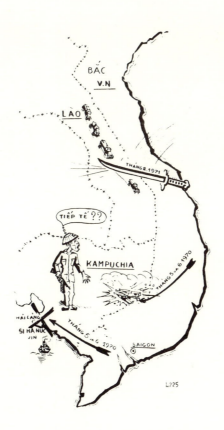

Since May 1970 the Communist sanctuaries have been destroyed and the Sihanoukville seaport has ceased to bring you supplies and equipment. You have been fighting in Cambodia for many months without enough supplies. Because of these shortages, Communist forces have suffered one defeat after another.

Now the Republic of Vietnam Armed Forces are raiding the Communist's last remaining supply route through southern Laos. Your situation will become worse and worse. If you continue to fight, you will die for an increasingly hopeless cause. Therefore, find a way to return to the Government of the Republic of Vietnam.

Source: U.S., JUSPAO, leaflet number 4225.

situation and help them evaluate the enemy and friendly
situations so that they clearly see our victories and the
coming enemy collapse."[10] A "Confidential" document
defined further countermeasures: "In the struggle
against the enemy psychological warfare and 'Chieu Hoi'
activities, the ideological leadership must be highly
emphasized, especially when the unit encounters much
hardship and difficulty in combat and the performance of
missions, or when the fight between ourselves and the
enemy becomes fierce or the unit sustains great
casualties after a battle."[11]

"Loss of faith" themes were very convincing.
Personal entreaties by ralliers in leaflets and
loudspeaker broadcasts were keys to its success. As the
intensity of fighting increased and Viet Cong defeats
multiplied, Chieu Hoi opened a way for divorce from the
side that appeared to be losing.

The fourth major appeal, concern for family, was one
of the most emotionally charged and effective propaganda
approaches used -- "Your family needs you now and is
waiting for you. You must live and not die
senselessly." Nostalgia, loneliness, and the desire to
return to home and loved ones were among the primary
factors motivating Communist soldiers to defect or
surrender. Many were concerned about the hardships their
families suffered due to the absence of the major
breadwinner. One leaflet asked, "What is happening to
your family how that you are hiding in the unhealthy
jungles? What will it do to your loved ones when you die
far away from your native home and are buried in an
unmarked grave?" Sketches of home life, with a husband,
or son missing, and poetry had potent effects -- "Only
through the Chieu Hoi policy will you bring unity to your
family" (Figs 4.16, 4.17). On an American loudspeaker
tape, a young boy's plaintive voice asked:

> "Daddy! Daddy! Where are you now? Are you
> fine, Daddy? Mommy is always thinking of you,
> and the family has been talking about you. All
> of us have been worrying about you. Daddy!
> Why don't you come back to dissipate our
> sadness? Mommy cries all the time, longing for
> you, Daddy. Come back to us, come back to us,
> Daddy."

These supplications often had the desired effect.
As one Viet Cong prisoner described his feelings: "When
I read the leaflets, I thought their message fitted the
situation I was in. . . . They said that our wives had
to toil day and night in order to support the children,
and, therefore, they appealed to us to return to our
homes and assume roles of supporter of the family. . . .
I was very touched by the leaflets' message . . . I

Figure 4.16
Family Hardships

Hãy trở về với gia đình !
Họ đang nhớ thương và cần đến bạn .

COMPATRIOTS: COME HOME!

    Your family needs you. They fear for your health and
welfare. They know you will die if you do not heed their plea. The
Government also wants you to come home. Contact the nearest
Government of Vietnam soldiers and officials. You will be well
treated, and both you and your family will be helped as soon as you
return to the Just Cause.

                    DON'T DELAY. COME HOME!
        RETURN TO YOUR FAMILY
        THEY MISS YOU AND NEED YOU.

_____

Source: U.S., JUSPAO, leaflet number SP-927.

Figure 4.17
Concern About Families

CHIÊU HỒI THẬT SỰ
CÓ NGHĨA GÌ ?

Chiêu Hồi có nghĩa là được sum
họp lại với những người thân
yêu và thoát khỏi cảnh cô-độc
ghê gớm...

SP-1252 A

WHAT DOES CHIEU HOI REALLY MEAN?

Chieu Hoi means being united with your loved ones. It means escape
from a terrible loneliness. . . . Chieu Hoi means friendship and a
chance to serve the fatherland.

Source: U.S., JUSPAO, leaflet number SP-1252A.

missed my family very much. . . . I think that everyone
believed the leaflets, and generally every one of us
tried to desert and go over to the Government of
Vietnam."[12]

Nonetheless, some potential defectors were reluctant
to rally for fear of Communist reprisals against their
loved ones. To resolve this dilemma, American
psychological operations tried to persuade their families
living in Viet Cong and contested areas to move into
government-controlled regions where they would be safe
from military activities and would enjoy the benefits
offered refugees. At the reception centers, efforts were
made to convince these displaced persons to induce
relatives serving the Viet Cong to rally and join them in
the "safe" government zones. Simultaneously,
psychological messages beseeched the Viet Cong soldier to
evacuate his family from areas threatened by combat
actions; and, once they were free from possible
retaliation, to join them through the Chieu Hoi Program
-- "Rally to the government and you will be given job
training and money. You will be able to move your family
to a safe areas. Think of your family's future and Chieu
Hoi." Female voices emanating from loudspeaker tapes
implored them to make their decision before it was too
late:

> "YOUR FAMILY IS IN DANGER IF IT IS LIVING IN
> VIET CONG-CONTROLLED TERRITORY!!! As the war
> rages over these areas there is no way of
> protecting your children, women, and elders.
> BUT THEY CAN BE MADE SAFE. Move them into free
> Government-controlled territory. After they
> have moved, use your National Safe Conduct Pass
> to join them under the Government's Open Arms
> Program, and YOUR FAMILY WILL BE SAFE."

This approach appears to be a circuitous route to
eliciting defection, but from all reports it was quite
successful. An added benefit was that because families
moved out of enemy and contested areas, Communists were
denied food, logistical support, and intelligence.

The "concern for family" messages addressed to
Hanoi's soldiers in the South were similar to those aimed
at the Viet Cong. In addition, the bombing of North
Vietnam was explained as being necessary to end the
war. Assurances were given that only military targets
were being attacked, but such avowals doubtlessly
heightened more that eased the soldiers' worries.

Finally, the disillusionment appeal was based on the
premise that the individual soldier might be able to
withstand the fears and hardships of the struggle as long
as he was convinced of the justness of Hanoi's aims, but
when he became skeptical of these goals, he would be more

prone to defect or surrender. This approach in many ways became the psychological coup de grace of American propaganda. Nagged by the constant threat of death, severities of life, and family concerns, the soldier suddenly was confronted with allegations that he had been duped and was being used by his leaders. One rallier, for example, asked his former comrades in a loudspeaker broadcast, "How can you blindly follow the distorted, demagogic propaganda of those who worship Communism and who capitalize on your blood and bones to achieve their personal purposes? If you want to live an adequate and happy life with your families, try to escape from these bloodthirsty people and rally to the Republic of Vietnam Government." Constrasting Hanoi's propaganda with the reality of widespread destruction and deaths of their compatriots in the South, some fighters were able to discern specific incongruities. The result was that many increasingly questioned their cadres' explanations. "Believe in what you have seen, but not the false statements by your leaders," one leaflet cautioned.

American psychological operations aimed at hammering as wide a wedge as possible between the Communist leadership and its followers -- "Do not allow the Party to drive you to your death to satisfy its unquenchable thirst for conquest." A leaflet produced in 1970, entitled "Stooges on a String," claimed:

> Since the day they took rein of North Vietnam, the Government . . . has acted as marionettes on a string for the Communists. They do not care about the interests of the Nation and its people. They care only about their own interests and those of their Communist masters. The Hanoi Government is completely dependent on its Russian/Chinese masters and cannot stand alone. The people of the North have become servants to the Communist stooges. . . . The enemies of the Fatherland are the very Communist leaders who are pushing you into this fratricidal war with the intent to make all Vietnam part of the Communist bloc. You must overthrow them in order to be the true fighters for Freedom, and a Democratic and Independent Vietnam.

Allegations of lies and betrayal were consistent themes -- "Your leaders have deceived you. To follow them will only lead you to a lonely death far from your home, your family, your ancestors" (Figs 4.18, 4.19). Ho Chi Minh's 1966 "Protracted War Thesis" of continuing the war as long as necessary to achieve victory was exploited in propaganda that showed the soldiers fighting a hopeless struggle in which the only prospects were

Figure 4.18
Betrayal by Communist Leaders

(Drawing depicting Communist political cadre): "According to the Party, the enemy's been defeated everywhere. Millions of enemy soldiers have been killed. Yet, why, after sending his troops into Cambodia, is he sending battalions and battalions of soldiers into Laos? We are being routed everywhere. What am I going to say to the comrade troopers now?"

The Party is always adversizing: "We've dealt deadly blows on the enemy," or, "The enemy is agonizing on his bed," or, "We've won, and the enemy is defeated." However, side by side with that, the Party is always repeating like a parrot: "However, the enemy is extremely perfidious, obstinate; he will not drop his dark plot of aggression, etc. . . ." And always concludes: "We have to carry on a long resistance and fight until final victory." . . . If the enemy is "agonizing on his bed," why are the Communists being harassed on the South Vietnam and Cambodian battlefields, and recently in Laos?

THE PARTY'S LOGIC IS PURE AND SIMPLE NONSENSE!

Source: U.S., JUSPAO, leaflet number 4229.

Figure 4.19
Communist Terrorism

 Hãy trở về với Đại Gia đình Dân Tộc để
được đón tiếp trong tình thương chân thành

DO YOU WANT TO EXTERMINATE THE VIET RACE?

The Government of the Republic of Vietnam has protested to the
International Committee of the Red Cross over the indiscriminate
rocket and mortar attacks on the Saigon area, calling these attacks
"deliberate genocide". . . .
Your leaders claim that they fire at military installations
only. The fact is only one soldier had died as a result of these
attacks. Most of the victims have been Vietnamese women and
children. . . .
Ask yourself this question: How much longer can you, as a
member of our race, continue to support the bloody murderers of our
own women and children?
You had better quit supporting this horrible people-destroying
activity and rejoin the Viet race, by coming in to our Government
under the Chieu Hoi Program. You will be received in people's love.

Source: U.S., JUSPAO, leaflet number 2742.

deprivation, family separation, and death: "If Uncle Ho has his way, will you ever see your child again? Will there ever be peace?" "Remember the fate of Mongolians in the thirteenth century? Do you wish your bones to rest far from home as theirs? Are you surprised free Vietnamese soldiers fight beside friendly foreign soldiers to help turn back you invaders? Refuse to die here . . . surrender!" In another case, after the Communist's 1968 Tet Offensive, enemy troops were told: "The cause you once thought noble has been betrayed! You are now fighting a war of aggression directed against the people. You are simply being used!"

A variation of the "disillusionment" appeal was initiated in March 1968 -- following President Johnson's offer to halt the bombing of North Vietnam -- to exploit the possibility of peace. Intelligence reports brought to light mounting concern by Viet Cong and North Vietnamese commanders about the likelihood of their troops becoming infected with "peace illusions" ("Ao tuong hoa binh"). They felt the soldiers' "fighting energy" or "fighting determination" might be sapped by the mistaken belief that the war could be settled through negotiations rather than on the battlefield.

The U.S. "peace" barrage highlighted the futility of dying when a truce is at hand, and rallying or surrendering as a way to ensure staying alive until the suspension of hostilities: "Peace is in sight, it could be so near. Ho Chi Minh says he has agreed to initial talks. Why die in the final days of the war? Soon you may be able to return to the North when peace is achieved or join the Chieu Hoi Program."[13]

American propaganda asserted that the accommodating proposals by South Vietnam's President Thieu would end the fighting and bring unity; President Nixon's peace overtures were said to reveal that only the Party in Hanoi stood in the way of a ceasefire and thus between the soldier's life and death. Finally, the U.S. and the People's Republic of China were shown as seeking a dialogue between them to bring peace to Vietnam. This last theme was used after Nixon's 1972 visits to Peking and Moscow in an attempt to isolate the Northern leadership, picturing it as the only group willing to continue the war and the accompanying death and destruction -- "American troops are withdrawing from Vietnam but the Party is urging you to continue fighting. Who are you fighting now? Your brothers of South Vietnam? Is that the 'Just Cause' advertized by the Party?" (Figs 4.20, 4.21, 4.22).

SPECIAL CAMPAIGNS AND TECHNIQUES

In addition to the general program centering around the five major psychological appeals, JUSPAO conducted

Figure 4.20
U.S. Proposal for a Wider Peace Conference

HOA KỲ ĐỀ NGHỊ MỘT HỘI NGHỊ MỞ RỘNG VỀ HÒA BÌNH

Ngày 7 tháng 10, 1970 Tổng Thống Nixon đã tuyên bố :

Tôi đề nghị triệu tập một hội nghị hòa bình Đông Dương. Tại cuộc hội đàm Ba Lê hiện nay, chúng ta mới đương hội đàm về Việt Nam mà thôi. Nhưng quân đội Bắc Việt vẫn tiếp tục thực hiện cuộc xâm lăng tại Lào cũng như tại Kampuchea.

Một hội nghị quốc tế là cần thiết để giải quyết cuộc xung đột tại tất cả ba quốc gia thuộc Đông Dương.

Những yếu tố cốt yếu của Hiệp Định Genève 1954 và 1962 vẫn có giá trị như căn bản của việc giải quyết những vấn đề giữa những quốc gia đó tại khu vực Đông Dương. Chúng ta chấp nhận kết quả của những thỏa hiệp đạt được giữa những quốc gia đó. 4068

On October 7, 1970, President Nixon said:

I propose an Indochina peace conference. At the Paris talks, we are talking only about Vietnam. But North Vietnamese troops are carrying on their aggression in Laos and Cambodia as well.

An international conference is needed to deal with the conflict in all three states of Indochina.

The essential elements of the Geneva accords of 1954 and 1956 remain valid as a basis for settlement of problems between states in Indochina. We shall accept the results of agreements reached between those states. . . .

Source: U.S., JUSPAO, leaflet number 4068.

Figure 4.21
Why Has the Party Rejected Peace?

On January 26, 1972, South Vietnam President Nguyen Van Thieu
proposed a comprehensive plan designed to bring a true and lasting
peace not only to Vietnam but also to Laos and Cambodia. . . .
    Yet the Party has rejected these proposals. It has rejected
Peace because it is interested only in conquest, in the subjugation
of the peoples of Indochina. It has decided that you, soldiers of
the North Vietnamese Army, will continue this horrible fratricidal
war, to cause death and destruction throughout Indochina, and to die
yourselves in the name of CONQUEST instead of PEACE.
    Ask yourselves why the Party is so adamantly opposed to
bringing peace to Vietnam? Why has it chosen to betray the desires
for Peace of the majority of the people in North and South Vietnam,
Laos and Cambodia? . . .

Source: U.S., JUSPAO, leaflet number 4483.

Figure 4.22
President Nixon's Visit to Peking

**MỘT CUỘC GẶP GỞ
LỊCH SỬ**

Mao trạch Đông, Chủ Tịch
Cộng Đảng Trung Hoa
thân mật bắt tay chào
mừng Tổng Thống Hoa Kỳ
Nixon khi đôi bên gặp
nhau trong buổi tiếp kiến
tại tư dinh họ Mao ở Bắc
Kinh ngày 21 tháng 2 năm
1972.   4485

A HISTORIC MEETING

Chinese Communist Chairman, Mao Tse-tung, receives U.S. President
Nixon in Peking. The two Chiefs of State exchange a friendly
handshake at their meeting in Mao's palace on 21 February 1972.

Source: U.S., JUSPAO, leaflet number 4485.

four special campaigns to support the Chieu Hoi bid. One
was distribution of safe conduct leaflets. Billions of
these official passes guaranteeing humane treatment upon
defection or surrender were scattered over the
countryside. A standard certification was used; it was
slightly altered in 1967 to include the flags of Thailand
and the Philippines as new Allies. In addition, the
serial number on the old version was dropped in favor of
President Thieu's signature and photograph as evidence of
official sanction for the safe conduct invitation (Fig
4.23). This use of a single, officially approved pass
avoided the complications experienced during the Korean
War where six different surrender certificates created
confusion among enemy soldiers who were unsure which was
genuine (In his excellent history of wartime leaflet
operations, Carl Berger cites an example of a man who
surrendered in Korea with several different safe conduct
passes in his possession; he said he didn't give up
earlier because he thought he needed the latest
edition).[14]

Both Viet Cong and North Vietnamese defectors and
prisoners gave Saigon's safe conduct pass high
credibility. Many cited it as an influential element in
their decision to lay down their arms. On the other
hand, several enemy soldiers believed a pass was needed
to ensure good treatment. A former civilian member of
the National Liberation Front reflected this outlook in
an interview: "When I was thinking about leaving the
Front I concluded that these safe conduct passes could
serve as a substitute for the GVN ID cards as a method of
identifying myself. . . . But when I fled, I didn't have
a safe conduct pass and I just had to take my chances."[15]

By 1969 American propagandists undertook measures to
counter this belief. Recognizing that the actual
presence of a leaflet gave a would-be defector added
courage to rally, they began to include the following
information in some Chieu Hoi messages: "You do not need
a safe conduct pass to rally, you may use this leaflet,
or any leaflet for safe conduct." It is doubtful,
however, that this suggestion was successful because of
the emphasis placed on the certificate as a means of
defection during the early years of the war. In any
case, the Vietnam experience proved once again the
usefulness of the safe conduct pass as a complement to
modern warfare.

Another special technique of the Chieu Hoi Program
was the "Rewards Campaign," which offered enemy soldiers
money for turning weapons over to Saigon when they
rallied. Leaflets and broadcasts instructed the
Communist troops to hide their arms before rallying and
promised remuneration when they were retrieved later by
the hoi chanh and government soldiers. Furthermore, a
bonus was offered to defectors who revealed the location

Figure 4.23
Safe Conduct Pass

SAFE-CONDUCT PASS TO BE HONORED BY ALL VIETNAMESE GOVERNMENT AGENCIES AND ALLIED FORCES

이 안전보장패쓰는 월남정부와 모든 연합군에 의해 인정된 것입니다.

รัฐบาลเวียตนามและหน่วยพันธมิตร ยินดีให้เกียรติแก่ผู้ถือบัตรผ่านปลอดภัยนี้.

SAFE-CONDUCT PASS TO BE HONORED BY ALL VIETNAMESE GOVERNMENT AGENCIES AND ALLIED FORCES

MANG TẤM GIẤY
THÔNG HÀNH
nầy về cộng tác
với Chánh Phủ
Quốc Gia các bạn
sẽ được :
● Đón tiếp tử tế
● Bảo đảm an ninh
● Đải ngộ tương xứng

NGUYỄN VĂN THIỆU
Tổng Thống Việt Nam Cộng Hoà

TẤM GIẤY THÔNG HÀNH NẦY CÓ GIÁ TRỊ VỚI TẤT CẢ CƠ - QUAN
QUÂN CHÍNH VIỆT - NAM CỘNG - HÒA VÀ LỰC - LƯỢNG ĐỒNG - MINH.

SAFE CONDUCT PASS

Return and cooperate with the Government of Vietnam with this Safe
Conduct Pass, you will be:
-- Warmly welcomed.
-- Your personal safety is guaranteed.
- Well treated.
SAFE CONDUCT PASS TO BE HONORED BY ALL VIETNAMESE GOVERNMENT
AGENCIES AND ALLIED FORCES

Source: U.S., JUSPAO, leaflet number 893B.

of Viet Cong arsenals and weapons caches -- "The government will pay you for the weapons you bring with you and will also pay you for all hidden weapons which you point out to the authorities" (Fig 4.24).
 This offer produced some amazing results. One hoi chanh contrived an ingenious scheme after reading leaflets and hearing loudspeaker broadcasts about the rewards: one night, as his squad went from door to door gathering rice in a hamlet, he gathered their weapons and rallied. Another good find occurred when a South Vietnamese unit, following a hoi chanh's directions to an arms cache location, instead found a Viet Cong base camp, including a large quantity of explosives and bomb-making supplies.
 In addition, the Republic offered up to $11,000 to any North Vietnamese who rallied with aircraft, ships, tanks, and similar weapons. There are no reports of any takers.
 A further overture was made to any person who would persuade members of the Viet Cong to rally. The monetary rewards, paid within three days of defection, were based on the rank of the hoi chanh -- from $25 for a lower-level soldier to $2,100 for a political commissar. Special bounties were offered to enemy troops who came in with at least two thirds of the members defected together (Figs 4.25, 4.26). These short-term, third-party rewards schemes were an immediate success and were extended through 1969. The official reason given for the eventual termination of these programs, financially supported by CORDS, was that the "South Vietnamese Government . . . considers inducement a civic responsibility that should be undertaken for reasons other than monetary gains."[16] However, the real reason for American withdrawal of funding may have been abuses said to be prevalent in the awarding of monies.
 A third special campaign carried out to support the Chieu Hoi Program was waged annually during Tet, the Vietnamese New Year. It exploited the soldiers' strong yearnings to return home, for Tet is an extremely sacred and sentimental time to renew memories, take part in family gatherings, and settle spiritual accounts. During the three- to seven-day holiday period, Vietnamese custom calls for paying social calls, exchanging gifts, wearing new clothes, and easing special foods. The central celebration of the New Year is the family festival, when all kinsmen gather to worship before the family altar, venerating their ancestors. An atmosphere of close communion prevails, and the spirits of forebearers are believed to be present.
 These Tet traditions heightened nostalgia, loneliness, and yearnings for loved ones among the enemy armed forces -- "Tet will lack its meaning and your family will be sad if you are not home." The holiday

Figure 4.24
Weapons Rewards Program

Figure 4.24 (continued)

THE GOVERNMENT WILL PAY YOU FOR THE WEAPONS YOU BRING WITH YOU AND
WILL ALSO PAY YOU FOR ALL HIDDEN WEAPONS WHICH YOU POINT OUT TO THE
AUTHORITIES

REWARD	WEAPON
1,200$	- Pistol, all types
3,000$	- Rifle, all types
5,000$	- Submachine-gun, all types
7,500$	- Automatic rifle, all types
17,000$	- Machine-gun, 7.62 mm
20,000$	- Machine-gun, 12.7 mm
50,000$	- Mortar or mortar barrel, 60 mm
60,000$	- Mortar or mortar barrel, 81/82 mm
75,000$	- Mortar or mortar barrel, 120/160 mm
40,000$	- Recoiless rifle, 57 mm
50,000$	- Recoiless rifle, 75 mm
60,000$	- Recoiless rifle, 82 mm
20,000$	- Bazooka, all types

Note: $ sign for piasters

_____

Source: U.S., JUSPAO, leaflet number 3339.

Figure 4.25
Third-Party Inducement Reward

DU-KÍCH-QUÂN

- Xã-đội-trưởng (Chính-trị-viên xã-đội)	25.000$
- Xã-đội-phó	20.000$
- Trung-đội-trưởng Du-kích	15.000$
- Trung-đội-phó Du-kích	10.000$
- Tiểu-đội-trưởng Du-kích	7.000$
- Tiểu-đội-phó Du-kích	4.000$
- Đội-viên Du-kích xã	3.000$

The award in cash will be paid within three days to the individual responsible for inducing the rallier, either at province or district level. The rights of the individual who induces a Communist to rally or a group to rally will be respected and not have his name disclosed.

Guerrilla
Village Company Commander	25,000$
Deputy Village Company Commander	20,000$
Guerrilla Platoon Leader	15,000$
Guerrilla Assistant Platoon Leader	10,000$
Guerrilla Squad Leader	7,000$
Guerrilla Assistant Squad Leader	4,000$

Note: $ sign for piasters

Source: U.S., JUSPAO, leaflet number 2991.

Figure 4.26
Group Rallying Rewards

TƯỞNG THƯỞNG ĐẶC BIỆT

    Những người có thành tích kêu gọi được tập thể cán binh Cộng Sản, tiền thưởng được tính riêng từng người cộng lại, sau đó gia tăng thêm từ 20 đến 70 phần trăm.

    Quyền lợi của người có công móc nối sẽ được đảm bảo cũng như danh tánh sẽ được giữ kín.

SPECIAL AWARD

    In cases where a Communist military unit is induced to rally as a group, the individual inducing the group to rally will receive not only an award for each individual in the unit, but also an extra bonus. . . .

    A unit will only be considered to have rallied as a group if the following conditions are met:
    -- It must consist of a minimum of three ralliers (one cell).
    -- They must all be from the same unit.
    -- They must rally together and at the same time.

    If the unit is a squad or larger in size, at least two thirds of its command cadre must accompany it as well as two thirds its combat number.

Source: U.S., JUSPAO, leaflet number 2992.

gave American propagandists an annual golden opportunity
to induce defections from the Communist camp by taking
advantage of the increased number of home leaves granted
the Viet Cong during this period (Fig 4.27).
     It is not surprising that virtually all
communication channels were pressed into service during
the New Year season, to reach not only the Communist
troops but the non-enemy populace of South Vietnam as
well. This last group was considered especially
important to the efforts during Tet because, once
civilians became convinced of the validity of the Chieu
Hoi summons, they had a strong influence in motivating
members of the Viet Cong to defect. A JUSPAO-sponsored
survey of 510 hoi chanh who came in during the 1966 Tet,
for example, indicated that forty percent were encouraged
to rally, or were helped to do so by their relatives, and
twenty percent deserted while visiting their native
villages. One-fourth stated that conditions for
defection were favorable during the holidays: lack of
supervision of lax security. Seventy percent reported
they had encountered no difficulties in coming over to
Saigon's side at this time.[17]
     Most themes developed for the Tet campaigns were
based on already existing appeals placed into the context
of the season. Leaflet and loudspeaker messages included
sketches of a happy family reunion, a pensive Viet Cong
away from home, and family longings for loved ones
serving the National Liberation Front. -- "On the New
Year the Government of Vietnam wishes you happiness and
peace so you can return to your family and freedom."
Loudspeaker broadcasts asked, "Will this be the last Tet
of your life? Will you spend Tet in the living hell of
the war you are losing? Away from your family -- your
lonely family? Oh! Come back now so that once again
there will be happiness in your family -- come now to the
open arms of your government so that you can be with your
loved ones during Tet." Leaflets for North Vietnamese
soldiers in the South sometimes included reproductions of
letters from their wives that had come into the hands of
the Allies:

> Following is an excerpt from a letter dated
> 7/2/71 by Bui Thi Minh Lan (a native of Hong
> Viet, Thai Binh, North Vietnam) to her husband
> Nguyen Tien Manh, APO 460.325 JX 33.
> My darling - the people at home had a great
> time celebrating Tet this year. Everybody was
> happy, but not me. How could I be happy
> without you my darling? In other families,
> wives happily welcomed back their husbands and
> sons. But as for me, you are so far away, far
> away. . . . We held a great feast during Tet,
> and mother kept talking about you, especially

Figure 4.27
Chieu Hoi During Tet

Tet is the best occasion to return and bring an end to the war.

Source: U.S., JUSPAO, leaflet number 2917.

during the Lunar New Year's Eve. And how sad I
felt when on the eve I found everything gloomy
because I felt no joy. I wondered, how and
where I could find you. That night I could not
stop thinking of you, and the thought of you
kept me from sleeping, I imagined I heard your
laughter and your voice talking to me. I can
never forget them.

                                        -- Your loving Lan,

     These communications proved to be very effective
during the days of celebration. But use of such appeals
also held a calculated risk. American Tet leaflets
frequently were not addressed specifically to Communist
audiences, and if intercepted by South Vietnamese
soldiers, these messages could have helped to bring about
their desertion (Fig 4.28). Nonetheless, such potential
"boomerang" communications were the exception rather than
the rule. In face, the imaginative Tet Chieu Hoi
campaigns were a major factor in the decision of many
Viet Cong to rally during the holiday festivities.
     A final special technique used was recruitment of
some hoi chanh for armed propaganda teams. These units
entered Communist-controlled and contested areas and
attempted, through distribution of printed materials and
personal testimonials, to persuade known Viet Cong and
their families to come over to the Republic's side (Fig
4.29). Many U.S. officials believed these endeavors were
among the most effective defection-inducement techniques
because they added a personal touch to the Chieu Hoi
invitations. One report tells how team members moved a
village audience to tears as they told of their previous
misdeeds as Communists and the good treatment they
received after rallying. The audience "believed that, as
former Viet Cong and soldiers who had been on both sides
at one time or another, they should know what they were
talking about."[18]
     In sum, these five major psychological appeals, and
their related special campaigns and techniques formed the
core of American attempts to convince the enemy soldiers
in South Vietnam to lay down their arms. The messages
were probably most effective on a strategic level, for
they created awareness among the Communist ranks of
defection and surrender alternatives. However, when
employed in conjunction with combat operations, these
efforts often left much to be desired.

TACTICAL MILITARY OPERATIONS

     Throughout the war the American military was
preoccupied with dropping leaflets and making loudspeaker
broadcasts. Using a "Sears, Roebuck" technique,
psychological operations officers assigned to combat

Figure 4.28
Loneliness at Tet

4451

COME BACK TO ME, MY LOVE!

This evening, in the cold and wild forest,
When the evening mist is brooding over the hills,
When monkeys are anxiously calling to another
    and birds are singing sorrowfully,
Do you feel the acute pang of homesickness?

Do you feel hope lingering in your heart like the evening mist
        hanging over the trees?
Do you feel sick thinking of your home and your native place?
Do you know that Spring has come, bringing Tet?
Do you feel downhearted at the thought of separation, my love?

Without you, no one at home will celebrate Tet.
And away from home, maybe you will feel no joy when it comes.
Come back home to me, O my love
To warm up our sad, cold hearts,
And bring spring light to war your people's hearts.

Source: U.S., JUSPAO, leaflet number 4451.

Figure 4.29
Armed Propaganda Teams

HAI HỒI CHÁNH VIÊN CAO CẤP ĐƯỢC
TƯỞNG THƯỞNG BỘI TINH TÂM LÝ CHIẾN

Trong một buổi lễ tại Phủ Thủ Tướng sáng ngày 7-12-67 Thủ Tướng Chánh Phủ đã gắn
huy chương cho hai Cựu Việt Cộng Hồi Chánh. Trung tá LÊ-XUÂN CHUYÊN và Trung tá HUYNH-CƯ. Trung tá LÊ
XUÂN CHUYÊN về hồi chánh năm rồi hiện được Chánh Phủ bổ nhiệm chức vụ " Chỉ Huy Trưởng Bộ Chỉ Huy Trung
Ương các Đoàn Võ Trang Tuyên Truyền" Được biết các Đoàn Võ Trang Tuyên Truyền có nhiệm vụ giải thích Chính
Sách Chiêu Hồi của Chính Phủ trong các từng lớp nhân dân trên toàn quốc. Trung tá HUYNH-CƯ Cựu Trưởng Phong
Quân Huấn Quân Khu V Việt Cộng về hồi chánh đầu năm nay được bổ nhiệm giữ chức vụ " Phụ Tá Đặc Biệt Tổng
Trưởng Chiêu Hồi " Chức vụ này nhằm giúp đỡ vị Tổng Trưởng về các vấn đề đặc biệt liên quan đến chương trình
Chiêu Hồi của Chính Phủ.

SP-2335

TWO HIGH RANKING HOI CHANH AWARDED PSYWAR MEDALS

In a ceremony at the Prime Minister's Building on the
morning of 7-12-67, the Republic of Vietnam Prime Minister
pinned medals on two former hoi chanh, Lt. Col. Le Xuan Chuyen
and Lt. Col. Huynh Cu. Lt. Col. Le Xuan Chuyen, a returnee at
last year was appointed as "Commander of Central Headquarters
of Armed Propaganda Teams." It is known that these Armed
Propaganda Teams have the job of explaining the Chieu Hoi
Policy to people all over the country. Lt. Col. Huynh Cu, ex-
leader of Viet Cong Training Section Zone V, a returnee of
early this year was appointed as "Special Assistant to Chieu
Hoi Minister" with the responsibility of advising the Minister
on special Chieu Hoi projects. . . .

Source: U.S., JUSPAO, leaflet number SP-2335.

Table 4.1
Military Leaflet and Loudspeaker Broadcast Operations

Aerial Leaflet Dissemination (in millions - 1969)

Source	January	February	March	April	May	June	July	August
U.S.	511.8	641.4	693.4	664.8	822.4	737.1	689.1	683.0
Republic of Vietnam	20.9	18.9	20.0	16.3	14.3	23.8	47.2	37.5

Airborne Loudspeaker Broadcasts (in hours - 1969)

U.S.	2064	2265	2405	1955	1982	2090	2054	1894
Republic of Vietnam	30	11	25	54	111	168	236	157

Source: U.S., MACV, PSYOP/POLWAR Newsletter, Vol. 4, No. 8 (August 1969).

units ordered preprinted leaflets and prerecorded
loudspeaker broadcast tapes from catalogues prepared
by JUSPAO and the MACV propaganda battalions.
Usually within two hours of the order from the
ground forces, standardized Chieu Hoi and surrender
leaflets and tapes, stockpiled at airfields, were
delivered by the Air Force over the specified target
area.
     The military's zealousness for dropping scraps
of paper and conducting loudspeaker operations is
shown in the dissemination statistics for the first
eight months of 1969; the figures also offer some
insight into the Americanization of the
psychological operations drive (Table 4.1).
     The vast majority of the American communications
contained standard Chieu Hoi and surrender appeals based
on general psychological receptiveness among the
Communist target audiences. Indeed, David Elliott
concluded from his 1967 investigation as a member of a
special Department of Defense-sponsored committee
studying the psychological operations campaign:

     The military PSYOP effort is obsessed with
     leaflets, loudspeakers, and ready-made
     materials. . . . The bulk of psychological
     operations carried on outside of Saigon tend to
     emphasize pre-packaged materials and
     standardized format. PSYOP activity in the
     field tends to be oriented around availability
     of materials (usually leaflets) and means of
     delivery (normally airplanes).[19]

American combat units also employed a limited number of "Quick Reaction" messages based on current mental vulnerabilities in the enemy situation and the nature of the particular Communist target group. Such "Quick Reaction" leaflets usually could be prepared by the propaganda battalions and disseminated by the Air Force within twenty-four hours after receiving a request from the field. One such leaflet implored a specifically targeted enemy unit: "ATTENTION MEN OF THE C-9 COMPANY, D-3 BATTALION, 84th ROCKET/ARTILLERY REGIMENT. We think that the defeats and hardships you have endured are sufficient to make you aware of your dire situation. Recently nine of your comrades, including one platoon leader, were killed. Besides an onslaught of bombs and bullets, you are exposed to malaria, scabs, and other dangerous diseases that can completely exhaust you. Death will become a certainty if you do not rally right now!"

One of the most credible and effective "Quick Reaction" techniques was the use of "personalized" leaflets prepared by hoi chanh. Typically, a rallier would write a Chieu Hoi or surrender plea to his friends in the enemy ranks and his picture would be taken. The appeal and photograph were then rushed to the supporting propaganda battalions for production and subsequent aerial delivery. These "Quick Reaction" testimonials often were addressed to the hoi chanh's previous unit and to his former comrades by name. The rallier would tell enough about himself to convince the recipients that he was alive and well -- the hoi chanh's own writing, bad grammar and all, and his signature were reproduced in many of the leaflets. In the remainder of the testimonial he told about the humane treatment he had received, followed by his personal, emotional tale of disaffection with the Communists (Fig 4.30).

Another useful "Quick Reaction" practice was "Earlyword" broadcasts by hoi chanh at the battle scene. Through ground radio link to nearby aircraft equipped with loudspeakers, a rallier would deliver personal entreaties to his friends still serving the Viet Cong; the orbiting psychological operations airplane would pick up the ground transmission and broadcast the message "live" to the enemy forces. This technique brought good results during the remainder of the war. As a North Vietnamese rallier explained the effect of these personal appeals: "I thought their content (that of the broadcasts) was true since I identified Phung's voice. He was a fighter in my company who rallied to the GVN. . . . That made me certain he was alive."[20]

In another case, a hoi chanh agreed to produce a tape addressed to friends of his previous company by name, urging them to rally. The tape was then broadcast

Figure 4.30
Hoi Chanh Rally Appeal

LÝ DO NÀO
ĐÃ KHIẾN CUỘC
TẤN CÔNG CỦA VC
VÀO ĐÔ THÀNH
BỊ THẤT BẠI ?

WHY DID THE ATTACK OF THE CAPITAL CITY FAIL?
Colonel Tran Van Dac, alian Tam Ha, former Field Grade Officer in
the National Liberation Front, New Area I, Military Zone 4, who
rallied to the Government of Vietnam on 29 April 1968, gives these
reasons:
    (1) The unexpected factor they intended to profit by during
Tet has been discovered, as they have been successfully fought off
by the Allied Forces and Army of the Republic of Vietnam.
    (2) Compared to the Viet Cong, the Allied and Vietnamese
forces are far superior, materially and morally. The Viet Cong's
defeat is now quite obvious, their lives are uncertain. If they
don't try to escape as Hoi Chanh, their lives will be threatened.
    (3) The people, with their experience in the previous attack,
did not stand up to support them but on the contrary hate them.
Whenever they venture into cities controlled by the government, they
are tracked down and captured by the people.

At first I also hesitated to rally but when I was here I was kindly
welcomed, and I have seen many old friends as well as my family, now
living in happiness. I do hope that you return to join your
families.

(Signature and name)

Source: U.S., JUSPAO, leaflet number 2627.

throughout the area where the unit was located -- within twenty-four hours eighty-eight members of the rallier's former comrades came over to Saigon's side.

Although specialized "Quick Reaction" messages were more likely to persuade defection or surrender because of their relevance to the experience and current situation of a specific target group, their use was the exception rather than the rule. The American military emphasized standardized, strategically oriented communications at the expense of the more effective and more difficult to produce "Quick Reaction" messages. Success in convincing the Viet Cong and North Vietnamese troops to give up the fight suffered accordingly.

Nonetheless, it is noteworthy that the armed forces places such emphasis on the psychological aspect of the war. General William C. Westmoreland, commanding general of MACV, undoubtedly was the motivating force behind the propaganda drive. His keen personal interest in the "hearts and minds" battle had a strong influence on the lower echelons. According to one account he ". . . even liked to dash off psyops messages of his own, jotting them down on a note pad when inspiration came."[21]

In spite of emphasis at the top, it was unfortunate that Americans turned so readily to ready-made materials. There were other problems too. Common to past wars in which the United States was involved were the attitudes of some field commanders toward the usefulness of the communications weapon. "A combat commander prides himself on his knowledge of tactics, formation, employment of supporting weapons, and leadership principles," writes one Army officer, "but until he knows psychological operations and how they fit into his military arsenal, he has not learned to use all of the tools of his trade."[22] The record in Vietnam was spotty.

Some commanders showed a distinct lack of appreciation for the role and capability of psychological operations, while a few held the propaganda tool in too high esteem and often were disappointed when their efforts did not produce immediate results. On the other hand, many were more interested in high body counts than in what the psychological instrument could do for them in defeating the enemy. The U.S. Army reported that, "The body count and kill attitudes was manifested in the remark of a unit commander who boasted that his Chieu Hoi program consisted of two 105mm howitzers -- one of which was marked 'Chieu' and the other 'Hoi.'"[23]

Then, too, some combat commanders simply gave lip-service support to the psychological battle and tended to measure their effectiveness in terms of the number of leaflets dropped. One propaganda company, for instance, reported more than one billion leaflets delivered during the first nine months of 1966; their usefulness was cited

by noting that over 6,000 Communist soldiers had rallied
in the areas where the fliers had been dispersed. No
attempt was made to correlate the number of ralliers with
their level of combat activity and the enemy environment,
two factors that undoubtedly played a major role in
spurring the defections. In some cases, boxes of
leaflets were delivered to combat units without English
translations. These were dutifully scattered about the
countryside by Americans who were ignorant of their
content and intended target audiences.

In assessing tactical psychological operations it is
especially interesting to note those techniques that
paralleled those used in the past and some new ones
developed during the Vietnam conflict. Ground
loudspeaker tactics, for instance, were similar to those
used during World War II and the Korean War. Typically,
a battle was initiated with artillery and aerial
bombardment. A lull followed during which all firing
stopped and Chieu Hoi and surrender pleas were delivered,
along with specific instructions on how to turn
themselves in. Ten to thirty minutes later there was
another display of firepower, followed by more
broadcasts, and, finally, the attack was consummated.
Loudspeaker-equipped helicopter gunships sometimes took
part in these operations, and personal urging by hoi
chanh were aired whenever possible.

Unlike previous conflicts, few leaflet artillery
shells and bombs were used because of the availability of
aircraft and helicopters for aerial dissemination. When
they were used, the procedures employed were those of
both World Wars and the Korean War. Each packed with 800
to 900 leaflets the artillery shells gave precise
accuracy with the message: "The next one may be an
explosive shell -- surrender now."[24]

Imitating World War I techniques, Army and Marine
Corps gunships often flew over enemy concentrations and
threw leaflets by hand out of the doors. Some dropped
small fused packages timed to explode in the air, or
slightly torn paper sacks stuffed with handbills were
snapped by hand, causing the bags to burst and the
contents to scatter to the ground.

Similar to practices in the American Indian wars,
some hoi chanh were recruited to serve as scouts for U.S.
combat units. These development grew out of a 1966
incident where Viet Cong propaganda cadres in one village
alleged that U.S. Marines had murdered several ralliers
who had accepted the Chieu Hoi offer. To counter these
claims, the former Communists were taken back to the area
to prove to the people that they were still alive. From
this incident emerged the idea to use hoi chanh on a
regular basis. The "Kit Carson Scout Program," with six
"Scouts," was initiated in October 1966; by 1969 their
numbers had burgeoned to over 2,000. The scouts served

as guides, helped with population control during battle
engagements, aided in interrogation of captives and
suspects, visually identified Viet Cong, and named dead
and wounded Communist soldiers. In addition, the
conducted psychological operations similar to those of
the armed propaganda teams.
During sweeps and patrols, the accompanying hoi
chanh often used hand-held megaphones to tell village and
hamlet audiences their story of disaffection with the
Viet Cong and the good treatment they received after
rallying. One American soldier saw a scout writing on
small scraps of paper and dropping them along a trail.
Suspicious of his intentions, the soldier retrieved one
of the notes and had it translated. It turned out that
the hoi chanh was running his own propaganda campaign,
telling the Viet Cong that he was well and asking them to
rally so that they, too, could become scouts.[25]
In addition, numerous gimmicks were used by the
Americans, some bordering on the bizarre:

Twenty-five thousand Japanese-produced,
strongly scented bars of soap, each containing
seven different Chieu Hoi messages printed on
interior layers, were delivered by hand during
the 1969 Tet campaign.
One infantry unit dropped white flags soaked
in a Vietnamese fish sauce called Nuoc Mam to
hungry enemy soldiers in an effort to persuade
them to rally.
Marines placed a Chieu Hoi leaflet and a
cigarette in plastic bags and floated them up
the mouths of rivers during evening tides;
similarly, plastic buckets containing a
washcloth, a half piece of elephant soap,
needles and thread, and a leaflet were drifted
into Viet Cong areas.
Marines nailed Chieu Hoi posters covered with
acetate on trees along trails and in hamlets; a
plastic bag containing leaflets was attached
underneath so enemy troops could take one as
they passed by.
Thousands of children's kites overprinted
with Chieu Hoi and other these were distributed
by CORDS; bumper stickers with amnesty slogans
were issued at government checkpoints; and
matchbooks with rally inducements were
distributed throughout the country.
A few enterprising soldiers painted in large
block letters the words "Chieu Hoi" on the
sides of water buffalo belonging to local
farmers.
Haircuts were given to Montagnard tribesmen
because the spectacle drew large crowds --

Chieu Hoi and other appeals were directed
toward the people assembled as American
soldiers clipped hair.
Finally, handwritten leaflets from <u>hoi chanh</u>,
wrapped in pieces of paper and fastened with
rubber bands, with geographical coordinates
inscribed on the outside, or "zip codes" as
they were called, were given to pilots to throw
out of cockpit windows when they were flying
over the specified areas; pieces of string were
attached to the elastics so that when the small
bundles of handbills were caught in the
slipstream created by the aircraft's propeller
the rubber band would snap off the leaflets,
allowing them to fall to the ground.

EFFECTIVENESS

In all communications efforts, effectiveness is the
essential goal but is difficult to prove. Psychological
operations in Vietnam were no exception. In the case of
the Chieu Hoi Program, success largely was contingent on
fulfillment of two fundemental communication
prerequisites: first, the Viet Cong and North Vietnamese
fighters and cadres had to receive and understand the
content of the propaganda messages; secondly, they had to
give some degree of credibility to the promises contained
in the communications before they would accept the
amnesty invitation.
Both of these factors played a role in what Ernest
and Edith Bairdain of Human Sciences Research called the
"Rally Decision Process." Acceptance of the Chieu Hoi
proposition normally evolved over a long period, lasting
from one to two years. Typically, disbelief of Saigon's
word of honor came first. There followed a slow
transition characterized by a recognition that the Chieu
Hoi offer was valid and confidence that the government
would keep faith with its guarantees of humane treatment
and resettlement. Once the amnesty policy was believed,
extracommunication or war-related factors motivating
defection came into play and led to the final decision
and act of rallying. As JUSPAO pointed out in 1967, "The
Chieu Hoi appeal is an important factor of persuasion,
but . . . very few . . . rallied because of it. Most
list excessive dangers and hardships or dissatisfactions
with VC policies and practices as their reasons."[26]
Based on the responses of 500 ralliers and prisoners
to specially prepared questionnaires, the Bairdains found
that both leaflets and airborne loudspeaker broadcasts
had been seen or heard by most of the respondents. Their
analysis also revealed that the communications played a
major part in the decision to rally: (1) leaflets were
read by nearly three times as many Viet Cong ralliers

(eighty-one percent) as prisoners (thirty-one percent) and more than twice as many North Vietnamese defectors (ninety-seven percent) as prisoners (forty-four percent); (2) almost all of the respondents who read the leaflets said that they understood the words in the communications and that they grasped the intent or theme of the messages; (3) while nearly all ralliers believed the propaganda appeals they received, prisoners, both Southerners and Northerners, gave them much less credibility; (4) almost two-thirds of the defectors testified that leaflets had a major influence on their decision to rally; and (5) thirty percent of the Viet Cong and forty-seven percent of the North Vietnamese hoi chanh said they would not have rallied if they had not read the leaflets.[27]

The Bairdains' study leaves little doubt that JUSPAO and MACV were successful in getting their Chieu Hoi and surrender communications to the Communist audiences, that the messages were understood, and that they helped to motivate some enemy fighters and cadres to defect. However, no matter how many leaflets and loudspeaker broadcasts were used, or how well the various appeals, themes, techniques, and special campaigns were integrated into the effort to exploit known psychological vulnerabilities among the Communist ranks, the ultimate effectiveness of the Chieu Hoi Program was largely dependent on how closely the guarantees made in the summons were followed up by the actions promised -- harmony of words and deeds. As if underlining this fundamental proposition, one rallier replied to a question about the best way to spread the news about the amnesty drive: "It's very simple. Very easy. They simply have to have good treatment in the Chieu Hoi Centers. The word will get back. This is what we call Radio Catinat, or the jungle grapevine. They'll speak to each other."[28]

Unfortunately, little information is available about the harmony of propaganda messages and the actions taken in carrying out the Chieu Hoi policy. But some judgments are possible by correlating the response to the campaign with the number and level of ralliers defecting. The major assumption here is that if the promises were not routinely redeemed by the South Vietnamese and their Allies; if ralliers were killed, mistreated, imprisoned or tortured, then the response would have been relatively low. On the other hand, a comparatively high response would suggest that the pledges, on the whole, were satisfied.

Although the Chieu Hoi campaign obviously was a success in terms of numbers of defectors (Table 4.2), most were among the lower-ranking and least ideologically motivated persons serving the Communists. Out of nearly 183,000 ralliers that came in through May 1971, only 171

high-echelon elite (division commanders, physicians,
professors, district Party chiefs) and 1,055 middle-
status cadres (deputy company commanders, nurses,
instructors, district party members) were counted.
Moreover, many of the low standing ralliers were simply
people who had somehow been caught up in the Communist
web without fully embracing its cause -- the Chieu Hoi
policy offered many an opportunity to escape service with
the Viet Cong and the accompanying hardships and threat
of death.

Table 4.2
Number of Ralliers*

Year	Number	Weapons Brought In
1963	11,248	276
1964	5,417	358
1965	11,124	1,222
1966	20,242	1,516
1967	27,178	1,536
1968	18,171	2,196
1969	47,023	3,091
1970	32,561	1,942
1971	20,357	unknown
1972	8,000 (est.)	unknown
Total	201,421	10,601

Source: Republic of Vietnam, Ministry of Chieu Hoi, The
Policy of Greater Unity of the People: Results of Chieu
Hoi Activities (Saigon: 1971), p. 130.
        *In addition to these official statistics, many
Vietnamese serving the National Liberation Front simply
quit the Viet Cong and returned to their villages without
going through the Chieu Hoi Program. See U.S., Senate,
Hearings Before the Committee on Foreign Relations,
Vietnam: Policy and Prospects, 1970. 91st Cong., 2nd
sess., 1970, p. 248.

      The North Vietnamese soldier, whose family was far
away, was more hesitant about rallying. Generally he
believed in the justness of the Communist goal of
"liberating" the South from American "colonialists,"
feared mistreatment at the hands of the Republic, equated
defection with dishonorable surrender, and tended to
reject messages alleging his leaders were wrong and that
Hanoi's military strength was inferior to Saigon's. In
1967, for instance, only 146 Northern troops rallied out
of an estimated 61,000 present in the South, and through
March 1970, a cumulative total of only 870 had gone over
to the Republic's side. And most of those rallying did

so because of the hardships attendant to the war not
because they thought the war was unjustified.

The Northern soldiers also demonstrated strong
resilience against surrender proposals. According to his
leaders he could not give up with honor even in a
hopeless situation -- he was expected to fight until he
was killed. Thus, many prisoners held in the South cited
a variety of circumstances on how they were captured
through no fault of their own (usually because of
incapacitation due to wounds).

To be sure, the low rank of most defectors and the
resistance by the North Vietnamese detracts from the
impressiveness of the number who took advantage of the
Chieu Hoi summons to "Come Home." But the fact that so
many did leave the Communists provides ample evidence
that the promises made in the amnesty messages were
largely lived up to. This credibility of the Chieu Hoi
Program undoubtedly was the key to the relative success
it enjoyed.

Nonetheless, as the following testimonies show, most
Communist soldiers remained firmly dedicated to the "War
of National Liberation" throughout the conflict.

A Viet Cong cadre outlined the reasons for his
perseverance:

> I am the son of the people. . . . The American
> aggressors came here and brought with them
> death and destruction to our people. . . . Our
> goal is to drive the American aggressors out of
> the country and restore freedom and
> independence for the country.

A private serving the National Liberation Front
assessed America's aims in Vietnam:

> I think the Americans want to conquer South
> Vietnam to make it their territory and to use
> the South Vietnamese people as slaves, like the
> Negroes in the United States. . . . I think
> the Americans are the number one enemy of the
> Vietnamese people.

A North Vietnamese private explained his view of
death:

> I never worried about getting killed. When I
> volunteered to join the Army, I had already
> made up my mind very clearly; I understand the
> problem of the country, and I accepted all
> kinds of hardships, and if it was necessary for
> the country to have independence, I would offer
> my life for the war. I knew that I could get
> killed when I joined the Army, but I strongly

committed myself to the cause of the salvation
of the nation, which is very sacred.

Another Northern private evaluated the impact of the
hardships endured by the Communists:

We all knew there was always hardships while
fighting a war. We disregarded them because we
were fighting for the country. . . .
Therefore, we never complained about the
hardships.

A Viet Cong cadre described his outlook on the Chieu
Hoi offer:

The Americans came to Vietnam and brought death
and destruction for our innocent people. . . .
The Chieu Hoi propaganda is nothing but a
demand for surrender. Since we know about
this, we do not let ourselves be influenced by
it.

Finally, a North Vietnamese cadre assessed Saigon's
(i.e., U.S.) psychological operations:

I do not believe the propaganda made by the
GVN. . . . In reality, the people were living
a miserable life, and their rice fields and
gardens left uncultivated. . . . The
Vietnamese people were being killed by bombs
and shells. . . . Due to these things we did
not believe any propaganda made by the GVN.
The more we saw the realities, the more logical
would be our struggle, and the more encouraged
we were.[29]

If this sampling of Viet Cong and North Vietnamese
attitudes can be used to generalize, there is little
doubt that the motivation and morale of the Communist
armed forces remained relatively high throughout the
war. But this conclusion must be reconciled somehow with
the fact that over 200,000 did take advantage of the
Chieu Hoi policy from 1963 through 1972. It appears
reasonable to suggest that, while the psychological
operations probably failed to persuade many enemy
fighters and cadres to defect, they were successful in
heightening the Communist soldier's awareness of his
fears, hardships, doubts, family concerns, and possible
disillusionment; the propaganda messages informed the
Viet Cong and North Vietnamese that there were
alternatives to his present situation -- rallying or
surrendering. War-related effects may indeed have been
ultimately responsible for motivating soldiers to give up

the fight, but the Chieu Hoi and surrender communications
informed them of the available options.

As propaganda specialist Konrad Kellen concluded in
his 1970 study for the Rand Corporation: ". . . neither
our military actions nor our political or psywar efforts
seem to have made an appreciable dent on the enemy's
overall motivation and morale structure" [emphasis
Kellen's].[30] Given the nature of the conflict, the
circumstances surrounding American involvement in the
war, and the ability by the Communists to maintain the
"justness" of their cause in the eyes of the great
majority of their followers, the slight degree of
effectiveness enjoyed in the Chieu Hoi and surrender
programs was probably all that was possible.

NOTES

1. South Vietnam Liberation Army, Tan Uyen District
Unit, "Communique" (December 20, 1966). In U.S., JUSPAO,
Psyops in Vietnam: Indications of Effectiveness
(Saigon: May 1967), pp. 21-23.
2. "Open Arms" is not a literal translation of
"Chieu Hoi" which may be best translated as "Summons to
Return." Moreover, "Chieu Hoi" is not a common
Vietnamese expression; it was created from two Chinese-
derived terms to characterize the amnesty program.
JUSPAO explains: "The word 'Chieu' . . . has an
honorable and traditional association with the side
possessing the mandate to legitimate, just and prevailing
power. To come over to the holder of that mandate has
never been considered unethical by the Vietnamese. The
word 'Hoi' means simply 'return' and has no connotations
to explore except the implication that the 'return' is to
a 'just cause.' The two together form the contemporary
and contrived term which serves as the label of the
program." See U.S., JUSPAO, "Connotations of Vietnamese
Words and Phrases Used Most Frequently in Appeals to
Enemy Audience" (Saigon: June 3, 1970).
3. U.S., JUSPAO, Psyops in Vietnam, pp. 75-76.
4. U.S., MACV, CORDS, Chieu Hoi Program, rev.
(Saigon: February 1971) and The Chieu Hoi Program:
Questions and Answers (Saigon: January 1, 1968). See
also U.S., MACV, Military Intelligence: Procedures for
Handling and Utilization of Returnees (MACCORDS) Chieu
Hoi Program, MACV Directive 381-50 (Saigon: February 22,
1971).
5. U.S., JUSPAO, "The Chieu Hoi Inducement Program"
Policy Number 16, (July 9, 1966) in Consolidation of
JUSPAO Guidance 1 Thru 22, Vol. I (Saigon: June 1,
1967), pp. 83-86.
6. Terence Smith, "The Mission of the B-52's," New
York Times (April 6, 1969), p. 18; U.S., Department of
the Army, Employment of U.S. Army Psychological

Operations Units in Vietnam, ACTIV Project No. ACG-47F, Final Report (APO San Francisco 96384, June 7, 1969), p. G-1.

7. U.S., JUSPAO, "The Use of Superstitions in Psychological Operations in Vietnam," Policy Number 36 (May 10, 1967) in Consolidation of JUSPAO Guidances 23 Thru 46, Vol. II (Saigon: October 1, 1967), pp. 75-77.

8. H. C. Bush, The Effectiveness of U.S. Psyops Leaflets: A Scale for Pretesting (Honolulu: Pacific Technical Analysts, Inc., January 1969), p. 16.

9. U.S., JUSPAO, Psyops in Vietnam, p. 115.

10. Ibid., p. 3.

11. Ibid., p. 39.

12. Ibid., pp. 117-18.

13. U.S., JUSPAO, "Peacetime Illusions: A VC/NVA Vulnerability," Field Memorandum Number 56 (July 31, 1968) in Consolidation of JUSPAO Field Memorandua 42 Thru 58, Vol. III (Saigon: n.d.), pp. 89-94.

14. Berger, Introduction to Wartime Leaflets, p. 61.

15. U.S., JUSPAO, Psyops in Vietnam, pp. 114-15.

16. U.S., JUSPAO, Chieu Hoi Dai Doan Ket National Reconciliation Programs, Policy Number 75 (December 18, 1968), and MACV, CORDS Chieu Hoi Operational Memorandum No. 32/68: "Chieu Hoi Nationwide Rewards Campaign (1 November 1968-31 January 1969)", (Saigon: October 31, 1968).

17. U.S., JUSPAO, Some Findings of the Survey of the Chieu Hoi Tet Campaign-1966 (Saigon: December 1966), p. 8, and 1967 Tet/Chieu Hoi Campaign Plan (Saigon: October 17, 1966).

18. U.S., MACV, CORDS, Questions and Answers, p. 5. See also Republic of Vietnam, Ministry of Chieu Hoi, APT Handbook, rev. ed. (Saigon: 1970), pp. 1-10.

19. David Elliott, "Comments on Psychological Operations," in Report of the ARPA-Supported Committee on Psychological Operations, Vietnam, 1967, Kenneth C. Clark, chairman, as amended by the Department of Defense, Advanced Research Projects Agency (McLean, Va.: Human Sciences Research, 1967), pp. C-1 to C-2.

20. U.S., JUSPAO, Psyops in Vietnam, p. 119.

21. "The War of Words," Wall Street Journal (December 5, 1969), p. 14.

22. Wallace F. Veaudry, "A New Look at Psywar," Army, Vol. 15, No. 1 (August 1964), p. 57.

23. U.S., Department of the Army, Psychological Operations United in Vietnam, pp. II-16 to II-17.

24. Beverly Deepe, "U.S. Unit 'Persuades' Viet Cong to Defect," Christian Science Monitor (October 15, 1968), p. 3.

25. Joe F. Steward, The Story of Kit Carson Scouts (Saigon: MACV, n.d.), pp. 9-48.

26. U.S., JUSPAO, Final Report on Ex-Hoi Chanh

Survey, Research Report (Saigon: March 19, 1967), p. 2.
    27. Ernest F. Bairdain and Edith M. Bairdain, Final
Technical Report: Psychological Operations Studies--
Vietnam, Vol. I (McLean, Va.: Human Sciences Research,
May 25, 1971), pp. 84-86.
    28. Quoted in Simulmatics Corporation, Improving
Effectiveness of the Chieu Hoi Program: Functional
Aspects of the Chieu Hoi Program, Vol. III (New York:
Simulmatics Corporation, September 1967), p. 285.
    29. Quoted in Konrad Kellen, Conversations with
Enemy Soldiers in Late 1968/Early 1969: A Study of
Motivation and Morale, RM-6131-1-ISA/ARPA (Santa Monica,
Calif.: Rand Corporation, September 1970), pp. 55, 96,
39, 13-14, 51, and 50-51.
    30. Ibid., p. vi.

5
The Psychological Offensive Against the North

The American psychological onslaught against North
Vietnamese morale was primarily an aerial operation.
Thousands of "leaflet bombs" were dropped from fighter-
bombers during attacks on military targets, and other
tons of leaflets were dumped from huge cargo aircraft
over international waters where the wind would take them
into the North. Small transistor radios were scattered
throughout the country or floated ashore from the Gulf of
Tonkin so that Northerners could listen to Saigon's
broadcasts.

There were other forms of air-delivered
communications too. Fact-filled propaganda newspapers
and news bulletin fliers were dispersed periodically to
help tell the American-South Vietnamese story; "money"
leaflets were used as an attention-getting device,
touching off charges by Hanoi of "economic warfare" and
"international crimes." The strange case of Nguyen Van
Be -- a widely acclaimed "dead" Viet Cong hero who turned
up alive in one of Saigon's prisoner-of-war camps -- also
was the subject of a special leaflet and radio
communications campaign.

The result of this intense psychological offensive
was a countryside littered with a billion pieces of
printed propaganda and thousands of homes penetrated by
endless hours of radio broadcasts. Its objective was
threefold: "to convince . . . both people and regime
that . . . aggression in South Viet-Nam would fail, to
motivate . . . peaceful settlement of the conflict, and

to warn the people to stay away from military targets because they were subject to air strike."[2]

LEAFLET CAMPAIGNS

Leaflets intended to exploit mental anxieties created by the 1965-1968 and 1972-1973 bombing raids were the cutting edge of the propaganda program. In addition, millions of circulars were strewn along the Ho Chi Minh Trail to increase the fears and worries of Northern soldiers infiltrating the South.

"Frantic Goat North"

America's first paper assault, dubbed "Frantic Goat North" (formerly the "Fact Sheet Campaign"), was kicked off on April 14, 1965, and continued until the partial bombing halt on March 31, 1968. Subsequent drops were restricted to the southern portion, or panhandle area of North Vietnam. This was the "Tallyho Campaign," which continued until all raids were terminated on November 1, 1968.

The primary aim of these psychological operations was to drive as broad a wedge as possible between the North Vietnamese people and the ruling Lao Dong Party (Figs 5.1, 5.2). American leaflets, most of which purported to come from the Saigon government, placed responsibility for the bombing squarely on the Ho Chi Minh regime. The population was informed that the air attacks were a response to the Party's aggression in the South. "Have you been told the truth concerning the bombing of military installations, supply depots, bridges and roads by the Republic of Vietnam and U.S. aircraft?," they were asked. "Do you know that these installations and depots as well as your roads have been used to support an aggressive war to kill your peace-loving kin and friends in South Vietnam? THOSE WHO SOW THE WIND WILL REAP THE WHIRLWIND."

These threats of continued bombing were reinforced by photographs of destroyed buildings, bridges, and the like: "If the Communists of North Vietnam continue their destructive war in the South, destruction as shown in these scenes will continue to be carried out."

Another divisive appeal was the charge that Northern leaders were misleading the people. One leaflet, for example, explained how Hanoi was concealing its military defeats: "Once again Hanoi radio is telling you of 'great victories' in Saigon and elsewhere in the South. . . . What is the true story? More than 2,000 of your relatives and friends have died in the futile fighting around Saigon. Here North Vietnamese Army soldiers lie dead in the streets of Cholon while an Army of the Republic of Vietnam soldier shows frightened

Figure 5.1
Victory Claims Are Lies

" CỘNG SẢN THUA TO "

Thương tá Trần văn Đắc, chi huy trưởng một đơn vị Việt Cộng tấn công Saigon trong dịp Tết Mậu Thân, đã ra hồi chánh tháng 4 thay vì xua đàn em vào những cuộc tấn công tự sát. Ngày 15-5 tại Saigon, ông nói: "Hai đợt tổng công kích của Cộng Sản đều bị thua to. Về mặt quân sự, họ đã không kiểm soát được mục tiêu quan trọng nào. Về mặt chính trị, họ đã không được dân chúng ủng hộ và hiện nay, nhân dân miền Nam tự do chán ghét Cộng Sản hơn bao giờ hết. "

• 133

COMMUNISTS SUFFERED BITTER DEFEATS

Col. Tan Van Dac, commander of a Communist unit that attacked Saigon at Tet 1968, rallied to the National Cause in April rather than lead his men in more suicide attacks. . . .

The Communist authorities in Hanoi, to hide their failures and delude the North Vietnamese people, have been falsely claiming "great victories" in the South. Their claims are fantastic, but it is difficult for the North Vietnamese people to learn the truth because they do not have any news except that prepared by Communist propagandists. The truth is that the people of South Vietnam and their allies have inflicted severe defeats on the Communist troops sent from the North. Thousands of Communist soldiers have been killed or captured. Many others . . . have realized that they have been misled and have rallied to the National Cause.

Source: U.S., JUSPAO, leaflet number 133.

Figure 5.2
North Vietnam Army Losses in the South

Ảnh thi thể T r u n g Tướng
Trần Độ nằm chết sau trận
đánh ở Chợ lớn trong cuộc
tấn công xảo trá của Việt
Cộng vào dịp Tết Mậu Thân.

96

Các bạn hãy đón nghe đài
TIẾNG NÓI TỰ DO

Đài phát thanh ngày thứ nằm Hàng
Tầm sóng sóng 650 kilo chu kỳ từ nửa đêm đến 7 giờ sáng
Tầm sóng sóng 650 kilo chu kỳ và 9670 kilo chu kỳ
từ 6 giờ mai đến nửa đêm

DEAR FELLOW CITIZENS IN NORTH VIETNAM:

Major General Tran Do was killed . . . in Cholon (on the outskirts of Saigon) while he was personally commanding the "general offensive" against Saigon and other cities in South Vietnam during the recent Tet holiday.

Together with the death of General Tran Do, from 30 January 1968 to 29 February 1968, over 42,000 North Vietnamese Regulars and Viet Cong soldiers were destroyed, 7,000 others captured alive, and over 12,000 pieces of assorted weapons seized. . . .

He who sows the wind reaps the tempest. . . . Fellow citizens, be determined to thwart all the attempts of the North Vietnam Communists who aim to send your children to die foolishly in South Vietnam.

Source: U.S., JUSPAO, leaflet number 96.

children where they can find shelter from the Communist
terrorists."
The Lao Dong Party also was depicted as needlessly
prolonging the war and the people's hardships through its
rejection of American-South Vietnamese offers of
reconciliation. "Why do your leaders continue to waste
the young men of North Vietnam in a hopeless war they
cannot win? Why do they refuse to sit down in honor with
the representatives of the Government of the Republic of
Vietnam and talk about peace," the public was queried.
"It saddens your friends in South Vietnam that the
strong, young men from North Vietnam have already died or
are needlessly dying from diseases or battle wounds. We
know it saddens you also. Ask your leaders to
reconsider." To substantiate these claims, the
propaganda often contrasted Allied peace proposals with
Ho Chi Minh's adamant refusal to negotiate -- "WHAT IS
THE FUTURE? MORE BOMBS, MORE DEAD SONS AND BROTHERS, OR
HONORABLE NEGOTIATIONS? The South Vietnamese and
Americans are ready to negotiate . . . but Hanoi
authorities refuse" (Fig 5.3).
Apparently peace overtures by the Allies, or the
communications about them, troubled Party leaders. They
responded defensively to the calls for accommodation by
launching vituperative counterpropaganda in an effort to
neutralize any positive inroads made by U.S. psychological operations among the populace. Radio Hanoi
vehemently denounced these "hypocritical" attempts to
weaken the will of the North Vietnamese: "The U.S.
imperialists have manifested greater boldness and cunning
in their war of espionage and psychological warfare.
. . . They have dropped leaflets . . . to threaten
intensification and at the same time rave about peace
negotiations with the aim of intimidating and deceiving
our people."[3] Quan Doi Nhan Dan, the Army's newspaper
added:

> The U.S. imperalists hoped to create an
> illusion about peaceful talks or U.S. aid, to
> sow division between the Vietnamese people and
> the people of other socialist countries, and
> brazenly to spread the myth of aggression of
> Vietnam by Vietnamese. From the big swindle of
> unconditional discussions and good will for
> peace, they have resorted to such contemptible
> tricks as spreading millions of leaflets to
> distort the truth about the struggle of the
> Vietnamese people and slander the DRV.[4]

Allegations of the Party's betrayal were further
reinforced by exploitation of a traditional Vietnamese
fear and mistrust of the Chinese, stemming from the

Figure 5.3
Lao Dong Party's Aggressive War

AI LÀ KẺ XÂM LĂNG ?

Có binh sĩ miền Nam tự do ở Bắc Việt không? Không!

Có hơn 100.000 binh sĩ Bắc Việt ở miền Nam tự do không? Có!

HÒA BÌNH SẼ ĐẾN VỚI TOÀN DÂN VIỆT NAM

KHI QUÂN LÍNH BẮC VIỆT TRỞ VỀ ĐOÀN TỤ VỚI GIA ĐÌNH.

134

WHO IS THE AGGRESSOR?

Are there any South Vietnamese troops in North Vietnam? No!
Are there more than 100,000 North Vietnamese troops in South
Vietnam? Yes!
PEACE CAN COME TO ALL VIETNAM WHEN NORTH
VIETNAMESE TROOPS GO HOME TO THEIR FAMILIES.

Source: U.S., JUSPAO, leaflet number 134.

latter's domination of the country for over a thousand years.

REMEMBER THE VALIANT STRUGGLE OF VIETNAMESE ANCESTORS.
Cartoon: "The Lao Dong Party brings the snake in to kill the people's own chickens" (based on an old Vietnamese saying).
Painted on the Snake: "Red China."
On the Commissar's Jacket: "The Lao Dong Party."

These psychological operations also accused the Ho regime of being a puppet of Chinese imperialism. Hanoi was charged with sending sons and husbands to the South to fight an unjust, fratricidal war on behalf of the Chinese who were willing to support the fight to the last Vietnamese (Figs 5.4, 5.5). Leaflets also claimed that Northern leaders were responsible for food shortages because they were trading rice for weapons: "The Lao Dong Party, prodded by their masters from Peking, and blinded by their thirst for conquest and dominations, are unmoved by the sufferings of the Vietnamese people, both North and South." Another contended:

Did you know that the 'Big Brother from the North' has pledged his full support to the Lao Dong Party's aggressive war in South Vietnam . . . until the last drop of blood?
Whose blood?
Vietnamese blood!
Demand the Lao Dong Party to stop the war against innocent people in South Vietnam and save your rice.

One handbill outlandishly charged that Peking's atomic bomb tests were contaminating North Vietnam's air and food, imploring the people to write protests to the Chinese Embassy.

Hanoi responded indirectly to the divisive themes by discrediting America's propaganda as a tool of its imperialist policy. An article appearing in the Lao Dong Party's theoretical journal, Hoc Tap, told its readers: "The U.S. imperialists have spread all kinds of rumors. They have tried to create distrust, pessimism or false optimism among the people. They have also tried to sow disunity . . . between the people and State, and between our people and fraternal countries."[5] A later account in the same magazine warned that, "The U.S. imperialists consider psychological warfare to be an important aspect of their aggressive policy. . . . The more they step up their policy of aggression, the more strongly their psywar machinery becomes and the more cunning and wicked their deceitful tricks will be."[6]

Figure 5.4
Lao Dong Party Controlled by Peking

"HE BROUGHT A SNAKE HOME TO EAT HIS
OWN PEOPLE'S CHICKEN"

" CÕNG

RẮN

VỀ

CẮN

GÀ

NHÀ "

Hôm 16 tháng hai lúc 9
giờ 25 tối, giờ Hà Nội, Đài
Phát Thanh Bắc Kinh tuyên
bố "Dân tộc Việt Nam mê say
tư tưởng của Mao Trạch Đông
... họ nhận rõ được sức mạnh
vô hạn của tư tưởng đó, họ yêu
thương những tác phẩm của
Mao Trạch Đông một cách vô
bờ bến và họ hết sức kính nể
tư tưởng bách chiến bách thắng
của Mao Trạch Đông" rồi Đài
Phát Thanh ấy cho tiếp theo
nhiều thí dụ để chứng minh
sự đó.

On February 16 Radio Peking . . .
said "The Vietnamese people cherish
ardent love for Mao Tse-tung's
thought . . . are fully aware of the
inexhaustible might of Mao Tse-
tung's thought, cherish boundless
love for Chairman Mao's works and
infinite respect for the all-
conquering thought of Mao Tse-tung,"
and then went on to give emphasis of
how this was true.

On February 17 . . . Radio Peking
said, "The Vietnamese people . . .
have boundless love and respect for
Chairman Mao Tse-tung . . ." and
then told several stories about
Vietnamese people weeping over Mao's
picture, naming babies after him and
swearing their children to love
China and Mao Tse-tung.

Over the centuries, China has
invaded and enslaved Vietnam. This
is the country that claims you have
"boundless love" for its leaders.
The Lao Dong Party, which is Chinese
controlled and follows the bidding
of its Chinese masters, was
responsible for the so-called Tet
offensive in the South that cost
more than forty thousand Vietnamese
lives on both sides. Was it
"Chairman Mao's thought" that made
all this possible?

The dragon on your border is
supplying you with arms, men and
"thought" to kill more Vietnamese.
Does this really evoke your
"boundless love?"

Source: U.S., JUSPAO, leaflet number 97.

Figure 5.5
Party Trades Rice for Chinese Weapons

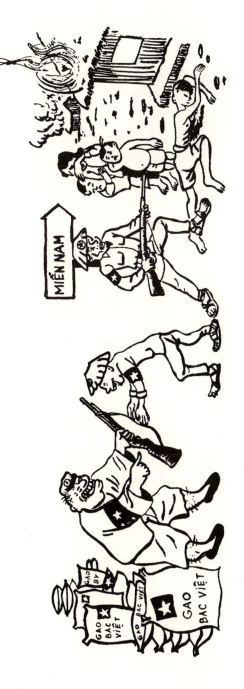

The Communist Government in Hanoi has taken the rice and paddy of the people to give to the Communist Chinese as an exchange for weapons and ammunition so that they can kill our innocent people in the South. . . .

Ask the Communist Government to keep the food and increase the rations so that the people of both North and South can earn their living in peace.

Source: U.S., JUSPAO, leaflet number 7.

Trying to undermine popular support for the Hanoi government was only one side of the American strategy. On the other side there was the attempt to create a favorable image of Saigon. To reinforce the divisive appeal positively, many communications contrasted the lives of the populace in the South with their Northern brethren (Fig 5.6). "Prosperity" leaflets, for example, pictured the good life enjoyed by South Vietnamese with photographs of well-stocked shops, streets filled with motorbikes, and busy docks and harbor areas, with the theme "In the Free South people are well-off, and there is no rationing." One leaflet queried, "Why does South Vietnam reject Communist rule? Because under the Free Democratic regime of the Republic of Vietnam the Southern people live in peace and prosperity. Almost everybody in the South has his own transportation. The cities are crowded with heavy traffic. Tall buildings spring up like mushrooms."

Other positively-oriented circulars took advantage of feelings of fraternity between the Vietnamese:

Dear Compatriots of North Vietnam:
The Trung Nguyen or Vu Lan holidays are approaching. This is the time when every Vietnamese would pause to burn a stick of incense in honor of our ancestors or as an act of mercy for the souls of those dead who have no one to honor their memories.
Faithful to our ancestral traditions, we in the South are burning incense and praying for the deceased. On this occasion, our thoughts go to you and the many sufferings, both material and moral, you are enduring under the ruthless regime of the Godless communists. We know that you are being harassed into abandoning your pious duty of honoring your dead. But our thoughts also go to the many dead who fall every day in South Vietnam under the murderous hands of the Viet Cong. How many wandering souls need our prayers and your prayers on this day of 'Pardon for the Dead?'
Compatriots, demand that the Lao Dong Party stop its war of aggression in the South so that no more innocent souls would have to join the already great numbers of innocent souls now wandering on this war-torn country of the South.

These fraternal appeals were reinforced by themes depicting the Republic's humanitarianism as shown by its warning the Northern public to stay away from military installations likely to be bombed (Figs 5.7, 5.8). "The Allied aircraft will bomb at night this whole area until

Figure 5.6
Prosperity in South Vietnam

Trên 100 nông dân từ chín làng đến viếng xã Hiệp Hòa để xem xét một thí điểm cấy Lúa Thần Nông đã thu gặt được 7,9 tấn lúa mỗi héc ta.

LÚA THẦN NÔNG CỦA MIỀN NAM TỰ DO

IR-8

TOÀN DÂN VIỆT NAM CÓ THỂ HƯỞNG ĐƯỢC LÚA NẦY KHI CÓ HÒA BÌNH

Tại một thí điểm ở xã Hiệp Hòa gần Sài Gòn, một phụ nữ đang bón phân trên cánh đồng cấy Lúa Thần Nông IR-8 của chi.

SOUTH VIETNAM IS EXPERIENCING A RICE REVOLUTION

Peace between North and South Vietnam would permit an exchange of scientific knowledge. . . .

More than 100 farmers from nine villages visit Hiep Hoa and inspect a test plot from which 7.9 tons of rice were harvested from each hectare. IR-8 SOUTH VIETNAM'S MIRACLE RICE. ALL VIETNAMESE CAN ENJOY THIS RICE WHEN PEACE COMES. . . .

With its resistance to diseases and its lack of sensitivity to the number of daylight hours it receives, the "miracle rice" can be grown in any season. IR-8 rice's short growing-season enables farmers to plan two or three crops a year. And one crop of IR-8 yields about three times more rice per hectare than the traditional varieties.

Source: U.S., JUSPAO, leaflet number 136.

Figure 5.7
Warning to Avoid Military Targets

Kho chứa dầu này gần Hànội
đã bị dội bom .

HÃY TRÁNH XA
NHỮNG MỤC TIÊU
QUÂN SỰ
NHƯ LOẠI NẦY

TO THE CIVILIAN POPULATION OF NORTH VIETNAM, WARNING!

    This oil storage area near Hanoi has been bombed. STAY AWAY
FROM TARGETS LIKE THIS.
    Bombing is not directed against you. Don't risk your life.
Stay away from all military targets such as OIL TANKS and other
petroleum storage areas. BRIDGES, HIGHWAYS, RAILROADS, and
WATERWAYS used to carry military supplies and troops, BARRACKS, GUN
EMPLACEMENTS, ALL MILITARY INSTALLATIONS, ELECTRICAL POWER STATIONS,
MILITARY POST FACILITIES.

Source: U.S., JUSPAO, leaflet number 54.

Figure 5.8
Reasons for Bombing

ĐỒNG BÀO
BỊ ÉP ĐI SỬA CHỮA
CẦU ĐƯỜNG
NÊN COI CHỪNG !

Compatriots who are forced to repair bridges and roads, BEWARE!
Roads and bridges will continue to be bombed to prevent the Lao
Dong Party from sending troops and weapons to attack the South. The
quicker they are repaired, the sooner they will be bombed again.
Compatriots, try to avoid working on roads and bridges. You will
save yourselves from a needless death.

Source: U.S., JUSPAO, leaflet number 51.

the supply for aggression in the South is stopped," they
were told. "Thinking of the life of innocent people, the
Government of the Republic of Vietnam and Allied forces
appeal to you to stay away from the sea zone and rivers
area. . . . Especially those who are fishermen, don't
move by boat on the rivers and at sea in this area by
night, Think of your life and don't give a hand to this
unjust war."
At the same time, other handbills were designed to
frighten people away from helping to restore damaged
facilities. Photographs of previously destroyed
buildings and bridges were used to intensify the image of
impending danger at military targets and the futility of
repair efforts. Some leaflets insisted -- true, but
probably doubted by the North Vietnamese -- that
significant attempts were made to avoid civilian
casualties. Sometimes American losses were admitted to
add credibility to the propaganda: "If civilians were
targets for bombing, all of your cities and towns would
now be in ruins. Allied pilots risk their lives by
flying low to try to avoid destroying anything but
military targets. This caution has been responsible for
the loss of many of the nearly 500 aircraft shot down
over North Vietnam. A heavy price has been paid to avoid
bombing civilians."
Strengthening the brotherhood theme still further,
toys and gifts were parachuted into the country or washed
ashore from the Gulf of Tonkin to show South Vietnamese
benevolence. In September 1965 alone, 9,000 packets of
toys were airdropped to celebrate Children's Day; they
included a pencil, sharpener, soap, plastic doll, other
small gifts, and a handbill bringing greetings from the
children of South Vietnam. In 1965 some 15,000 gift
kits, containing a towel, T-shirt, comb, needles, cloth,
tablet, and an appropriate message, were air-delivered
during November and again on Christmas Eve.
Hanoi's response to this American gambit was
unsurprisingly venomous. One newspaper reported:

Many children have torn to pieces the leaflets
dropped on the fields by enemy aircraft.
Whenever the enemy dropped toys or clothing,
the people immediately collected items and
brought them to the local administration or
fighters of the People's Security Armed Forces
nearest them. Old Kinh, a Catholic in Bui Chi
Diocese, Nam Dinh province, said: "The U.S.
imperialists are like a wild beast mortally hit
by bullets. They bite wantonly and might do us
some harm, but they cannot escape final
death."[7]

Periodically, special newspapers and bulletins were

used to counter the Party's one-sided propaganda. In
1965, for example, some 340,000 copies of <u>Nhan Van</u>
("Humanist Knowledge" or "True News"), an American
propaganda newspaper named after one banned by Hanoi,
were scattered across the countryside. Articles about
the South typically featured agricultural, economic,
political, and military events. The South Vietnamese
were portrayed as staunch anti-Communists, inflicting
defeats on the Viet Cong, who were "returning" in droves
to the "just cause" of the Republic. Also highlighted
were progress reports on the Paris Peace Talks and
international news with an anti-Communist angle.
Cartoons, too, were featured to extend the psychological
messages to illiterate persons.[8]

"Field Goal Operation"

In April 1972 leaflet raids against the North were
re-initiated, coinciding with the renewed bombing of the
country. Called the "Field Goal Operation," this second
paper assault was essentially a sequel to the earlier
"Frantic Goat North" campaign; the American psychological
goals and strategy were strikingly similar to those in
the 1965-1968 propaganda offensive. However, to meet the
changed circumstances of the war, the emphasis placed
earlier divisive appeals and the image of the Republic of
Vietnam was shifted.

The anti-Chinese theme was dropped, mirroring Sino-
American rapprochement following President Nixon's visit
to the People's Republic in February. Peace was now the
predominant theme. Allegations of lies and betrayal by
Party leaders received less attention, while greater
stress was placed on the charge that Hanoi stood in the
way of the truce -- "The U.S. and China want peace, the
Lao Dong Party wants war!" (Fig 5.9).

The renewed bombing and the mining of harbors had to
be explained. In this context, the Party again was
labeled as the aggressor, prompting the U.S. once more to
rain bombs on the country -- "Air strikes will continue
in order to prevent the Lao Dong leadership from
succeeding in its aggression" (Figs 5.10, 5.11).
American propagandists hoped to push the North Vietnamese
public to pressure the Hanoi government into seeking
peace -- "Demand that the Party immediately stop its war
of aggression, its insane effort to enslave the people of
the South." "The war can end when the Lao Dong Party
negotiates seriously," they were told. Hanoi was again
said to be needlessly prolonging the war and the
suffering in both parts of the nation -- "Since the 1
April 1972 invasion of South Vietnam there have been over
20,000 casualties, including women and children, in the
cities which the North Vietnamese have shelled in wanton
disregard of human life." Another leaflet asserted, "The

Figure 5.9
Lao Dong Party Prolongs War

(Cartoon showing two North Vietnamese soldiers observing a group of
wounded straggling back to camp.) One soldier says to the other:
"Over there are remnants of a battalion returning to the base area
after a 'brilliant victory' in the South. If we continue to win
such 'victories,' there will be none of us left."

The more the Lao Dong Party prolongs the war, the more likely
it is that the young generations of North Vietnamese will be
completely destroyed. You should encourage your young men to refuse
to serve the Lao Dong Party's plot to take over the South by
choosing one of these means:
  1) Go home if possible.
  2) Find some way to stay in the rear.
  3) After you reach South Vietnam, remember that the people of
South Vietnam will receive you with open arms if you decide to come
to them in peace as a brother.

Source: U.S., JUSPAO, leaflet number 4563.

Figure 5.10
Why Renewed Bombing?

**Tổng Thống Hoa Kỳ
Richard Nixon**

Tổng Thống Hoa Kỳ
đã nhắn nhủ các nhà lãnh
đạo Hà Nội như sau :
« Nhân dân quý quốc đã
quá đau khổ vì quý vị
theo đuổi cuộc chinh
phục. Xin đừng gia tăng
nỗi thống khổ của họ với
sự tiếp tục kiêu căng
của quý vị. Thay vì thế,
quý vị hãy chọn con
đường hòa bình để đền
bù những sự hy sinh của
quý vị, đảm bảo nền độc
lập thực sự cho quý quốc,
và khai sinh một kỷ
nguyên hòa giải».

4505

The U.S. President noted in his 8 May 1972 speech that the recent military actions taken in North Vietnam were necessary in response to the massive invasion of the Republic of Vietnam on 1 April 1972 by the Lao Dong leaders. He further stated that the U.S. never would abandon the 17,000,000 South Vietnamese people to communist tyranny and terror. If the Lao Dong leaders want these new military actions to cease they must agree to releasing all American prisoners of war and an internationally supervised ceasefire throughout all Indochina. The U.S. will promise to withdraw all U.S. troops from Vietnam within four months after the ceasefire takes effect.

The U.S. President stated in direct remarks to the leaders of Hanoi: "Your people have already suffered too much in your pursuit of conquest. Do not compound their agony with continued arrogance. Choose instead that path of a peace that redeems your sacrifices, guarantees true independence for your country, and ushers in an era of reconciliation."

Source: U.S., JUSPAO, leaflet number 4505.

Figure 5.11
Sacrifice by North Vietnamese People

(Drawing of North Vietnamese soldier thinking of his wife and mother).

NORTH VIETNAMESE TROOP'S MOTHERS AND WIVES!

For over the past sixteen years, (as the war rages on) you have conscientiously fulfilled your duties as mothers and soldiers' wives. You have made great sacrifices in allowing your husbands and sons to go to fight in South Vietnam, and taking their places in the production field. But what have your great sacrifices brought?

-- Nothing! Your husbands and sons have left, never to return. Not only have they not achieved victory, but they have failed to "liberate" anything because they have fought for the Party's deceitful policy of "liberating South Vietnam." The majority of them have been killed and left unburied on the battlefields in the face of the South Vietnamese Army's and population's courageous might.

The Party's foolish dream is to dominate South Vietnam. Although it has sustained defeat after defeat, the Party still wants to deceive you by urging you to make more sacrifices by giving up your men. You know yourselves what the result will be. At once stop making sacrifices for the Party, so it will no longer be able to prolong this fratricidal and unjust war against the South and thus cause more bloodshed and death.

Source: U.S., JUSPAO, leaflet number 4492

longer the Party continues this war, the more people will
have to endure hunger and hardships."

A substantial number of fliers also dealt with the
progress of the war in the South (Figs 5.12, 5.13,
5.14). Emphasis was placed on the success in thwarting
Hanoi's invasion, achievements of the surrender and Chieu
Hoi programs, and popular support for the Saigon
government: "The people of South Vietnam, though longing
for peace, are determined to oppose the North Vietnamese
invasion of South Vietnam and the Party's scheme to
enslave the people of South Vietnam. Everybody - young
and old, big and small, male and female - is motivated by
the common goal of driving the invaders away to defend
their own freedom and happiness."

In October and November 1972, with a ceasefire
pending, U.S. propaganda informed the North Vietnamese
that peace was at hand (Fig 5.15). Coupling the up-
coming Tet New Year with the nostalgic desire to be
reunited with loved ones, leaflets proclaimed that "the
waiting is over" -- Northern troops imprisoned by the
Republic soon would be released, and those in Laos,
Cambodia, and South Vietnam also would return home --
"This will be the happiest Tet in memory."

The peace barrage was buttressed by news items
picturing the Lao Dong Party as isolated in its refusal
to seek a negotiated resolution to the conflict. Some of
the most prominent articles featured the re-election of
President Nixon, the Strategic Arms Limitation agreement
between the U.S. and U.S.S.R., the American-Soviet
agreement on peaceful uses of atomic energy, the food
crisis in the Soviet Union, Nixon's visit to Peking, and
the continuing Sino-Soviet dispute. One bulletin
reported that, "250,000 Soviet citizens recently staged a
three-hour protest march past the Chinese Embassy in
Moscow following a border clash between Soviet and
Chinese troops. Mao Tse-tung was hanged in effigy by the
demonstrators. The Soviets accuse the Chinese of
committing horrible atrocities. Anti-Soviet
demonstrations have been staged by millions of Chinese."

The intensive "Field Goal Operation" also produced
one of the most controversial issues of the psychological
offensive -- the use of a facsimile dong, the North
Vietnamese medium of exchange. The trouble began in 1972
when inflation of the dong prompted USIA's propagandists
to produce imitation banknotes to attract attention and
reinforce an attached message intended to increase
popular discontent about rising prices (Fig 5.16).

This ploy "boomeranged" when Hanoi responded with a
burst of specious charges that the U.S. was guilty of
forgery and attempts to undermine North Vietnam's
economy. Domestically, the government said inflation was
due to the bogus dong notes flooding the country;
globally, it damned President Nixon culpable of the
"international crime" of counterfeiting. The foreign

Figure 5.12
Why Don't You Ask the Party to Repay Its Debts?

Xe tăng Bắc Việt do Liên xô chế tạo bị phá hủy tại mặt trận Trị Thiên đầu năm 197... Thép còn chẳng chịu được bom và tên lửa thì thử hỏi xương thịt con người làm sao chịu nổi. 4584

A North Vietnamese tank destroyed by the Armed Forces of the Republic of Vietnam at the Tri-Thien Front. Steel cannot withstand rockets and bombs; what will such weapons do to flesh and bones?

The "liberation of the South" is like a game of chance played by the Lao Dong Party leaders against the Government and people of South Vietnam. It has been almost twenty years since the Party leadership began to play, and with every year it has claimed loudly that it is winning, that its adversary surely will be defeated. But every year they have come back to the people of North Vietnam and demanded further sacrifices. Every year, more North Vietnamese young men are lost foolishly by a losing gambler. . . . The Hanoi leadership is up to its neck in debts, like the Prince of Debtors. Don't believe it any longer. You should ask that it repay its debts. The Party leaders are gambling with your happiness and your future in a game which cannot be won. You should lend more of your blood and bones.

Source: U.S., JUSPAO, leaflet number 4584.

Figure 5.13
Soviet-American Relations

*Tổng Thư Ký Đảng Cộng Sản
Liên Xô Leonid Brezhnev nâng
ly chúc mừng Tổng Thống Hoa
Kỳ Richard Nixon sau khi thỏa
ước hạn chế vũ khí chiến, lược
được ký kết ngày 26 tháng 5 vừa
qua giữa Hoa Kỳ và Liên Xô*

**Cùng nhân dân miền Bắc
Việt Nam**

— Tổng Thống Hoa Kỳ Richard Nixon đã đến Mạc Tư Khoa ngày 22-5-1972 vừa qua để bắt đầu một cuộc viếng thăm 8 ngày.

— Tổng Thống Hoa Kỳ và các nhà lãnh đạo Liên Sô đã ký sáu thỏa ước lịch sử nhằm đi đến sự hợp tác giữa Hoa Kỳ và Liên Sô.

— Đặc biệt đáng chú ý là Hiệp Ước Hạn Chế Vũ Khí Chiến Lược được ký vào ngày 26 tháng 5 vừa qua mà Tổng Thống Nixon và Tổng Thư Ký Đảng Cộng Sản Leonid Brezhnev hoan hỉ cho rằng để *ngăn chặn cuộc chạy đua về vũ khí nguyên tử giữa Hoa Kỳ và Liên Sô*.

— Đồng thời một số thỏa ước khác cũng đã được ký kết, liên quan đến các lãnh vực Hợp Tác Không Gian, Bảo Vệ Khung Cảnh Thiên Nhiên, Y Tế, Khoa Học Kỹ Thuật và những vụ Rắc Rối ở Biển.   4508

Soviet Communist Party Secretary General Leonid Brezhnev drinks a toast to U.S. President Richard Nixon after signing the agreement on Strategic Weapons Limitation on May 26, 1972.

(Reverse side.)

WARNING: On 9 May 1972, mines were laid in the harbors and mouths of rivers of the Democratic Republic of Vietnam. These mines are dangerous to large and small boats, including fishing craft. You are advised to avoid navigation in all harbors and mouths of rivers.

Source: U.S., JUSPAO, leaflet number 4508.

Figure 5.14
South Vietnamese People Support the Government

Hình bên mặt là những người tình nguyện gia nhập đoàn
Nhân Dân Tự Vệ để bảo vệ xóm, làng. Nhân dân miền
Nam tuy yêu chuộng hòa bình, nhưng cương quyết đánh bại
cuộc xâm lăng của quân Cộng Sản Bắc Việt và mưu mô
nô lệ hóa miền Nam của Đảng. Già, trẻ, lớn, bé nữ hay nam
đều một lòng đánh đuổi quán xâm lăng Bắc Việt để bảo vệ
tự do, hạnh phúc.

4504

CONTINUED SUPPORT PROMISED

The photograph at right shows volunteers who have joined the
People's Self-Defense Force to defend their villages and hamlets.
The people of South Vietnam, though longing for peace, are
determined to oppose the North Vietnamese invasion of South Vietnam
and the Party's scheme to enslave the people of South Vietnam. . . .
In an 8 May 1972 message to the people of South Vietnam, the
President of the United States promised them continued firm support
in resistance against aggression. The population of the Republic of
Vietnam are united in their resistance to North Vietnamese
aggression. . . .

Source: U.S., JUSPAO, leaflet number 4504

Figure 5.15
A Ceasefire is Pending

VUI HƯỞNG THANH BÌNH

Những chiều Trường Sơn núi rừng cô quạnh,

Mẹ hiền ơi, con chợt nhớ quê mình.

Khói lam chiều, giàn mướp lá lên xanh,

Con bướm nhỏ, mái đình xưa nhớ quá.

Những câu này trích trong bài thơ của một chiến sĩ gửi cho mẹ là bà Trần Thị Phần. Chiến sĩ này từng tham dự nhiều trận đánh và đã tử trận cách đây vài năm.

Nhưng nay hòa bình đã đến với nước Việt Nam. Tất cả chiến sĩ có thể trở về quê nhà. Trong vòng 60 ngày sau khi ký kết thỏa hiệp, số ít binh sĩ Hoa kỳ còn lại sẽ rời Việt Nam.

Các bạn chắc chắn sẽ sớm về quê nhà trước Tết Quý Sửu (1973).

Trong vòng 60 ngày sau khi ký kết thỏa hiệp ngừng bắn, tất cả các lực lượng Hoa Kỳ sẽ rút khỏi Việt Nam. Các chiến sĩ Quân đội Nhân dân Việt nam chắc chắn sẽ sớm về quê nhà trước Tết Quý Sửu (1973).

Tết này sẽ là một cái Tết hạnh phúc nhất ghi sâu trong lòng mọi người.

TO ENJOY PEACE

Within sixty days of the signing of the ceasefire agreement, all American forces will be withdrawn from Vietnam. The soldiers of the Democratic Republic of Vietnam will be home long before Tet Quy Suu [Year of the Buffalo]. This will be the happiest Tet in memory.

Source: U.S., JUSPAO, leaflet number 4591.

Figure 5.16
Dong Banknote

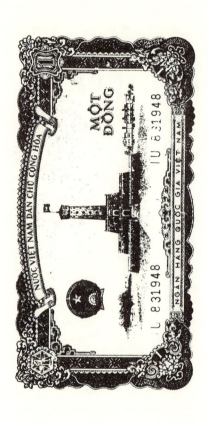

Hãy coi chừng

một cuộc cải cách

tiền tệ nữa.   Các

bạn có thể mất

tất cả tài sản,

công lao mồ hôi

nước mắt của bạn.

Dear Comrade,

You may lose all your property earned by your hard work, sweat, and tears. The Party is wasting the money-property of the people in the desperate war. While the war is going on, you don't feel like buying anything, but when the war is over, the country devastated, the money which the people are saving will be worthless.

Be alert for a currency exchange -- It may happen again.*

Source: U.S., JUSPAO, leaflet number 4743.

*Reference to a "currency exchange" apparently refers to the possibility of another devaluation of the dong similar to the one in 1959. In that anti-inflationary measure, the regime called in existing currency at a rate of 1,000 old to one new and virtually eliminated private savings throughout the country.

press echoed the Party's allegations around the world, and the U.S stopped distribution of the <u>dong</u> leaflet. It is not clear whether some of the circulars were passed off by some persons as real money, but as one American official explained, "It's not currency as such. . . . It's simulated currency likely to attract attention to our propaganda. I suppose with a scissors you could cut it out and if someone had dull vision or the light were bad you could pass it."[9]

Ho Chi Minh Trail Campaign

During the Indochina War the 6,000 mile labyrinth of concealed roads and paths stretching through the eastern portion of Laos became known worldwide as the "Ho Chi Minh Trail." With feeder routes extending into Cambodia and South Vietnam, it long was Hanoi's major lifeline to the war against Saigon. Calling it a "Trail," however, was one of the great misnomers of the twentieth century. In many areas the unpaved roads were in such excellent condition that truck convoys could travel at speeds of sixty miles per hour. The maze of roads making up the "Trail" rivaled Los Angeles freeways in intricacy and design.

The trek South along this route was a long a hazardous one for the Northern infiltrators, since American aircraft struck the "Trail" day and night trying to cut Hanoi's umbilical to the Viet Cong. Psychological operations supplemented the bombing and served as a propaganda bridge between the "Frantic Goat North" and "Field Goal Operation" campaigns and the Republic's Chieu Hoi and surrender programs. Most of the appeals were similar to those which exploited mental vulnerabilities of enemy soldiers in the South -- fears, hardships, loss of faith in victory, concern about families, and disillusionment with the Communist cause. Laotian rally overtures were also airdropped to the Northern troops. These American leaflets, purporting to be of Laotian origin, encouraged infiltrators to turn themselves over to the authorities before it was too late -- "The Royal Laotian Government invites you to rally to the Royal Army and save yourself from hardships and possible death" (Fig 5-17).

The psychological operations placed most emphasis on the soldier's <u>fear</u> of being killed, and, as so often was the case, these threats were linked with nostalgia and loneliness themes trying to sap both morale and the will to continue infiltration (Figs 5.18, 5.19). Many North Vietnamese believed they were given a one-way ticket for the journey south. As one intelligence account explained, "In Hanoi's military terminology, South Vietnam is known as the B Zone. Getting sent to South Vietnam is called 'taking a B.' Taking a trip down the

124

Figure 5.17
Lao Safe Conduct Pass

Trên đây là Giấy Thông Hành của chính phủ Vientiane. Hãy trình giấy này với bất cứ người lính hoặc viên chức nào của chính phủ Vientiane. Các bạn sẽ được đón tiếp nồng hậu.

YOUR FUTURE FATE

Because of the deceitful propaganda of the Lao Dong Party leaders you have been misled into believing that your "international obligation" includes violating the sovereignty and neutrality of the brotherly Khmer nation. Surely you realize by now that you comrades who believed in this Party falsehood are being fiercely opposed by the combined military might of the Vietnamese people of the South and their American allies. To protect our peace and prosperity we are determined to halt your aggressive fratricidal designs on your Vietnamese brothers. At this very moment your future Cambodian sanctuaries are now battlefields littered with your dead and wounded comrades. Your future fate will be a similar if you continue to follow the so-called "liberation path" to your beloved Vietnam of the South. The time to act is now. You must escape this future tragedy. If you wish to live in peace, show this leaflet to any official of the Vientiane Government. You will be welcomed and well treated.

Source: U.S., JUSPAO, leaflet number T-5-SPC.

Figure 5.18
Fear of Death

TẠI SAO LẠI PHẢI HY SINH TÍNH MẠNG XA QUÊ HƯƠNG CHO CẤP CHỈ HUY KHÔNG NHÌN NHẬN MÌNH ?

● ● ●

 CHÍNH PHỦ V.N.C.H. MONG ƯỚC NHỮNG NGƯỜI
CON LẦM LẠC TRỞ VỀ

The Government of Hanoi has sent South Vietnam complete divisions with weapons and ammunition causing more suffering for the people for nearly eight years. Now, in front of the world press, Xuan Thuy of the North Vietnamese Delegation in Paris made the statement: "North Vietnamese troops never exist in South Vietnam."

Why does Hanoi deny this sacrifice on the part of your soldiers in the South? You have come South to fight for a Communist Cause. And now Hanoi does not want to recognize that.

After you complete your infiltration, return to the welcome of the people and Army of South Vietnam. Your efforts will be respected and rewarded properly.

The Government of Vietnam needs and wants all of its sons and daughters.

Source: U.S., JUSPAO, leaflet number 2660-T.

Figure 5.19
Loneliness Along the Trail

Figure 5.19 (continued)

TAKE A HUSBAND, MY LOVE

Listen to me, my love.

Take a husband, my love, for my life is fast ebbing. Although I must lie to myself when giving you this advice. But, my darling, I must think of your future.

Have courage, my love. Don't delay, for the fires here in the South burn fiercely (the war rages on). My arm is torn from the body and with my life's blood I write this last plea.

Please listen, my darling, don't refuse. That I may die in peace without remorse. Darling, please have no anger for me and don't resent your fate. Rather, turn your anger and resentment on those who have driven me into this senseless war.

Oh, please, do as I say and this is all I ask, Darling. Bury our memories so that our love can melt away with the sinking sun. And my image and all there was of me shall fade forever from my homeland in the North.

Farewell sweetheart. We found no enemies here. Rather, it was I who opened fire first. My death is one deserved and I pay for my sin. It is you who remain behind who must suffer.

I am committed. And Eternal bitterness is my lonely fate. Oh, listen to my aching heart. And seek your ideals in love.

Source: U.S., JUSPAO, leaflet number T-84

Ho Chi Minh Trail has been called a 'death journey' in
many captured diaries."[10] Thus one handbill said, "This
trail is a one-way street -- you have been sent South to
fight until you die."

Burial themes were also aimed at heightening worries
of impending death: "Will you die in Laos far from your
ancestral home?" Another leaflet exploited beliefs in
ancestor worship with a photograph of a dead North
Vietnamese soldier and asking,

> IS THIS A GRAVE?
> Unfortunately it is not. But it is this
> soldier's final resting place, many thousands
> of kilometers from the graves of his ancestors.
> His body cannot be identified, his grave cannot
> be marked, and his soul will never find rest.

Some fliers reinforced the anti-Chinese theme used
in the "Frantic Goat North" campaign; photographs of
corpses were accompanied by the question: "Do you want
to be used as a Chinese bulletshield and die in vain like
this?"

Lack of food, medical case, shelter, and clothing
were highlighted in leaflets which exploited the severe
hardships along the "Trail." Another primary topic was
disease, since many infiltrators suffered from malaria
and dysentery. "When we first arrived in the South," a
Northern private summarized, "we were tired and many of
us had malaria. I think that this was because of our
long and hard trip to the South."[11] One imaginative
circular, therefore, offered some health tips:

HEALTH HINTS FOR THE TRAIL

You are facing 90 days of hard marching through
dense disease-infested jungle. Here are some
suggestions to help keep you alive and healthy
throughout the ordeal.
1. Keep your feet dry. Jungle infections
and fungus grow on moisture.
2. Disinfect and bandage all cuts and
scratches promptly. Inflammation born in cuts
can easily spread through your body.
3. Don't sleep in wet clothes. You may
wake up with a fever.
4. Never forget to take malaria pills.
One out of every three men who have preceded
you down the trail have succumbed to malaria.
5. Eat plenty of food. You will need the
strength to keep walking and resist disease.
Your food ration should be supplemented along
the trail if supplies have not been bombed or
stolen.

If you follow these rules you may live to die
in South Vietnam.

"If you are not sick from disease now," another
message warned, "you probably will be by the time you
reach South Vietnam. . . . The way ahead is hopeless.
Only the seriously wounded or fatally ill are sent back
to North Vietnam -- many of them will die along the
trail."

The loss of faith appeal was used primarily to
highlight Communist defeats (Fig 5.20). Although many
fighters still in Laos undoubtedly did not believe claims
that the Army had suffered heavy losses in the South,
JUSPAO hoped that once they arrived and experience
corroborated these claims, propaganda credibility would
be enhanced. Furthermore, once they were in the South,
Hanoi's soldiers were bombarded by leaflets and
loudspeaker broadcasts contrasting Party propaganda with
reality. These communications were followed up by safe
conduct passes, as well as hard-sell rally and surrender
appeals that took advantage of their surprise at the
conditions they found: These persuasive themes
frequently were linked closely to claims of lies and
betrayal by their leaders (Fig 5.21).

An early "Trail" leaflet illustrates this
coordinated approach:

SOLDIERS GOING SOUTH
DON'T BELIEVE YOUR CADRE
LOOK AROUND YOU IN THE SOUTH
BELIEVE YOUR OWN EYES

WHAT TO LOOK FOR IN THE SOUTH:
-- Are the people happy or unhappy?
-- Are they well clothed or not?
-- Do they have to attend political meetings
   (except for those areas temporarily under
   the control of the Hanoi authorities)?
-- How much does a bicycle cost, or a radio, or
   a meter of cloth? Is there rationing?
-- Are there travel controls and 'letters of
   introduction' (except in Party controlled
   areas)?
-- Are the people free to sell all that they
   raise or make? Are the people forced to
   join cooperatives?
-- Do the people want to be liberated?
-- Is 4/5th of South Vietnam 'liberated' as the
   cadre say?
-- Have any district or provincial capitals
   been 'liberated'?

Figure 5.20
Communist Losses in the South

CUỘC TẤN CÔNG

Cuộc tấn công của Đảng Lao Động vào dịp Tết ở miền Nam Việt Nam đã không thu được một thành tích quân sự nào theo ý chúng muốn cả. Lực lượng Việt Cộng do Đảng Lao Động chỉ huy, bất chấp những giờ phút thiêng liêng nhất của buổi đầu Xuân, đã tấn công Saigon và 43 thị trấn khác vào đêm Giao thừa. Chúng đã làm cho bao người

bị thương và chết chóc. Nhà của bao nhiêu đồng bào vô tội bị tiêu hủy. Dân chúng đã không ai trợ giúp những kẻ đã tấn công; trái lại dân chúng đã phụ

giúp lực lượng quân đội Việt Nam Cộng Hòa. Dân chúng miền Nam không cần bọn Cộng Sản giải phóng

vì chính họ đang sống tự do và hạnh phúc. Và bây giờ đây dân chúng miền Nam thù ghét lực lượng Cộng quân miền Bắc hơn bao giờ hết.

Đảng Lao Động cai trị miền Bắc đã bảo với các đồng bào rằng hàng triệu người ở miền Nam đã nổi dậy xung vào hàng ngũ Cộng Sản. Chuyện ấy đã không bao giờ xảy ra được. Vì làm sao mà giải phóng được một dân tộc đã sẵn có tự do?

Trong cuộc tổng tấn công vào dịp Tết của cộng quân, Quân Đội Việt Nam Cộng Hòa và Đồng Minh đã tiêu diệt hơn 65,000 cộng quân và bắt sống hơn 12,000. Các bạn đang bị đưa vào Nam để thay thế những người đó. Đa số các bạn sẽ chết xa nhà và thây bị chôn vùi dưới những nấm mồ vô chủ. Các bạn đừng nghe những lời dối trá của chính quyền Bắc Việt. Hãy tìm cơ hội rời bỏ đơn vị bạn và bước sang hàng ngũ của chính phủ Việt Nam Cộng Hòa.

95-T

THE COMMUNIST TET OFFENSIVE FAILED

Your Party-controlled government has been telling you that millions of people in the South rose to join the Communist ranks. This never happened. A free people cannot be liberated.

During the Communists' Tet offensive, the Army of the Republic of Vietnam and the Allies killed more than 65,000 Communist troops and captured more than 12,000. You are being sent South to replace them. Most of you will be killed far from home and buried in unmarked tombs. Don't listen to the lies of the regime in North Vietnam. Seize the first opportunity to leave your unit and come over to the ranks of the Republic of Vietnam.

Source: U.S., JUSPAO, leaflet number 95-T.

Figure 5.21
Lies and Betrayal by the Northern Leadership

(Cartoon showing two concealed North Vietnamese soldiers observing a prosperous South Vietnamese town.) One soldier says to the other: "We came South to liberate our compatriots. But after seeing how free and well-off they are, perhaps we should return North and help improve the lives of our people."

The leadership cadres often lie, saying the people of the South lead miserable lives and are awaiting your liberation. The truth is that the people of the South are free, happy and prosperous. They don't need your liberation and are determined to resist you everywhere.

Source: U.S., JUSPAO, leaflet number T-28.

Figure 5.22
Hardships Suffered by Family

CUỘC CHIẾN
TRANH ĐIÊN RỒ
MÀ CÁC LÃNH
TỤ CỘNG SẢN
BẮC VIỆT ĐANG
THEO ĐUỔI TẠI
MIỀN NAM CHẲNG
GIẢI PHÓNG ĐƯỢC
GÌ CẢ, MÀ LÀ ĐỂ
PHÁ VỠ MỌI GIA
ĐÌNH, NỀN TẢNG
CỔ TRUYỀN
CỦA XÃ HỘI
VIỆT-NAM.

RETURN TO YOUR FAMILY

The crazy war the North Vietnamese Communist leaders have been pursuing does not liberate anyone; it is a war that destroys traditional foundations of Vietnamese society.

You must return to your family now that you realize you were falsely deceived by your political cadre. You were told to go South to liberate, but instead you will be causing suffering and death to your compatriots in the South who would otherwise be enjoying a peaceful and free life. Therefore, your cause for fighting is not just! . . .

Find a way to leave your ranks so that you can return to your native village to live with your family. Your father and mother, your wife and children . . . are in need of you.

Source: U.S., JUSPAO, leaflet number T-10-SPC.

-- Are you free to have contact with the people
or must you hide in the forests? Will the
cadre let you go to towns and villages?

      YOU WILL SEE WHAT THE TRUTH
         IS IN THE SOUTH.
    IF THE CADRE HAVE LIED TO YOU
       ABOUT CONDITIONS IN THE SOUTH,
       CAN YOU BELIEVE ANYTHING THEY
       SAY?

"Why are you laboring in the jungles of Laos?," another
circular asked. "Your leaders claim great victories are
being won in the South. But wouldn't you be enjoying
yourself in Saigon, or any other city of South Vietnam,
if their claims were true?"

Interwoven with these themes was the <u>concern about
families</u> appeal (Fig 5.22). Many messages were aimed at
heightening the troops' concerns about the safety of
their families during American air strikes. Once again
the bombing of North Vietnam was linked to the Party's
aggression in the South. While placing the ultimate
blame on Hanoi, leaflets also pointed out that the
soldiers' willingness to fight was bringing greater
dangers to their loved ones: "As you part from your
family to start your long trek to the South, you leave
behind more than any empty place in the family circle.
You leave behind greater danger for your loved ones
because your invasion of the South is what makes the war
continue."

One unusually effective leaflet described the fears,
hardships, loss of faith, family concerns, and
disillusionment of one hapless infiltrator as he moved
down the "Trail." Air-delivered by the millions in both
parts of the nation, it contained a poem take from the
diary of a North Vietnamese soldier killed in August
1965. Subsequently, many ralliers and prisoners taken in
the South could recite the verses from memory, except for
the punchline added by JUSPAO at the end.

A POEM TO MOTHER

(A North Vietnamese youth spills out his heart)

From the day I left you, O mother,
To follow my companions in this trip through
    Laos to Central Vietnam,
I have endured the hardships of climbing up
    the green mountains
And marching through rain and shine.
Although at my young age life could have
    blossomed like a flower,
For the sake of Peace I don't mind

Enduring hardships and dangers.
For several months, I marched during the day
    and rested at night.
My shoes' heels have worn out and the cloth
On my shoulders was rubbed thin where the cold
    seeps in.
When the evening comes,
Besieged by loneliness in the heart of the
    Truong Son range,
O mother, I missed our home,
I missed the blue smoke, the gourd arbor,
The little butterfly, the old temple roof,
    O I missed them all
Here I am, though on strangers' soil
But the South is also my country,
With the same green-leafed coconut trees, the
    same roads
Filled with the scent of rice paddies,
The same blue smoke filling the evening sky,
The buffalo returning to its shelter,
The sound of a flute making one feel homesick.
As I got over my feeling of estrangement,
I began to look around and wondered what there
    was here to liberate.
The market was crowded with people in gay mood,
The rice fields were green with rice plants.
From a curve-roofed pagoda came the sound of a
    worship bell.
The class rooms were full of cheerful children
Singing a song in chorus.
And in a plot of garden the small butterflies
    were busy.
On the yellow cabbage flowers.
Peace and joy reigned throughout the country.
But why they ordered me to burn the villages,
    destroy the bridges,
Lay mines to sow death around?
Often my hands trembled
While laying a mine, because later on I saw
People blown up and blood sprayed around.
Whose blood was it?
It was the blood of our people, those like
    mother and me.
That night, my eyes were filled with tears
and sleep with nightmares.

The above poem was written by a North
Vietnamese youth to his mother, Mrs. Tran Thi
Phan of Hai Duong. This misled youth was
killed in the battle of Duc Co but undoubtedly
his soul is still blaming the Lao Dong Party
for having sent him to the South as a tool of
the Party's aggressive war against South

Vietnam. With due respect to the deceased, we
print this moving poem as a legacy to all our
young friends of North Vietnam who are in the
same situation as this unfortunate youth.

RADIO BROADCASTING

Many of the appeals and themes used in the leaflet
campaigns were supplemented by the radio commentaries of
South Vietnam's U.S.-sponsored "Voice of Freedom" and
USIA's "Voice of America." While featuring light music
and dramatic programs to gain and hold listening
audiences, selected news accounts were interspersed as
the most important persuasive channel. This was in
keeping with the axiom that news is the "first weapon of
propaganda" -- "The appeal of credible fact is universal;
propaganda does not consist of doctoring the fact with
moralistic blather, but of selecting the fact which is
correct, interesting, and bad for the enemy to know."[12]
By providing carefully chosen, non-editorialized and
ungarnished facts, American psychological warriors hoped
to establish the authenticity of their broadcasts,
enhancing the credibility of subsequent propaganda. As
Britisher R. H. S. Crossman says, "If you give a man the
correct information for seven years, he may believe in
incorrect information on the first day of the eighth year
when it is necessary from your point of view, that he
should do so."[13]
To increase the listening audiences, thousands of
miniature transistor radios were distributed in the
North. Parachuted into the country or washed ashore from
the Gulf of Tonkin, they were pre-set and functioning so
their noise would attract passers-by. The North
Vietnamese called them "Hoho-Hoho" machines, mimicing
their static bark. In addition, schedules of the
American radio stations and other non-Communist networks
were dispersed over the country (Fig 5.23). One leaflet
asked:

WHERE IS THE TRUTH?

For so long, the compatriots in North Vietnam
hear only through the Party's ears and see only
through the Party's eyes. Thus how can they
know what they want to know? If you want to
know the objective truth and all the news,
whether good or bad, concerning the war in
Vietnam and the situations of world affairs,
just tune in to

THE VOICE OF FREEDOM

Saigon's Ministry of Defense operated the Voice of

Figure 5.23
Radio Broadcasting Schedule

TIẾNG NÓI HOA KỲ

Tần số	Giờ phát thanh (giờ Hà Nội)
19-25-31-263	5g30-6g hằng ngày
16-19-25	11g30-12g hằng ngày
263-19-25-31	18g -18g30 hằng ngày
19-25-31-263	18g30-19g hằng ngày
25-19-31-263	20g -20g30 hằng ngày
25-31-19-263	21g -22g hằng ngày
19-25-31 190-263	23g -23g30 hằng ngày

VÔ TUYẾN TRUYỀN THANH VTVN

Tần số	Giờ phát thanh (giờ Hà Nội)
345	10 phút mỗi đầu giờ
62	
49	
31	liên tục từ 6g đến 6g 10
25	từ 7g đến 7g 10
491	.....
41	

B.B.C.

Tần số	Giờ phát thanh (giờ Hà Nội)
12	6g30-7g hằng ngày
14	6g30-7g hằng ngày
17	6g30-7g hằng ngày
19	6g30-7g hằng ngày
25	6g30-7g hằng ngày
31	6g30-7g hằng ngày
42	6g30-7g hằng ngày

TIẾNG NÓI TỰ DO

Tần số	Giờ phát thanh (giờ Hà Nội)
362	5g-7g hằng ngày
	13g-23g hằng ngày
	23g-23g30 hằng ngày
31	13g-23g hằng ngày
	23g-23g30 hằng ngày

Phát thanh trong bóng
10 phút mỗi đầu giờ

DO YOU KNOW THE TRUTH ABOUT THE PARIS PEACE TALKS?

The bombing of your area continued because Lao Dong Party leaders are using your land as a road to send North Vietnamese troops to attack the people of the South. Will the peace talks in Paris bring an end to the bombing? Do Lao Dong leaders care what happens to you? You can keep yourself informed about the progress of the peace talks by listening to radio broadcasts in the Vietnamese language. News schedules are listed above. (Schedules for Radio Saigon, Voice of Freedom, Voice of America, and the British Broadcasting Corporation.)

Source: U.S., JUSPAO, leaflet number 132.

Freedom located at Hue. Broadcasting began in 1964; in
the beginning substantial American financial, technical,
and advisory assistance was provided to make up for the
lack of Vietnamese expertise. Over the years a dynamic
formal instruction and on-the-job training program
successfully raised the level of competence of the native
employees. As they became more adept at radio work, U.S.
support for the station gradually was phased out; all aid
was terminated in 1972.
     Initially, taped programs were aired for about two
and one half hours daily over a relatively weak 20-
kilowatt transmitter which reached only the southern-most
provinces of North Vietnam and the coast to the Chinese
border. This limited coverage continued until 1968 when
two 100-kilowatt transmitters, mounted in tandem at the
mouth of the Pearl River near Hue, made possible an
increase to twenty-one hours daily. Prime time for the
Voice of Freedom was between 10 P.M. and 1 A.M. Since
most people worked all day and were required to attend
political indoctrination meetings at night, late evening
was the only time when most were free. Moreover,
darkness provided cover for covert listening.
     The programming featured both news and music. These
included a special women's show, reviews of scientific
developments, reports of progress and prosperity in the
non-Communist world, readings from romantic or political
short stories and books banned in the North, traditional
music from all regions of Vietnam featuring well-known
singers, Vietnamese folk music, "golden music" or popular
love songs banned by Hanoi but in demand by the young,
and neo-classical dramas. In addition, Voice of Freedom
had its own symphony orchestra, and a chorus of twenty-
three voices was selected from its employees.
     The following 1970 highlights provide an overview of
the radio station's content:

     Newscasts -- Aired every hour on the hour (twenty-
     one news reports daily) and headlines delivered on
     the half hour;
     Special Events -- Accounts of happenings in South
     Vietnam as recorded by two-man field teams which
     traveled about the countryside;
     Commentary and Analysis -- A five-minute political
     commentary and a brief news analysis (three or four
     times daily);
     "Bridge of Love" -- Names and addresses of North
     Vietnamese soldiers who were killed or who defected
     in the South (broadcast to their relatives in two
     nine-minute segments, each four times daily);
     "Words in the Night" -- A disc jockey show,
     conducted by a well-known vocalist, which included
     light political and social commentary interspersed
     between music (forty minutes in two sections, aired

twice between midnight and dawn);
"Sentimental Letter" -- Letters written by ralliers
to their relatives in the North (nine minutes, four
times daily);
"Hoai Phuong Show" -- Music and a soft-spoken girl
talking with Northern soldiers about life in the
South (twenty minutes, three times daily);
"To Sing a Song" -- Words to popular songs read very
slowly to allow copying; North Vietnamese youths
formed clubs to copy and disseminate words to pop
music broadcast by the Voice of Freedom (twenty
minutes weekly);
"Tran Quan Show" -- Vietnamese popular music aired
by a male disc jockey;
"On the Way to Liberation" -- Testimonials by
defectors of the dangers and hardships suffered
while trying to "liberate" the South (fifteen
minutes weekly);
"Confidential Friend of Northern Troops" -- Anti-
French resistance period music, popular in the North
but banned by Hanoi, featuring a well-known female
vocalist talking with Viet Cong prisoners and
Northern ralliers (twenty minutes weekly);
"Open Arms" -- Experience of hoi chanh, often
including poetry and songs written and sung by
defectors (twenty minutes, twice weekly);
"Our Villages and Hamlets" -- Interviews with the
rural populace concerning their everyday life, work,
and betterment as provided by Saigon's pacification
program (fifteen minutes, twice a week);
"World of Little Huyen" -- A children's program
written in drama form, depicting the life of South
Vietnamese youngsters (fifteen minutes weekly);
"Propaganda and Truth" -- Hanoi's policy confusion
as shown through exposure of contradictions taken
from Communist publications and broadcasts (twenty
minutes, three times a week); and
"Think on These Things" -- Errors and contradictions
in Communist theory and practice pointed out to
Northern cadres by authoritative persons from the
South (ten minutes, three times weekly).

Although such radio broadcasts could reach audiences
over great distances, this also increased the problems of
assessing effectiveness. Throughout the war, the Voice
of Freedom was uncertain about the size of its audience
and extent of its influence. Listening to the broadcasts
was forbidden by Hanoi, but some Northern prisoners
reported they had eavesdropped on a few of the programs
before infiltrating. Such feedback was useful in judging
the radio station's importance, but a time lag of six
months to a year between a soldier's hearing a broadcast
in the North and his trek down the Ho Chi Minh Trail,

being captured or defecting and questioned, obviously impaired accurate recall.

Another indication of effectiveness came in 1970 through use of an evaluation panel: Vietnamese of varied backgrounds, who had either lived or spent considerable time in the North, analyzed and evaluated a random sample of Voice of Freedom's daily programmed. They generally rated the propaganda very effective and made few criticisms. The panel gave especially high marks to the use of forbidden traditional music as symbolic of pre-Communist Vietnamese philosophy. The "Bridge of Love," which gave the names of soldiers killed in action, was also regarded as a potent factor in gaining and keeping a widespread audience.[14]

In addition to the Voice of Freedom there was USIA's Voice of America. It identified itself openly as the radio organ of the United States and featured music, news, and editorials. Troubles in the Communist world and the Sino-Soviet rift received primary emphasis. During the North's invasion of South Vietnam in 1972, Voice of America commentaries, aired eighteen hours daily, focused on the attempts to restore peace. Like the Voice of Freedom, the names of captured and killed North Vietnamese soldiers were broadcast to increase listenership.[15]

THE STRANGE CASE OF NGUYEN VAN BE

One of the more unusual special psychological operations campaigns of the Indochina War concerned a Viet Cong soldier around whom the Communists had organized a "hero emulation" campaign.[16] The tale of Nguyen Van Be was intended to instill a spirit of self-sacrifice in the youth of North Vietnam and, to some extent, of the South as well. But, after Hanoi had conducted a six-month political indoctrination drive stressing the "revolutionary zeal" of this "martyred hero," the hapless Nguyen Van Be turned up alive in one of Saigon's prisoner-of-war camps. The Allies immediately launched an extensive communications barrage aimed at exposing the Communist fabrication. Predictably, Hanoi responded with vitriolic counterpropaganda.

According to the Lao Dong Party, Be was born in 1946 to a poor peasant family living in the Mekong Delta region of South Vietnam. He had been a member of the Viet Cong's "People's Youth League" and later joined the "Liberation Army." There Be became a model of "revolutionary zeal" as an ammunition carrier. He was captured on May 30, 1966, while moving explosives through a canal network. He was taken to the town of My An where American and South Vietnamese officers crowded around him to see the grenades, mines, and ammunition he had been transporting. One of the officers asked Be how the mines were operated. In response, Be

. . . bent down and lifted the mine which weighed twenty pounds. . . . Hatred increased his strength tenfold. Raising the mine above his head, his eyes shining with a terrible fire, he shouted: "Long live the National Front for Liberation. Down with American imperialists." There was a general stampede: the terrified officers and men tried to flee. But it was too late. Be smashed the detonation against the body of the nearby armored vehicle. A terrible explosion was heard. . . . Thus 69 enemy personnel were killed, among them 12 Americans (one captain) and 20 puppet officers. . . . From that day, the local people would burn incense sticks in honor of the hero who had sacrificed his life to win such glorious victory. Everyone passing through the city could hear the legendary story of the N.L.F. fighter Nguyen Van Be.[17]

The Viet Cong and North Vietnamese began telling his "legendary story" in the fall of 1966. He was a perfect subject for extolling revolutionary virtue because of his poor background and earlier membership in the Communist youth activities. In the North, Be's "martyred death" was the subject of several pamphlets, plays, poems, and newspaper and magazine articles. Radio broadcasts also discussed the "dead" hero as an inspirational example for all Vietnamese youngsters. Additionally, an opera was written about his supposed exploits, at least two statues were erected in his honor, over four million people took part in a six-weeks course devoted to studying "the legend of his valiant life and heroic death," and the Viet Cong awarded him the posthumous title of "Indomitable Loyalty and Magnificent Bravery."[18]

In February 1967 a prison guard noticed a striking resemblance between a humble prisoner named Nguyen Van Be and pictures of the "hero martyr" appearing in Communist publications. After this startling discovery was brought to the attention of the authorities, questioning and observation confirmed that Be the prisoner and Be the dead "hero martyr" were one and the same. Agreeing to cooperate, he was presented at a press conference on March 13, 1967, in Saigon to relate the actual circumstances of his capture. According to Be, the battle was over in minutes and he had had no chance to get his hands on a gun to fight back. After four of his comrades were killed, he dove into the canal and attempted to swim underwater to the other side. A South Vietnamese soldier jumped on him and pulled him out by

his hair. He struggled, but was beaten into submission.
     The Be episode gave the Allies a unique opportunity
to undermine and discredit the Communist indoctrination
programs. They mounted a closely coordinated
counterpropaganda campaign about the "live 'dead'
hero." Initial exploitation was aimed at establishing
the fact that he was alive. By July 1967 JUSPAO had
publicized the Be affair for Southern audiences through
the production of more than thirty million leaflets,
seven million cartoon leaflets, 465,000 posters, a
special newspaper in 175,000 copies, 167,000 photographs
for community displays, 10,000 songsheets, several motion
pictures, and numerous radio and television programs
featuring Be, his family, and his hoi chanh friends.
Material was provided the international press, and
extensive exhibits were shown in the cities and
countryside. The Voice of Freedom covered the "live
'dead' hero" extensively in its programs beamed to the
North, and millions of leaflets (twenty million alone in
April 1967) informed the Northern populace that Be was
alive and well (Figs 5.24, 5.25).[19]
     The Communists, on the other hand, responded to Be's
reappearance with intensified indoctrination efforts,
urging youths to emulate his model of self-sacrifice. On
May 30, the anniversary of his supposed death, the
Central Secretariat of the Vietnamese Labor Youth
directed that "major theme study meetings" be conducted
concerning the "revolutionary" exploits of Be and a
heroic anti-aircraft gunner of the North. These
assemblies were aimed at bringing some four million young
people into "youth forums, cultural and drama activities
and action campaigns bearing the name Nguyen Van Be." In
addition, extensive newspaper accounts, films, a third
statue, and a full-length book were named after the
"hero-martyr."
     A second Communist response was a harsh denunciation
of the "clumsy and stupid" American-South Vietnamese
"swindle." Three days after Be's initial press
conference, Radio Hanoi told its Southern audience:

        In the past few days psychological warfare
        organs of the Americans and their lackeys in
        Saigon employed every propaganda trick to
        invent a story about the reappearance of Hero
        Nguyen Van Be in their prison before they
        released the news that Nguyen Van Be had been
        arrested and was living safe in their claws
        without being tortured. . . . Their trick
        about Hero Nguyen Van Be is an insolent offense
        to all the Vietnamese people. They dared
        offend an outstanding hero who represented the
        revolutionary heroism of the anti-U.S. national
        salvation generation. Southern compatriots,

Figure 5.24
Be Episode: For the South Vietnamese

"LIỆT SĨ" BÉ GẶP LẠI CÁC ĐỒNG CHÍ CŨ

NGÀY 15 THÁNG 7 NĂM 1967

Anh Nguyễn-Văn-Bé đã gặp lại ba đồng chí cũ, những người đã cùng thời gian
với anh phục vụ trong Mặt Trận Giải Phóng. Trong hình từ trái sang phải :
Nguyễn-Văn-Ba, Trung Đội Trưởng kiêm Chính Trị Viên Trung Đội B4 thuộc 860 × 16,
Nguyễn-Văn-Tho Tiểu Đội Trưởng A1, B2 thuộc Đơn Vị 332 × Y2 và
Nguyễn-Văn-Bé, người mà Mặt Trận Giải Phóng đã phong là "LIỆT SĨ".
Anh Bé đang cầm tờ Tiền Phong, tờ báo đã đăng tải câu chuyện của anh xuất
bản tại Hà-Nội. Mặt sau là hình tờ báo.   SP- 2138

BẠN CÓ THỂ DÙNG TRUYỀN ĐƠN NÀY NHƯ
MỘT GIẤY THÔNG HÀNH.   KHÔNG CÓ THÔNG
HÀNH BẠN VẪN ĐƯỢC TIẾP ĐÓN NỒNG HẬU.

"MARTYR-HERO" BE MEETS AGAIN HIS OLD COMRADES

On 15 July 1967 Nguyen Van Be met again his old comrades who
had served the same length of time with him in the Liberation
Front. . . . Be is holding a copy of the Tien Phong newspaper,
which published his story in Hanoi. . . .
The Party can make a newspaper hero. But it cannot admit a
mistake. If you are really interested in reading closely, you can
see the size of their error.

Source: U.S., JUSPAO, leaflet number SP-2138.

southern youths, and especially liberation combatants, comrades of Nguyen Van Be, will surely not forgive them and will punish them severely.[20]

The foreign audience also was addressed. Radio Hanoi's international service in English alleged,

The falsification of South Vietnam Hero Nguyen Van Be's story by the United States and its Saigon henchmen is sheer knavery showing how they are afraid of his great example of patriotism. . . . But the clumsy forgery about Hero Nguyen Van Be cannot dim the light spread by his sublime act nor minimize the great educational effect of his sacrifice among the South Vietnamese youths and people who are rushing to avenge him and bring nearer the day of complete victory.[21]

In June 1967 an article from Doc Lap ("Independence"), a weekly North Vietnamese newspaper oriented toward the Southern population, informed its readers:

To us, youths and students of Da-Nang, we are grateful and esteem Be, our beloved friend, elder brother and comrade. In memory of him we are determined to follow his heroic example and pledge to trail him in the struggle to sweep off the American invaders and the traitors to regain independence, freedom for the people and our youths.[22]

For Northern consumption, the Lao Dong Party's newspaper, Nhan Dan, claimed plastic surgery was used to create a person looking like Be.

It is almost one year now since Nguyen Van Be sacrificed his life for this country. Now his mine has exploded once again and this time it burst right at the American throat. . . . From Saigon, the Americans started a coup d'etat against Nguyen Van Be. It is not necessary to look for Be's replacement in the bulky documents and files of the CIA. Zorthian merely resorted to the Hollywood technique of selecting actors and the medical art of changing facial traits as applied in Hongkong and Japan.[23]

In July 1967, the Communists offered two million piasters, or about $16,950, for anyone who "cancelled"

Figure 5.25

Be Episode: For the North Vietnamese

145

Figure 5.25 (continued)

THE "LATE HERO" NGUYEN VAN BE READS ABOUT HIS OWN DEATH

A very strange story indeed. According to the Communists, Nguyen Van Be died a glorious death in the service of the cause. Supposedly after he was captured by Army of Republic of Vietnam forces he detonated a mine killing himself and 69 Americans and Government of Vietnam troops. Glowing accounts of his death were printed in Communist newspapers and read over Radio Hanoi and Liberation Radio. Many poems and songs were written about his exploits. A statue was even built in his honor. But, as can be plainly seen, he is very much alive. He is shown reading about his own death in the Hanoi newspaper Tien Phong of December 7, 1966. The Communists say that Be chose a hero's death. Be says that he never fired a shot and did not even think about exploding a mine.

Source: U.S., JUSPAO, leaflet number 66.

the "false" Be permanently. They increased their
pressure on the populace around his home area in the
Mekong Delta and threatened to shoot "on the spot" anyone
who said he was alive. Several hoi chanh who had
defected because of the "live 'dead' hero" were reported
to have been put on the Viet Cong's "blood debt" list.[24]
    Because of Hanoi's specious condemnation, Allied
propagandists tried to provide positive proof that Be was
alive by taking him to his home hamlet, hoping to film
his reunion with family and friends. But, having never
seen his home from the air, he directed the helicopter to
the wrong location. Meanwhile, the Viet Cong had
obtained a statement from his parents saying that the man
claiming to be their son was an imposter. However, when
the actual reunion did take place a few days later,
mutual recognition was "immediate and positive."
    That was still not the end of the Be story -- each
year on May 30, the anniversary of his claimed death,
Allied psychological operations exploited the "live
'dead' hero" incident with a variety of propaganda
messages to show him as being alive and well. Annual
Voice of Freedom broadcasts to the North also brought up
the live "hero martyr." Despite all these efforts, Louis
Steed, senior U.S. advisor during 1968-1972, believed
that after the initial successes in 1967, Hanoi had
probably succeeded in convincing most people that the
individual claiming to be Be was a person made up to look
like him.
    Indeed, the strange episode of Nguyen Van Be
illustrates and reaffirms the axiom that, in an
international propaganda duel between countries, people
tend to believe their own government over foreign ones.

EFFECTIVENESS

    American air attacks against the North caused
special problems for JUSPAO's leaflet and radio
propagandists. The North Vietnamese were severely
punished for continuing the conflict in the South as
countless bombs flattened the country's war-supporting
industry, disrupted its agriculture, and ravaged its
major transportation arteries. But infusion of large
amounts of economic and military aid from the Soviet
Union and Chinese People's Republic sustained Hanoi's
determination and capability to withstand the bombardment
and carry on the war. While the air strikes devastated
the North's primary transportation system, the ingenuity
and tenacity of its people ensured continuing movement of
men and supplies to South Vietnam. A 1966 draft
memorandum from Defense Secretary McNamara to President
Johnson summarized the military and psychological effects
of the bombing campaign:

The increased damage to targets is not
producing noticeable results. . . . No serious
transport problem in the movement of supplies
to or within North Vietnam is evident. . . .
The raids have disrupted the civil populace and
caused isolated food shortages, but have not
significantly weakened popular morale. Air
strikes continue to depress economic growth and
have been responsible for abandonment of some
plans for economic development, but essential
economic activities continue. The increasing
amounts of physical damage sustained by the
North Vietnamese are in a large measure
compensated by aid received from other
Communist countries.[25]

Clearly, there was little that leaflets and radio
broadcasts could say that was effective. Moreover, a
psychological "boomerang" effect resulted from the air
strikes; a "burst of patriotism" rather than despair
followed the initial bombing. The Party adroitly fanned
the fires of anger from these attacks and channeled the
people's ire toward hatred of the United States and
dedication to driving the "foreign invaders" from
Vietnam. A U.S. Army research group reported in 1966
that, "occasional reports by non-Communist visitors to
North Vietnam, although fragmentary, suggested that most
of the people became highly conscious of their Vietnamese
identity and that generally they seemed to support the
regime. The same sources also suggested that after the
initiation of United States air attacks in 1965 the
popular attitude toward the United States 'toughened.'"[26]
     Nor should this account be surprising; a 1966 report
by the Institute for Defense Analysis pointed out that
Americans failed, ". . . to appreciate the fact, well-
documented in the historical and social scientific
literature, that a direct, frontal attack on a society
tends to strengthen the social fabric of the nation, to
increase popular support of the existing government, to
improve the determination of both the leadership and the
populace to fight back, to induce a variety of protective
measures that reduce the society's vulnerability to
future attack, and to develop an increased capacity for
quick repair and restoration of essential functions."[27]
In short, the negative lessons of World War II saturation
bombings of German cities had been forgotten.
     Hanoi's answer to the bombing and psychological
assaults was an immense "Hate the U.S." campaign combined
with shrewd calls to Vietnam's past. Just as Stalin
appealed to pre-revolution Russian nationalism as the
Germans rolled toward Moscow, Ho Chi Minh turned to
traditional Vietnamese nationalism as the Americans
stepped up air attacks against the North. Setting the

theme in an April 1965 address to the National Assembly, Ho implored: "To oppose the United States and save the country is the most sacred task of every Vietnamese patriot."[28] Subsequently, the Party's propaganda and indoctrination apparatus went into full swing; newspapers were filled with captions such as "Hanoi Full of Hate." Anti-American slogans were spread throughout the country. -- "Defeat the United States Imperialist Aggressors," "Hammer in One Hand and Rifle in the Other," "Work for Reunification of the Fatherland," "Struggle for National Salvation."

The intensified ideological catechism pictured the populace as a "heroic people," maintaining industrial and agricultural production despite the bombing. The public's efforts were praised as bringing about "inevitable Communist victory" and reunification of North and South Vietnam. These claims were further supported by allegations that the Viet Cong was winning in the South, the Saigon government's "puppet army" was disintegrating, the anti-U.S. struggle by the Southern population was intensifying, and American forces were said to have poor morale and to be soft and that they could be beaten by the "people's war" despite their technological advantages.[29]

Wire-diffusion radio networks, the press, periodicals, books, posters, banners, murals, drawings, motion pictures, exhibits, lectures, meetings, and demonstrations all carried the anti-American theology to the people.[30] The Lao Dong Party's control of communications was total, and no segment of North Vietnamese life escaped its crusade against the new "foreign invaders."

Face-to-face indoctrination by Party cadres was the most important communications channel employed in this "Hate the U.S." campaign. Party propagandists personally carried Hanoi's line to every community, cooperative, work site, factory, hospital, and school in the country. Systematic ideological instruction fostered public support for the Communist political and social order, while mobilization drives and "hero emulation" movements helped neutralize psychological inroads made by U.S. propaganda. For instance, an "Each One Works As Two" campaign called upon the people to help neutralize the effects of American bombing by working harder to support the "revolution" in the South. A "Three Ready" movement urged North Vietnamese youth to be "ready to fight," "ready to join the Army," and "ready to go anywhere" they were needed "to defeat the enemy." A "Three Responsibilities" drive exhorted women to take up work normally performed by men now in military service, care for their families and those of soldiers at the front, and join the local militia.

The regime's attempts to rally the popular support

for the "greatest patriotic war of our history" was made
easier because of the bombing. The success of the
Party's indoctrination was evident in comments by North
Vietnamese held prisoner in the South:

> At first, the people . . . were frightened
> because of the air attacks. They hated the
> Americans a great deal for it. . . . The
> people got very mad and cursed the Americans a
> great deal.
> All the construction works the people had
> completed in ten years by tightening their
> belts were destroyed by the Americans. So,
> they hated the Americans a lot.
> The people hated the Americans because to them
> the Americans were the cruel enemy who had
> bombed the civilian population.[31]

Although Party leaders found it relatively easy to
convert popular loyalty and devotion to Vietnam into
support for the war by resurrecting historical
nationalism, they carefully maintained the essential
elements of Communist doctrine as well. Thus, patriotic
sentiments were often couched in Marxist-Leninist
terms. "Revolutionary heroism," for instance, provided
the key to linking Vietnamese nationalism and Communism
together. It included calls on the people to maintain
the dual tasks of building a socialist society while
resisting the "imperialist" invasion -- the "anti-U.S.
patriotic struggle" and "revolutionary heroism" were
considered as interdependent and mutually reinforcing. A
June 1970 editorial in Nhan Dan summarized the essence of
this nationalist-Communist motivational appeal: "This
revolutionary heroism consists in being loyal to the
party and to the people's democratic state, selflessly
defending the fatherland and the revolutionary
undertaking, serving the people unconditionally,
respected them, uniting together to assist them relying
on them to fulfill tasks, possessing a high spirit of
organization and discipline, being self-conscious,
seriously implementing the Party's lines and policies,
the state's laws, and the upper echelon's instructions
and orders, and possessing the revolutionary ethics of
being thrifty, honest, impartial, industrious, creative,
resourceful, valiant, active, strenuous, careful,
concrete, and exact."[32] A truly "revolutionary
combatant" was cast as an individual dedicated to both
pre-colonial Vietnamese nationalism and twentieth century
Marxism-Leninism.
     Within the People's Army of Vietnam the Party's
political catechism was aimed primarily at inculcating
its troops with fervid patriotism and loyalty to inspire
self-sacrifice and dedication to the "struggle for

national salvation." Indoctrination of the soldiers also included appeals to motivate their struggle against the class enemy on the political and ideological fronts; i.e., a "working class" viewpoint. Their oath of allegiance ("Ten Honorary Oaths"), for example, included both nationalist and Marxist-Leninist content. Swearing "under the glorious flag of the Fatherland," their first pledge was:

> We solemnly swear to sacrifice everything for the Vietnam Fatherland, struggle for the future of the people, Democracy and Socialism under the leadership of the Vietnam Labor Party and the Democratic Republic of Vietnam Government in order to build up a rich and strong Vietnam country, achieve Peace, Reunification, Independence and Democracy, and contribute efforts to the safeguarding of peace for South-East Asia and the World.[33]

A central feature of the Party's efforts to inspire and motivate its troops was "revolutionary heroism" as applied to the military. "Hatred of the U.S." was the heart of their fighting creed. This theme formed the core of the soldiers' training and was constantly reinforced through frequent indoctrination by political officers assigned to the Army units. One group of researchers believed that "Party propagandists were attempting to attach qualities of almost supernatural power to this hatred theme." Quan Doi Nhan Dan outlined its essence:

> Hatred is a revolutionary sentiment which is very important in fighting. It is the explosive power of our heart. It is the soul of each bullet and is the bayonet pointing against the enemy. It transforms the steel and iron in our hands into invincible strength . . . with hatred one is bold, with the flame of hatred burning their hearts, our fighters would not fear difficulties and would not retreat in the face of death.[34]

The effectiveness of this motivational approach was reflected in the comments by Northern prisoners captured in the South. One private, for instance, gave a poignant explanation for his hatred of the U.S.:

> When I was still in the North I heard about . . . the miserable life the Vietnamese people in the South had to suffer, about the American bombardment damaging the country, killing the people, and I felt that as a young man of the

country which is being invaded by the
foreigners, and I must do something to give the
South Vietnamese people a hand to liberate the
country . . . after arriving in the South I
understand more about the miseries of the
people there, I hated the enemies and I became
very enthusiastic to fight.
Another private added:
If we don't fight, the Americans would conquer
our country. Moreover, after the Americans
dropped bombs on North Vietnam to destroy our
economy, to kill the children in the schools
and patients in the hospitals, our willingness
to fight increased considerably.[35]

In sum, the Northern Soldier's political
socialization and "Hatred of the U.S." combined with the
psychological controls exercised by the Party served to
solidify and sustain his morale and dedication to driving
the "foreign invaders" from Vietnam. He expected the war
to be a long one, but he accepted his fate of having to
fight a materially superior "aggressor" in a "people's
war." He considered it his moral and patriotic duty to
fight for the "liberation of the South from American
imperialists."
In short, American psychological operations were
forced to use impersonal scraps of paper and radio
broadcasts to penetrate the all encompassing, intricate
ideological shield thrown-up around the North's
population and armed forces. In competition with the Lao
Dong Party's communications monopoly and its personalized
political indoctrination as well as the public's natural
love for homeland, the U.S. propaganda first had to get a
hearing and then to sap the will of the military and
motivate the people to pressure their rulers to end the
conflict. Clearly, the odds were overwhelmingly in favor
of Hanoi; failure of the psychological offensive could
have been foretold of the beginning.
On the other hand, the leaflet and radio appeals
undoubtedly did score some successes; they raised
questions which the leadership would have preferred left
unasked. The propaganda surely created some friction,
divisiveness, and discontent among the North
Vietnamese. However, stirring up such troubles was a
long way from convincing the Party to cease its military
activities and agree to a negotiated settlement. In
final analysis, neither American bombing nor
psychological operations had any measurable effect either
on undermining Northern morale or willingness to continue
the fight. As Robert Shaplen, noted journalist and
trenchant observer of the Indochina War, summarized in
1970:

The North Vietnamese are still deeply dedicated
to their cause of the 'liberation' of the South
and hold a continuing staunch belief in the
advantages of Communism in the North.   This
belief . . . entails acceptance of the harsh
regimen and strict security measures imposed on
the North by the war, and a conviction that the
war in the South has been a legitimate drive
for 'national salvation' -- a natural and
logical sequel to the struggle against the
French that began in 1945.[36]

Indeed, the military and psychological
ineffectiveness of the self-restrained bombing, coupled
with immense infusions of Soviet and Chinese aid and the
Party's successful ideological motivation campaign, were
hurdles too great for the American propaganda to
overcome.

NOTES

1.   U.S., JUSPAO, "Operation Memorandum: Newspaper
Nhan Van (NP-3) for Airdrop in North Vietnam" (Saigon:
October 29, 1965).
2.   U.S., JUSPAO, General Briefing Book (1968), p.
27.
3.   U.S., JUSPAO, Psyops in Vietnam, pp. 44-45.
4.   Ibid., pp. 46-47.
5.   Ibid, p. 53.
6.   Tran Van, Hoc Tap (Hanoi: September 1967).
7.   U.S., JUSPAO, Psyops in Vietnam, p. 47.
8.   U.S., Department of the Army, Area Handbook for
North Vietnam, Pamphlet No. 550-57 (Washington, D.C.:
Government Printing Office, June 1967), p. 241.
9.   "USAF Dropping 'Money' Leaflets on N. Vietnam,"
International Herald Tribute (September 20, 1972), p. 2,
and "Americans Drop Forged Banknotes on N. Vietnam," The
Times (London: October 10, 1972), p. 7.
10.   George McArthur, "Hanoi's Army: Good Soldiers
But Human," Washington Post (April 23, 1972), p. B4, and
"The Ho Chi Minh Trail: A Spidery, Constantly Shifting
Route," New York Times (February 5, 1971).
11.   Quoted in Kellen, Conversations with Enemy
Soldiers, p. 15.
12.   Linebarger, Psychological Warfare, p. 137.
13.   R. H. S. Crossman as quoted by William E.
Daugherty, ed., "The Creed of a Modern Propagandist,"
Psychological Warfare Casebook, p. 38.
14.   U.S., JUSPAO, "Panel Evaluation of Voice of
Freedom Broadcasts," JUSPAO Memorandum (Saigon:
September 9, 1970) (mimeographed).
15.   Richard Reston, "U.S. Steps Up Its Propaganda
Aimed at N. Vietnam's Morale," International Herald

Tribune (August 3, 1972), p. 2.

16. The core of the Vietnamese Communist motivation doctrine was formed by the hero emulation program or, in Hanoi's terms the "cult of revolutionary heroism." They had been very successful in using this technique in the past by capitalizing on the exploits of dead heroes. Stories concerning the heroic sacrifices made by the martyrs were repeated in hundreds of daily group meetings and discussed throughout the mass media. During the group discussions, after the heroic story had been repeated, everyone was required to tell how he could apply the "spirit of revolutionary heroism" to his own life. In the present case, the peak of achievement and glory could be attained by emulating Nguyen Van Be.

17. Quoted in U.S., JUSPAO, _Further Exploitation of the Nguyen Van Be Case_, Policy Number 42 (Saigon: July 27, 1967).

18. U.S., USIA, _Viet Cong Haunted By Still Living "Dead Hero"_, USIA Feature Number 67-SM-95 (Washington, D.C.: August 1967).

19. JUSPAO was fully aware of the importance ". . . that our campaign does not assume that because truth is on our side, most of the battle is won," and that JUSPAO ". . . should not imply the Vietnamese youth are not capable of heroism." Rather, "Our stance is to suggest that the Communists have now insulted the memory of many genuine Vietnamese heroes throughout history." See U.S., JUSPAO, "Viet Cong Live 'Dead' Hero," Field Message Number 144 (Saigon: April 1, 1967).

20. "A Dirty Psychological Warfare Trick," Radio Hanoi in Vietnamese to South Vietnam (March 16, 1967).

21. "Nguyen Van Be," Radio Hanoi international service in English (March 21, 1967).

22. "A Big Cheat," _Doc-Lap_ (Hanoi), Issue Number 2 (April 1967).

23. "The Guerrilla's Mine," _Nhan Dan_ (Hanoi: May 21, 1967).

24. Robert A. Erlandson, "Reds Offer $16,950 for 'Dead Hero,'" _Baltimore Sun_ (July 21, 1967).

25. Sheehan, _Pentagon Papers_, pp. 554-55.

26. U.S. Department of the Army, _Area Handbook for North Vietnam_, p. 251.

27. Sheehan, _Pentagon Papers_, p. 506.

28. Ho Chi Minh, _On Revolution_, p. 362.

29. U.S., USIA, _Vietnamese Communist Propaganda Offensive: 1965 (North Vietnam and the Viet Cong)_, R-62-66 (Washington, D.C.: March 1966), pp. 6-10.

30. The North Vietnamese employ a wide-ranging wired-diffusion network similar to Communist China. This system consists of a transmitting station connected by wire to a number of loudspeakers located in areas where group listening is most likely, e.g., factories, offices, schools. The network is not as expensive as the usual

radio, it can be used in areas not having electricity,
and its provides a captive audience for Party
propaganda. The transmitting stations receive Voice of
Vietnam (Radio Hanoi) broadcasts by radio link and re-
broadcast them over the loudspeakers. See U.S.,
Department of the Army, Area Handbook for North Vietnam,
p. 229.
    31. Quoted in Konrad Kellen, A Profile of the PAVN
Soldier in South Vietnam, RM-5013-1 (Santa Monica,
Calif: Rand Corporation, March 1967), pp. 10-11.
    32. "For the Fatherland's Security, People's
Security Combatants are Determined to Fulfill All Tasks,"
Nhan Dan (Hanoi: June 16, 1970).
    33. Quoted in U.S., Department of the Army, The
Communist Insurgent Infrastructure in South Vietnam: A
Study of Organization and Strategy. DA Pamphlet No. 550-
16 (Washington, D.C.: Government Printing Office, 1967),
pp. 153-54.
    34. Quoted in U.S., Department of the Army, Area
Handbook for North Vietnam, p. 250.
    35. Quoted in Kellen, Conversations with Enemy
Soldiers, pp. 57-58.
    36. Robert Shaplen, The Road From War: Vietnam
1965-1971, rev. ed. (New York: Harper & Row, 1971), pp.
334-35.

6
Winning "Hearts and Minds" in the South

> When bulls and buffaloes battle,
> flies and mosquitoes die.
>
>   -- Vietnamese Proverb

The tragedy of the Indochina War lies in what happened to the South Vietnamese people. Caught between Hanoi and Saigon, they sought shelter from the conflict by "bending like the bamboo." They took the Confucian middle path between extremes, giving allegiance to neither side. "It is not shameful to avoid elephants," goes a local saying. Although both protagonists tried strenuously to win their "hearts and minds," most remained ambivalent, waiting for the battlefield to determine the victor before choosing sides.

Following its intervention in 1965, the U.S. entered this Vietnamese war of ideas when it attempted to create a strong anti-Communist nationalism by winning the people's loyalty for the Republic.[1] The American-inspired and financially-backed Pacification and Rural Development Program was the cutting edge of the psychological sword in this political-economic "other war." Exalted as a means of defeating the Communists at their own game, "pacification" was the sum total of political, economic, social, security, and psychological measures taken in both cities and rural areas to enlist and retain popular support. This was seen as an important first step in "nation-building," the creation of a modern central government held together by new social sinews replacing outmoded traditional relationships.[2]

According to American pacification theory, Vietnamese would abandon their "wait-and-see" attitude if they were provided security from attack and persuaded, through propaganda of word and deed, that the Republic would best serve their personal interests. Once safeguarded by a "shield" of military force, a host of reforms designed to improve the quality of life and encourage participation in local and national affairs from the rice roots up. would give the people a personal stake in victory by the Republic. However, these efforts could pay off only under conditions of sustained protection from Viet Cong retribution. As one exasperated government pacification officer poignantly explained, security was of paramount importance to the "hearts and minds" battle:

> This hamlet is too insecure to be pacified.
> . . . The pacification Cadre was not here long enough to accomplish anything; but even if they had been here much longer, they could not have changed the people's attitude, because the people are afraid . . . there are other people in the hamlet who would inform to the VC when they come through. There are many people in the hamlet who really sympathize with the Government: but they <u>are afraid to identify themselves to the Cadre</u>. They are afraid to say anything good about the Government. And that is still true, after ten weeks work.[3] [emphasis in original]

Pacification foundered in 1965 and 1966 when large-scale operations against the Communist armed forces were given priority. But some progress was achieved through "Revolutionary Development" teams organized by the CIA. Dressed in the black pajama-like clothes of the peasant and armed for self-protection, these 59-member companies were sent into newly won areas. There they attempted to consolidated Saigon's control by organizing the public for self-defense and eliminating any remaining Viet Cong. When security was somewhat assured, they undertook political, economic, and social reforms to improve the peasants lives and enlist their allegiance for the Republic.

However logical in theory, these early efforts were in fact plagued by both inefficiency and lack of motivation on the part of most government cadres. As a result, enemy presence often remained strong, several pacification troops were killed, and as many as one in four deserted for the safety of the cities. But the root cause of failure was the lack of adequate protection from Communist attack. Daniel Ellsberg, a special assistant in the nation-building enterprise in 1967, outlined the major problems:

> Even in areas of relative security -- usually based on local saturation with friendly regular forces -- there had been little success in inducing people to make this commitment to the

GVN or to resisting the VC: because the GVN
did not attract their support . . . and because
security from VC retaliation was only relative
and looked temporary to most people. But in
the 'contested' areas where Cadre tended to be
assigned, the VC presence often was so
obtrusive that it was quite hopeless to
persuade people to risk their necks, rather
than to cooperate with both sides (depending on
which side was represented at the moment by
'the man with the gun:' generally away from
outposts and main roads, the VC).[4]

Urged by Americans, Saigon took two additional
security measures in 1967 to improve the protective
screen for the rural development endeavors. One was to
retrain locally-based paramilitary Regional and Popular
Forces, to equip them with better weapons, and to provide
them with extensive advisory assistance from the U.S.
Army Special Forces ("Green Berets"). The second
approach initiated the then-still-secret Phung Hoang
("Phoenix") Program to root out and destroy the Viet
Cong's underground political and administrative network.
        During the summer of 1968 the People's Self-Defense
Force (local militia) was formed to involve the populace
in their own protection. In November, with substantial
U.S. financial and advisory aid, Saigon kicked off the
"Accelerated Pacification Program" aimed at recouping
widespread losses suffered during the Communist's Tet
Offensive of the previous February. By year's end,
security had been reestablished in many areas. The
Communist underground had been damaged or eliminated in
several locales, and pacification actions had been
initiated in over a thousand rural hamlets.
        The improved military "shield" in 1969 meant
increased attention could be given to nation-building
efforts. To guide the over-all campaign, President Thieu
formed the Central Pacification and Development Council,
with himself as chairman. Elections were held in many
villages and hamlets, bringing about strengthened local
self-government. Village councils were given increased
responsibility for local self-defense and betterment,
including control over the budget and taxes, Popular
Forces, People's Self-Defense units, and police. The
47,000 Revolutionary Development cadres were re-organized
into smaller, 30-member teams. Working under village
chief direction, they were closely integrated into local
efforts, bringing a new dynamism and hope to the
Republic's "hearts and minds" winning enterprise.
        By 1970 the war had changed from a struggle for
control of territory to one for internal security and
consolidation. The Communist strategy of protracted
guerrilla warfare, terrorism, and covert political

penetration had not stalled the American-South Vietnamese
pacification drive. With relative safety assured, it was
possible for Saigon to put more emphasis on revitalizing
the village community through locally-determined
improvement projects. Increasingly, the Rural (formerly
"Revolutionary") Development cadres -- now divided into
10-member teams -- took on the role of political
organizers on behalf of the Thieu government.

In March the first major land reform ever undertaken
in South Vietnam was enacted -- the "Land-to-the Tiller"
law. Its aim was to reduce the number of tenant farmers
from about sixty percent of the country's growers to zero
over a three-year period. This U.S.-bankrolled
redistribution was seen, by Americans, as a way of giving
more Vietnamese a personal stake in Republic victory --
the coup de grace of the nation-building campaign.

In 1971 the U.S. accelerated its troop withdrawal
and the dismantling of its own pacification bureaucracy,
while Saigon placed major emphasis on "self-reliance."
By the year's end, the government claimed that only
25,000 people in thirty-seven hamlets were not under its
control.

With the Communists on the defensive and with
significant strides being made in the countryside, the
stage was set for the fierce North Vietnamese onslaught
in March 1972. The success or failure of Allied efforts
to win the people's "hearts and minds" would be
determined by subsequent events.[5]

PSYCHOLOGICAL GOALS

Throughout the war, the ubiquitous American
leaflets, posters, and broadcasts extolled the virtues of
the various reforms of the Pacification and Rural
Development Program. Calculated to evoke strong feeling
of nationalism, intense antipathy for the Viet Cong, and
a broad appreciation of the U.S. role in Vietnam, the
propaganda appeals were designed to win the people's
"hearts and minds" by creating three interrelated
psychological images:

(1) Image of the Republic -- To persuade the South
Vietnamese that government victory was inevitable and
that Saigon -- the legitimate successor to Vietnam's pre-
colonial past -- was moving toward the modern social
revolution, offering the people "the only true and
realistic hope for the achievement of national and
personal aspirations;"

(2) Anti-Communist Image -- To make the people
"fully aware that the Viet Cong leaders are conscious
instruments of a foreign power, Red China, and that the
rank-and-file members are misled or unwitting instruments
of these leaders;"

(3) Image of the United States -- To convince the

populace that the presence of the U.S. and other "Free
World Nations" would help them defeat a common threat to
them all -- Communist aggression -- and aid them in
building a better life.[6]
During the efforts to build a genuine South
Vietnamese nationalism, Americans took over too much of
what the government should have done itself by going
directly to the people with propaganda. In effect JUSPAO
became a surrogate Republic ministry of information.
Without doubt it could have contributed significantly to
building national cohesion and support against the
Communists, had its psychological operations been closely
harmonized with Saigon's actions in the vital
pacification undertaking. Indeed, the ultimate success
of its image-creating propaganda largely depended on the
government carrying out the advertized political,
economic, and social reforms. But over that factor
Americans had very little control.

IMAGE OF THE REPUBLIC

The Rural Development Program was the focal point of
the U.S. psychological operations. They were designed to
convey a positive image of the Saigon government by
picturing the pacification drive as a major effort to
improve the economic and political life of the people.
All of the mass media publicized its practical results.
Major emphasis was placed on actions that were taken
to raise the peasants' standard of living. Government
pacification workers were portrayed as standing side-by-
side with the populace, selflessly striving to improve
their well-being. Banners throughout the country
proclaimed: "Revolutionary Development Cadres Serve the
Nation by Helping the People," "The Rural Pacification
Program Will Answer the People's Desire for Freedom and
Happiness." "Scenes of Progress" were depicted in
posters showing cadres and peasants working together:
"Enthusiastic support of the people in the Revolutionary
Development Program is rapidly achieving dramatic and
permanent results - results which spell progress toward
lasting peace, economic growth, and national unity."
Efforts to provide the populace with medical care
and schools also were cited as evidence of Saigon's
desire to serve and help them (Fig 6.1). Photographs
were used to reinforce these concerns. One leaflet,
depicting a cheerful mother cradling her child, had the
message: "This mother has a happy smile because
Government of Vietnam medical aid has saved the life of
her baby. The Communists only promise to help the
people, but the Government of Vietnam does truly help the
people." Pictures of rural betterment projects were used
to contrast what Saigon was doing for the population and
what the Communists were doing against them:

Figure 6.1
Government Provides Education Facilities

HỌC SINH TỰ TAY XÂY CẤT, SỬA CHỮA TRƯỜNG
HỌC BẰNG VẬT LIỆU DO CHÍNH PHỦ CUNG CẤP

SCHOOL CHILDREN, THE NATION SPROUTS

A nation is strong and prosperous, not due to the might of its arms but thanks to the educational level of its population. Thus, education is the essential condition to build a strong and prosperous nation.

The Government of Vietnam advocates the policy of strongly pushing forward national education through the building of more schools and training of more teachers to meet the learning requirements of the rising generations. . . .

Government of Vietnam materials and student labor provides learning facilities.

Source: U.S., JUSPAO, leaflet number 2935.

THE GOVERNMENT OF VIETNAM HELPS

Vietnam and allied nations join hands to build
a better life. The true revolution of the
Government of Vietnam: Roads, schools,
hospitals and wells being hope and progress.

THE VIET CONG DESTROY

The false revolution of the Viet Cong: Empty
promises, deceits, death, destruction and
poverty.
THE GOVERNMENT HELPS THE PEOPLE - SUPPORT THE
GOVERNMENT OF VIETNAM

Children were special targets for psychological
exploitation. For them, JUSPAO produced a variety of
contents for "Patriotic School Kits" which appealed to
the young (and impressionable) -- hand puppets,
flexagons, flags, songsheets, bookmarkers, and similar
items (Fig 6.2). A bookcover, for instance, was
overprinted with the inscription: "You must learn the
duty of a citizen and form a united morale to grow up and
participate in the community life, built the Fatherland,
and create happiness together. You are the chaste,
unripe seeds, like the new-risen moon, like the new-
budding flowers, comprising all of the promise of the
future. The future of the country -- good or bad, win or
lose, rising or declining tomorrow, remaining or being
lost -- depends on the generation of children."
A leaflet, in the red and yellow national colors
with a flag on one side, urged youngsters to be good
citizens by informing on the Viet Cong and convincing
their parents to participate in village pacification
programs: "THE NATIONAL FLAG IS A SYMBOL OF NATIONAL
SOUL BECAUSE YOU HAVE TO CAREFULLY MAINTAIN IT IN ORDER
TO PROVE THAT YOU ARE A PATRIOTIC SON OF FREE AND
DEMOCRATIC VIETNAM."
Another aspect of the campaign to popularize the
Saigon government were attempts to enhance the images of
its local militia, armed forces, and police. As JUSPAO
noted, "Self-defense is obviously a Vietnamese concern,
and for the U.S. to urge it visibly would be counterproductive." Nevertheless, Americans widely publicized
the formation of the People's Self-Defense Force as an
action of the population in their anti-Communist struggle
(Fig 6.3). This propaganda promoted a citizen-soldier
image of its members, emphasized civic responsibility in
supporting the program, and outlined the benefits that
would accrue for the country: "Since the launching of
the people's self-defense movement, you have held fast to
your villages and expelled the sabotage of the Communists
from their original area of activites. As a matter of

Figure 6.2
Children's Bookmarker

LOVE THE COUNTRY
YOU ARE THE KEYSTONE AND THE FUTURE OF THE COUNTRY
VIETNAM

HẤY YÊU MẾN
QUÊ HƯƠNG
TỔ-QUỐC

CÁC EM LÀ
RƯỜNG CỘT TƯƠNG-
LAI CỦA NƯỚC
NHÀ

(Extract from the song: "Vietnamese Mother".)

Vietnam, Vietnam knows when we were born. Vietnam is two words on our lips. Vietnam is our country! Vietnam is called out by those who die. Vietnam here is a beautiful land. Vietnam brings freedom and justice and eternity. Vietnam is a peaceful nation. Vietnam appeals to affection and love. Vietnam dislikes war. Vietnam builds happiness for the present and the future.

Sacred fire illuminate the world and show that Vietnam is determined to keep up the struggle for life. Affection is the weapon. Vietnam is the voice to build human love. Vietnam, Vietnam, Vietnam is a bright country. Vietnam, Vietnam Eternally

Source: U.S., MACV, 10th Psychological Operations Battalion, PSYOP Catalog, leaflet number 10-512-68.

Figure 6.3
People's Self-Defense Force

MỖI NGƯỜI HÃY NHẬN LẤY
TRÁCH NHIỆM BẢO VỆ XỨ SỞ

LET US JOIN TOGETHER TO PROTECT OUR NATION

The purpose of the People's Self-Defense Plan:
a. To mobile the entire population for participation in the war.
b. To create a force to defend our villages and cities in order to increase the availability of troops to the armed forces at the front.
c. To unify the people's will to defend the National Righteous Cause in the political struggle against the enemy.
d. To create a popular force which supports the voice of the nation at the international conference table.
e. To support every aspect of an all-out, long and difficult war in order to advance towards self-sufficiency, self-reliance, and self-determination. . . .
It is everybody's responsibility to protect our nation.

Source: U.S., JUSPAO, leaflet number 2799.

face all of you now hate and consider them robbers and hoodlums. . . . Let our countrymen actively take part in the program and annihilate the Communists and rebuild your villages in freedom and democracy."

(As a side note, the local militia groups were not only "defense" organizations. With some four million members in mid-1971 -- only a quarter of whom were in combat elements -- they also provided a means of politically involving the populace in the anti-Communist struggle. In addition, they gave President Thieu a forum to enhance his personal image and consolidate his political position.)

Battlefield successes over the Communists also were given widespread publicity to enhance the prestige of the South Vietnamese military. These psychological operations tried to bolster the idea of inevitable victory and to foster national pride in the armed forces (Fig 6.4). "The Army of Vietnam soldier is dedicated to achieving the final victory for the Government," the people were told. "The Army is strong enough to protect you and your family," and the soldiers are "Proud that they can maintain the war against the Viet Cong to protect the people while the Allied forces return home."

In addition, JUSPAO attempted to build a public service image of the National Police, praising their loyalty and staunch determination to protect the populace. Other propaganda explained the necessity for roadblocks and waterway barriers to halt the movement of Communist supplies (Fig 6.5). A handbill for distribution at the stopping points explained: "The National Police must make checks for your protection. They help to maintain security for yourself and your family by preventing the Viet Cong from carrying weapons and explosives into towns to kill innocent people. . . . Checkpoints are necessary to carry out the task of helping the government and patriots win a final victory which would assure the independence of Vietnam."

A U.S. AID-sponsored public health campaign was used for propaganda purposes, too. Millions of posters, leaflets, and handbills were produced in a nation-wide education program dealing with prevention, symptoms, and treatment of various diseases (e.g., polio, malaria, typhoid fever) -- "In order to prevent infectious disease, the people should: BE INNOCULATED AGAINST CHOLERA AND PLAGUE." An anti-rat crusade was conducted to stop the spread of bubonic plague -- "Rats Are Very Dangerous To Your Health." Other topics explained how to build a toilet (together with an exhortation -- "USE TOILET ROOM WHEN YOU NEED"), how to prepare purified water, how to dispose if garbage ("This Is Your Home, Keep It Clean. Please Put Trash in Trash Cans"), and how to brush teeth. Banners exhorted the populace "Not To Spit" (spreads tuberculosis), "Wash Your Child With

Figure 6.4
South Vietnamese Armed Forces

THE ARVN SOLDIER....ON CONSTANT ALERT....PROTECTING THE PEOPLE

Over all the country the image of ARVN servicemen is present
everywhere to defend our people against all oppressions, arrests and
terrorist acts of the Communist aggressors and their lackeys in
South Vietnam.

Even in the most remote areas, the Republican fighters are
there to raid and destroy the inhumane dishonest Communists who are
always looking for every means to do harm to our people.

Bringing peace and happiness to the entire population are the
two biggest objectives of the Army of the Republic of Vietnam.

Source: U.S., JUSPAO leaflet number 2932.

Figure 6.5
Why Are There Check Points?

KHI ĐẾN TRẠM KIỂM SOÁT

Bạn hãy nhớ làm những điều sau đây :

1. Nên giữ trật tự khi lên và xuống xe ;
2. Trình thẻ căn-cước cho nhân viên Cảnh-Sát;
3. Nên chuẩn bị những gói, cặp hoặc xách tay mà bạn mang theo mình để Cảnh Sát làm phận sự.

Đồng bào vui lòng áp dụng nhiều điều kể trên để việc kiểm soát được kết thúc nhanh chóng.

Check points are used to serve the people:
    1. To protect your families and your homes, the police set up check points to prevent the Viet Cong from transporting bombs and other explosives to kill innocent people.
    2. Check points are established in order to enforce law and order, so that you and other innocent people can live in security. Check points may delay your business a little, but they will also help us achieve a final victory.
WHAT TO DO WHEN YOU ARE AT A CHECK POINT:
    1. Keep in line and maintain order when you get off and on a vehicle.
    2. Present your identification card to the police.
    3. Get your packages or handbags ready for the police to check.
Please follow the above instructions in order to speed up the check.

Source: U.S., JUSPAO, leaflet number SP-2216.

Soap," "Wash Vegetables Before Eating Them" and "Wash Your Hands Before And After Meals." Most of the propaganda sheets made it clear that the public health information was provided by the government because of its concern over the people's well-being (Figs 6.6, 6.7).

In addition to the general appeals, attention was given to major political events. One was land reform. It was by far the most important pacification action taken and crucial to creation of a favorable government image. Beginning in 1967, JUSPAO trumpeted Saigon's "gigantic" strides toward economic and social regeneration, citing its 1969 cost-free distribution of formerly French-owned property, and rent and land occupancy freezes as steps leading to meaningful land redistribution. Finally, in March 1970, the long awaited "Land-to-the-Tiller" bill was passed by the South Vietnamese Assembly. It set into motion no-cost transfer of more than 2.5 million acres of riceland -- over half of the country's total acreage -- to the actual tillers.[8]

Working closely with the VIS, American propagandists enthusiastically publicized the new program -- "'Land to the Tiller Bill' is a Social Reform Objectives of the Second Republic" (Fig 6.8). Peasants were urged to apply for land and the benefits of private ownership were illustrated -- no rent, a better life for the farmer and his family, greater agricultural production, and national self-sufficiency. Banners in hamlets throughout the country proclaimed:

WELCOME THE NEW RULE JUST COME INTO BEING
'THE FARMER HAVING LAND'
EVERYWHERE SAFETY

BROTHERS RETURN TO YOUR HAMLET AND VILLAGE
WE HAVE LAND TO CULTIVATE
RELATIVES ARE FREE FROM WORRY

Inevitably there were problems. For some peasants the Land-to-the-Tiller law made little difference; they had not seen a landlord nor paid rent for years. In some cases, the tenants liked the owner and were reluctant to claim the land. A few, as a matter of preference, continued to pay fees as before.

Nevertheless, the importance of this redistribution cannot be overemphasized. After years of promises, Saigon had finally delivered land to the tenant farmer. In one sweep, it took away one of the Communist's most successful appeals to the rural population. His own land gave the peasant a tangible reason to support Saigon against the Viet Cong. The ordinary rice farmer could now benefit personally by government victory. As Michael Arnsten and Nathan Leites, writing for the Rand Corporation in early 1970, described its potential

168

Source: U.S., MACV, 10th Psychological Operations Battalion, <u>PSYOP Catalog</u>, poster number 10-423-68.

Figure 6.6
Rats Spread the Plague

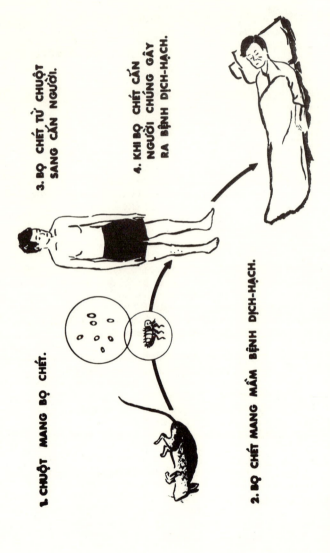

CHUỘT GÂY BỆNH DỊCH-HẠCH NHƯ THẾ NÀO?

1. CHUỘT MANG BỌ CHÉT.

2. BỌ CHÉT MANG MẦM BỆNH DỊCH-HẠCH.

3. BỌ CHÉT TỪ CHUỘT SANG CẮN NGƯỜI.

4. KHI BỌ CHÉT CẮN NGƯỜI CHÚNG GÂY RA BỆNH DỊCH-HẠCH.

Figure 6.7
How to Brush Your Teeth

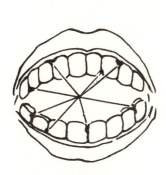

SAU KHI ĂN, CÁC
THỨC ĂN THƯỜNG
MẮC TRONG CÁC KẼ
RĂNG NẾU KHÔNG
ĐƯỢC LẤY RA, RĂNG
CÓ THỂ BỊ SÂU VÀ
CÁC CHỖ SÂU SẼ LỚN
DẦN RA, LÀM CHO
TA ĐAU—ĐỚN VÀ SẼ
PHẢI ĐI NHỔ RĂNG.
CÁC HÌNH VẼ KẾ
BÊN CHỈ CHO CHÚNG
TA CÁCH NGĂN—
NGỪA CÁC NGUYÊN
NHÂN SÂU RĂNG ĐÓ.

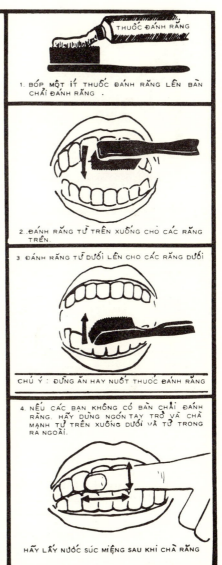

THUỐC ĐÁNH RĂNG

1. BÓP MỘT ÍT THUỐC ĐÁNH RĂNG LÊN BÀN CHẢI ĐÁNH RĂNG.

2. ĐÁNH RĂNG TỪ TRÊN XUỐNG CHO CÁC RĂNG TRÊN.

3. ĐÁNH RĂNG TỪ DƯỚI LÊN CHO CÁC RĂNG DƯỚI

CHÚ Ý : ĐỪNG ĂN HAY NUỐT THUỐC ĐÁNH RĂNG

4. NẾU CÁC BẠN KHÔNG CÓ BÀN CHẢI ĐÁNH RĂNG, HÃY DÙNG NGÓN TAY TRỎ VÀ CHÀ MẠNH TỪ TRÊN XUỐNG DƯỚI VÀ TỪ TRONG RA NGOÀI.

HÃY LẤY NƯỚC SÚC MIỆNG SAU KHI CHÀ RĂNG

Source: U.S., MACV, 10th Psychological Operations Battalion, PSYOP Catalog, poster number CC-040-69.

Figure 6.8
Land Reform

cc-289-70

LAND-TO-THE-TILLER

(In Cambodian language for ethnic Khmers in Mekong Delta.)
To the farmer:

The President of The Republic of Vietnam has promulgated the law "Land to the Tiller."

From now on the regime of "sharecropping" is eliminated from Vietnamese society.

Landlords are compensated quickly and fairly.

Farmers will get land without having to pay anything.

We work our own land. Our people enjoy a good life, construct their hamlets and villages.

Source: U.S., MACV, 10th Psychological Operations Battalion, PSYOP Catalog, leaflet number CC-298-70.

impact: "The beginning of a new program of land reform in Vietnam will provide the GVN opportunity -- through extension of land ownership to heretofore landless families -- to increase the rural population who can be persuaded that their self-interest is inconsistent with an NLF victory."[9]

The economic and social improvements brought about by the pacification drive often were linked with an image of political progress. By casting the Republic as the people's guardian, U.S. propagandists tried to foster ardent patriotism (Fig 6.9). The formation of the Vietnamese Constitution was widely advertized: "The adoption of the Constitution marks an important step for our people on the way to freedom and democracy;" President Thieu was pictured taking the oath of office and saying, "I solemnly swear that I shall defend the nation, respect the Constitution and serve the people's interests."

American pacification theory also said that democracy would play a vital role in winning "hearts and minds." As JUSPAO put it, "The balloting . . . will not only restore the tradition of village and hamlet self-government, it can play a decisive role in winning popular support for the revolutionary development program by giving the people's elected representatives the main voice in their own affairs."[10] However, this view overlooked the fact that the ideals of democracy, as known in the United States were not widely shared by the Vietnamese. Douglas Pike's observation is probably closer to the mark:

> Most Vietnamese, North and South alike, if candid, will tell you they are skeptical of the notion that the proper way to divide political power is to have people go into a little booth and drop pieces of paper in a box. This is not the traditional way it has been done in Vietnam. Further, they add, there is something starkly un-Vietnamese about the process. The all-or-nothing, win - lose character of an election ignores the imperative of group harmony, they argue. It tears society apart, drives the losers to desperate measures because they get nothing, whereas in the traditional Vietnamese system of 'private arrangements,' the loser would get something.[11]

Nonetheless, Vietnam's 1967 Constitution set into motion a series of elections for a variety of national and local officials. JUSPAO attempted to avoid giving the impression of taking part in the political process. Americans were prohibited from printing literature on behalf of the candidates, from providing them with

172

Figure 6.9
Democracy and Prosperity

SINH HOẠT CỦA NHÂN DÂN VÙNG TỰ DO

Phong trào chăn nuôi gia súc như gà, vịt, heo...v...v... đang được bành trướng mạnh tại vùng Tự Do.

Nhiều gia đình đã có thêm được một số tiền lời hàng tháng nhờ phong trào chăn nuôi gia súc này.

SINH HOẠT CỦA NHÂN DÂN VÙNG TỰ DO

Nâng cao trình độ văn hóa để phục vụ đắc lực cho nền kỹ thuật và khoa học hiện đại là một điều cần thiết. Do đó, ngoài giờ làm việc ở các xí nghiệp, nhà máy, công trường... anh chị em công nhân sống trong vùng tự do còn được học tập văn hóa.

Cả đến những người từ bỏ Cộng Sản trở về với chính phủ VNCH cũng được giúp vốn để trở thành người chăn nuôi gia súc như hai nư cán bộ CS trên đây.

Để kiện toàn nền hành chánh hầu phục vụ nhân dân nông thôn một cách hữu hiệu, các công sở xã đã được gấp rút xây dựng. Dưới chính thể Dân Chủ Tự Do, nhân dân được luật pháp bảo vệ khỏi những sự áp bức bóc lột. 3007

To improve the educational level to serve usefully the modern science and technology is a necessary condition. Therefore, workers living in Free Area have actively studied literature after finishing their work at factories, enterprises, work camps, etc.

To improve the administration system in order to serve the people in the countryside effectively, village government offices have been built very quickly.

Under the Free and Democratic regime, people are protected by the laws against oppression.

Source: U.S., JUSPAO, leaflet number 3007.

transportation, from printing ballots, and from rendering
financial support. They were also warned to stay away
from campaign gatherings and polling stations on election
days. However, the U.S. propaganda machine did provide
the Vietnamese with civic education in the workings of
Western democracy. Cartoon books instructed in the
workings of Western democracy. Cartoon books instructed
the populace in the democratic process, including the
rights and obligations of citizens, duties of a
representative government, and explanations of the
logical thought processes in selecting the best
candidate. In addition, all media were used to urge the
people to vote and to explain how their participation
would be beneficial -- "Participating in the Village
Popular Council Elections Contributes to the
Reconstruction of the Nation" (Fig 6.10). Or, as
explained by one leaflet,

> To the whole people:
> In order to maintain the democracy in South
> Vietnam, the province and city council will
> be elected on 29 June 1970. Election is
> the right of every citizen in a free and
> democratic country. The people should go
> to vote in large numbers in order to
> protect their right. Choose a talented and
> virtuous person to represent you and to
> control the public action for you. Vote in
> order to set up freedom and democracy.

Touted as steps toward "revolutionary and social
reforms," the balloting was followed up by substantial
publicity concerning their success. They often were
linked with Chieu Hoi appeals for Communist target
audiences (Fig 6.11).

Although the voting outwardly suggested democracy in
action, a host of irregularities plagued the electoral
process, leaving the popular base of the Thieu government
open to question. Through its province chiefs Saigon had
an important part in selecting which candidates would be
allowed to run for political office. Prior to the land
reform, landowners controlled village leadership in areas
where there were a large number of tenants; they had a
say in how the people voted. Both Joseph Buttinger and
Robert Shaplen, two incisive critics of the Republic,
pointed out several irregularities in the 1967 President
and National Assembly balloting. Shaplen contended that
the lethargic Vietnamese reactions to the elections
". . . can be attributed partly to national cynicism but
much more to the enduring conviction that the whole
elective process is simply an American-directed
performance with a Vietnamese cast." President Thieu,
after being re-elected unopposed in 1971, abolished

Figure 6.10
Leaflet - Voting Card

ĐI BẦU 3-9-67

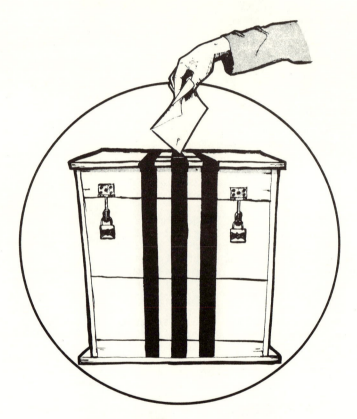

ĐI BẦU 3-9-67

VOTE 3 - 9 - 1967

You must possess a voting card in order to vote. Obtain your card early and put it in a safe place. On election day (3-9-67) vote early - 7:00 AM to 4:00 PM.

Source: U.S., JUSPAO, leaflet number SP-2044

Figure 6.11
Elections and the Chieu Hoi Program

NHÂN DÂN XÃ ẤP
CHỌN BẦU
NGƯỜI ĐẠI DIỆN
CHO MÌNH

3686

PEOPLE IN VILLAGES AND HAMLETS VOTING FOR THEIR REPRESENTATIVES

There is a significant development that marks a decisive
turning point for the people of the Republic of Vietnam in the
countryside. Elections of village councils and hamlet chiefs are
being carried out in accordance with democratic principles. All
citizens can select their own representatives, by writing the names
of their chosen candidates on their votes to elect government
officials of the local administration.

Friends still remaining on the other side. The fact has proved
to you that only under a democratic regime can the people actually
enjoy full rights of their citizenship. Coming back to the people
of South Vietnam, you will enjoy all the rights of citizenship, and
the freedom to live a peaceful and happy life.

Source: U.S., JUSPAO, leaflet number 3986.

hamlet elections through the country and took other steps
to limit local self-government in August 1972. These
measures were taken to consolidate his control in prelude
to the expected post-ceasefire political struggle with
the Viet Cong. As he summed-up his attitude: "I never
denied independence and democracy. . . . I must complain
that our government has allowed us to enjoy too much
democracy too soon."[12] In short, the wholesale transfer
of American democratic concepts, based on the American
experience and American values did not fit the Vietnamese
circumstance.

In addition, special campaigns were waged to win the
allegiance of the country's Montagnards (aboriginal hill
tribesmen) and Cambodians (Khmers). Stressing the
Republic's interest and actions in advancing the social
and economic status of the minorities, propaganda
promised respect and encouragement of divergent cultural
traditions within the context of Vietnamese
nationality. Heavy emphasis was placed on how the
national government would better serve their interests.
A special cartoon booklet with simple caricatures and
captions in one tribal dialect was used to promote the
village self-development program -- Saigon's assistance
was said to indicate its true concern in helping the
Montagnard people. Similarly, one leaflet, entitled "A
Man Should Be Proud of His White Hairs," promoted
unity: "The old man you see in the picture seems very
happy. Perhaps he is thinking that despite the ravages
of war, the Vietnamese - Montagnard people are making
progress toward a better life. . . . Let us honor and
show love to the old people who have made such great
contributions to our personal welfare and to the cause of
Vietnamese - Montagnard unity under the red and yellow
flag of the Government of Vietnam."

The host of refugees was another special target
group for propaganda. The war produced millions of
homeless persons -- a peak of 1.5 million on 1969 -- who
left their villages in Viet Cong and contested areas to
escape the bombing and shelling, search-and-destroy
operations by Allied forces, and Communist harassment.
As Ralph K. White points out, the movement of people into
government regions could hardly be considered support for
Saigon or "voting with your feet" because there was
little evidence to indicate whether they were "escaping"
from the Viet Cong or trying to avoid the consequences of
military activity.[13]

The refugee program, used to lure people out of
Communist-controlled areas, offered many inducements to
leave home. A 1967 JUSPAO poster, highlighted by
photographs, outlined the benefits. They were so
numerous and extensive that it is a wonder people were
not lined up a hundred deep waiting to get in at the camp
gates. But was it believable?

VOCATIONAL COURSE FOR THE REFUGEES FROM COMMUNISM
IN DINH TUONG PROVINCE

BENEFITS OF REFUGEES:
Period of temporary resettlement: Coming
from the unsafe zone and settling at the
temporary camps, each head is provided 10
piasters for daily meals during a month. Every
family is also issued commodities such as
cloth, mosquito net, milk, individual bag,
cooking oil and soap.

Period of permanent resettlement: When
refugees build houses in the safe zones
(refugee hamlet), each family is funded 5,000
piasters for the house, and approximately 4,000
piasters for feeding during 6 months. Rice
ration: Adult: 15 kg of rice per month,
Children: 10 kg per month.

Self-help development: After being
resettled, each family is issued a pig, fish
for raising, seeds and fertilizer for
planting. Capable relatives of refugees will
be sent to the vocational school to learn the
classes of electricity, motor, driving, tailor
. . . so they'll be able to take care of
themselves and their family. Local authorities
have built installations of education and
health to educate relatives of refugees and
take care of their health.

In order to enable the relatives of
refugees to get a good life in the future, the
local Refugees' Service has cooperated with the
My-Tho vocational school to open free classes
in building, car motor, outboard motor, water
pump, radio, and particularly tailor for the
female.

That was not the only instruction received, for once
refugees came under Saigon's control they were important
targets for political indoctrination and psychological
exploitation. Normally, they were received at temporary
centers, screened for intelligence, and provided with
food, shelter, sometimes clothing, and medical care.
Once their local area was secured by Allied forces, they
were either returned to their homes or resettled in
government regions.

While at the camps, propaganda publicized Saigon's
efforts to ease the refugees' plight and put the blame
for their homelessness squarely on Hanoi and the National
Liberation Front (Fig 6-12). A multiplier effect was

Figure 6.12
Refugee Resettlement Program

ONE OF THE MOST SUCCESSFUL PROGRAMS

"One of the most Successful programs of the Government of
Vietnam is the anti-Communist refugee resettlement program."
This is the declaration of Lt. Col. Vu The Quang, Mayor of Cam
Ranh. He revealed that actually there are five refugee camps at Cam
Ranh. Recently on 12 and 20 December 1968, more than 193 families
have been resettled at My Ca village, 15 kilometers from Cam Ranh
city. This resettlement shows that the right cause of the
Government of Vietnam has won over the dictator regime of the
Communists.

Source: U.S., JUSPAO, leaflet number 3064.

hoped for when word-of-mouth news of good treatment and benefits at the refugee centers would be passed back into Communist areas. Next, in the American theory, greater numbers of Viet Cong would defect under the Chieu Hoi Program, and when the populace heard of the government's generosity, they, too, would leave their homes, thus denying the Communists their support.

But there were serious barriers to creating a favorable image of the Republic. One was the dilemma of having to fight a war amidst the very population Saigon was trying to pacify. As communications specialist Ithiel de Sola Pool observes, this situation made the Allies' use of firepower an inherent paradox: "The side that wins the war in Vietnam is likely to be the side that is most restrained in its use of force, and is least violent in its chosen means."[14] On the other hand, such constraint frequently produced American casualties and home-front concern. As a result, commanders placed increased reliance on the use of artillery and aerial bombardment, since they had not been able to crush the elusive Viet Cong and North Vietnamese soldier by other means. Despite stringent self-imposed rules of engagement, civilian casualties inevitably mounted. In the end, as Buttinger and White note in their studies, more deaths and misery probably were brought about by Allied firepower than Communist terrorism.[15]

The Republic's image suffered as a result, for the National Liberation Front was quick to take advantage of the people's resentment over the death and destruction wrought by Allied military operations. For instance, in August 1968, Americans fired on a friendly hamlet after being ambushed by the Viet Cong. Several innocent civilians died. Subsequently, the Communists increased the villagers' anger by spreading rumors that the "foreign troops" had fired without provocation. Since they could not tell the difference between friend or foe and shot at anyone wearing black pajamas, the Americans were no better than the French. Other stories claimed that the hamlet had been caught in a crossfire fight between South Vietnamese and American soldiers, and others said that U.S. helicopters had "callously" machinegunned the area.[16]

JUSPAO tried to escape this paradox of having to support both a violent war and a positive image of Saigon by placing responsibility for fighting in populated areas on the Viet Cong (Fig 6.13). Moreover, to minimize civilian casualties and to show the government as the true guardian of the people, the rural populace normally was forewarned of impending aerial and artillery strikes. Specific evacuation instructions were provided and the population was given time to escape (along with many Viet Cong). "As soon as you receive this paper you must move your family right away from this area," they

Figure 6.13
Viet Cong Cause Government Attacks

THE GOVERNMENT WANTS TO PROTECT THE PEOPLE

   The Viet Cong are misusing your land and your homes for hostile activities against the people. The Government of Vietnam must destroy the Viet Cong. It will destroy them unless they see the light and come to the cause of justice of the Government of Vietnam.
   Because the Viet Cong are hiding in your homes and your land, you might be affected by the Government effort to destroy the Viet Cong. The Government of Vietnam does not want to hurt you. As best you can, stay away from the Viet Cong; do not shelter them or help them, so that you will not be hurt when the Government of Vietnam destroys the Viet Cong. Protect yourselves. Support the just and winning cause of the Government of Vietnam.

Source: U.S., JUSPAO, leaflet number SP-2316.

were warned. "VNAF and USAF will come to destroy the
Viet Cong who hiding themselves here. We don't want to
kill you by accident. The National Government always
looks after the safety of the civilians." American
Marines provided similar admonitions:

> Respected Villagers -- Your hamlets are
> completely surrounded by United States and
> Vietnamese forces which will shortly advance to
> destroy to Viet Cong who oppress and endanger
> you and your families. In order to protect you
> from danger, we urge you to follow the
> instructions broadcast by loudspeakers. . . .
> For your safety please cooperate with us. Act
> immediately, as we advance in a few minutes.

Other leaflets and loudspeaker broadcasts outlined
curfew rules -- "You must remain in your homes during
curfew from 8 at night to 5 in the morning. Anyone
traveling the rivers and canals during these hours might
be mistaken for the Viet Cong." And the harmless effects
of tear gas, used to flush the Communists from their
hiding places, were explained -- "Tear gas is not
harmful, it will only cause irritation to your eyes."
Warnings of attack were especially effective when,
after reestablishing its authority, government forces
remained and seriously undertook pacification efforts.
For instance, in a small operation in late 1966, some
200,000 "evacuation" leaflets were airdropped near a
village in hostile territory. The circular announced an
on-coming military sweep, identified specific evacuee
assembly points, provided instructions for what to do,
and outlined the benefits of the refugee assistance
program. More than 2,000 persons responded -- nearly the
total population -- and sixty-seven Viet Cong took
advantage of the situation to defect.
With civilians out of the way, the area was
occupied, remaining enemy soldiers were eliminated, and
the people returned to their homes within two months and
were provided resettlement aid. Rural Development cadres
were dispatched to the village, and pacification programs
were initiated behind the "shield" of security provided
by the armed forces. Similar small-scale operations were
repeated again and again in attempts to minimize civilian
casualties while the struggle to dislodge insurgents
continued.[17]
Explaining defoliation of the countryside was
another nettlesome JUSPAO task which got in the way of a
positive government image. Conducted on and off since
1961, "spray aircraft" operations were greatly increased
in 1967. By eliminating dense vegetation from possible
ambush sites, they helped provide security for military
posts, roads, waterways, and other transportation

arteries. Defoliants also were used to remove jungle
concealment from Communist base areas and infiltration
routes. JUSPAO attempted to ease popular concern over
these practices by explaining, in good rational terms,
the tactical advantages of defoliation. Assertions that
the herbicides were non-poisonous and that sprayed food
and water could be consumed without danger were common
themes. One loudspeaker broadcast explained,

> Dear Citizens:
> The Viet Cong usually take advantage of
> dense and lush terrain, and its thick
> vegetation in order to:
> - Place mortars to bomb and kill honest
>   people.
> - Infiltrate provincial capitals to
>   conduct barbarous actions against
>   innocent people.
> So the Government of Vietnam sees that is
> is necessary to spray chemicals to make the
> leaves fall and so destroy the jungle and thick
> bushes and prevent the enemy from using them as
> hiding places.
> Set your mind at ease, because these
> chemicals do not harm your health or lives.

Unfortunately, such explanations probably fell on
deaf ears, since the population's doubt was based more on
emotion than on reason. Some illnesses were reported as
a result of the herbicides, but Americans diagnosed these
symptoms as associated with hysteria and suggestive in
origin. Regardless of the actual cause of the maladies,
the important psychological point was that the sick
believed themselves to be ill from the defoliant
chemicals. Moreover, this belief prevailed among the
other people in the same local area.

Predictably, the National Liberation Front enjoyed
substantial success fanning fear and indignation over the
defoliation undertaking. Overt and whisper campaigns
were common, alleging the herbicides were harmful to
people and livestock. For instance, a Communist grammar
school text had tucked among its nursery rhymes: "We
children hate Americans who are cruel. They scatter
poison to destroy our paddies and vegetables."[18] Hugh
Mulligan describes an incident of Viet Cong exploitation
of these practices in his book, No Place To Die: A young
American medic, after correctly diagnosing an epidemic of
encephalitis in the Montagnard village, risked his life
by helping to treat the ill, and "While Sergeant Gregg
was busy with his outbreak of the dread Asian sleeping
sickness, Viet Cong messengers were moving through the
valley spreading the word that the disease actually had
been caused by rice spoiled by defoliation
chemicals. . . ."[19]

In spite of the problems, these many attempts to build a positive government image enjoyed some success. But they constituted only part of the U.S. campaign to win "hearts and minds." The other side of the propaganda was aimed at fashioning a negative image of the National Liberation Front.

ANTI-COMMUNIST IMAGE

To create a sinister picture of the Viet Cong, American propaganda focused on what the insurgents were doing against the people. But, as Arnsten and Leites pointed out in their Rand Corporation study, it is difficult to portray Communists unfavorably among the rural populations of Asia because it is hard for the people to see how their personal position would deteriorate under their rule. In Vietnam, this difficulty was compounded by the predominant role Ho Chi Minh's followers played in driving the French from the country.[20] To overcome these obstacles and show how a Viet Cong victory would be against the people's best interests, Communist exploitation of the peasantry and the effects of their terror activities on innocent civilians were emphasized. A secondary focus was placed on elimination of the Liberation Front's political underground, the Chieu Hoi Program, and a variety of rewards offers.

Most anti-Viet Cong appeals portrayed them as oppressors of the people. Evidence of their "persecution" was widely publicized: destruction of property, forced taxes, and taking the peasant's rice (Figs 6.14, 6.15). As one leaflet explained:

YOU ARE **NOT** SLAVES!

You should not work and sweat all day to pay the Viet Cong illegal taxes. We are proud Vietnamese who have rights and freedoms which your government is determined to maintain.

Do not fear the evil Viet Cong. Just inform the nearest Government authority when the Viet Cong try to collect taxes and the Government of Vietnam will defend your rights.

Another showed "before" and "after" photographs of a building destroyed by Viet Cong shelling: "After the Communists received continuing heavy defeats by the Republic of Vietnam armed forces, they resorted to shelling into crowded civilian areas, such as: work projects, hospitals, schools, churches, homes, and shrines. . . ." Yet another depicted a young boy weeping at their "cowardly" destruction: "The Communists are

Figure 6.14
Viet Cong Rice Taxes

WHY ARE THE VIET CONG RICE TAXES SO VERY HIGH?
BECAUSE THE VIET CONG ARE LOSING THE WAR!

The Viet Cong are now desperate for rice. In the North, the Chinese are pressing them continually for more rice to pay for their guns and ammunition. Here in the South, it is becoming much more difficult for the Viet Cong to supply their forces in the field, since the Government forces are seizing more of their supply and storage areas. As the Chinese squeeze Uncle Ho in the North, the Viet Cong soldiers are starving in the South, and the Viet Cong intended to make us starve with them!

Source: U.S., JUSPAO, leaflet number SP-806.

Figure 6.15
Viet Cong Rob the Peasants

ROBBERY

The Viet Cong have been reduced to forceful taxation in order to exist. Desperate for food and money they now have to resort to taking the food from your families. You and your children must suffer.

Protect your loved ones . . . notify at once, your nearest Government of Vietnam or Allied official of any attempted taxation by the Viet Cong.

Source: U.S., MACV, 246th Psychological Operations Company, Leaflet Catalogue, leaflet number 334.

cruel and atheistic, and also cowardly! When they are surrounded by Republic of Vietnam armed forces, they don't allow you to run. Instead, they use you to deflect bullets! . . . Then the Communists burn your houses to provide themselves a way to escape. Because of these actions, the Communists are the enemies of the people."

By painting the Viet Cong in such sinister terms, JUSPAO hoped to transform public fear of attack into animosity and a desire for revenge against their terror activities. Once that psychological conversion was made, it was hoped to channel anger and vengefulness into active support for the government. One method of doing this was to exploit civilian injuries and deaths resulting from enemy assaults (Fig 6.16). A photograph in one leaflet showed a bandaged and suffering small boy lying in a hospital bed with the message:

> The Viet Cong say they are building a better life under Communism. But look at the little boy in the picture - and see how the Viet Cong helped him live a better life; they shot him. When a small band of Viet Cong terrorists crept into the refugee village of Duc Phong and shot wildly at defenseless women and children and when little Nguyen Van Ba fell to the ground, bleeding and crying, the Viet Cong didn't care.

In addition, a photographic poster with the title, "The Desperate Acts of the Losers," showed specific examples of Communist terrorism which resulted in injuries to the innocent: "The more they are defeated, the more savage the Viet Cong become. They murder, force youth to join their military units, destroy bridges, mine roads and busses -- make misery for the people. The Viet Cong commit more and more atrocities against the people but in the end they will perish and lose."

JUSPAO wisely did not exploit assassinations of government officials and other selective targets; this would have reinforced the Liberation Front's image of being able to strike at any time despite Saigon's countermeasures. Citation of Communist terrorism was normally limited to the area where the acts were perpetrated to avoid spreading their propaganda effects.

For instance, in June 1970, the Viet Cong attacked a "pacified" hamlet in one of the northern provinces of South Vietnam. After a heavy mortar barrage, they over-ran the hamlet, destroying about seventy-five percent of the buildings, killing more than seventy men, women, and children, and wounding a like number. Many of the civilian casualties occurred when the Communists, after pinning down a small defending force, threw satchel bombs into the people's shelters. Initially, the psychological reaction of the populace was dismay that Saigon's

Figure 6.16
Communist Terrorism

BẠN THÍCH CẢNH NÀO ?

4384

(One cartoon illustrating a peaceful scene; another showing
destruction caused by the Viet Cong and North Vietnamese.)

The Republic of Vietnam pacification and development programs
have brought security and prosperity to the people in the villages
and hamlets. They are now enjoying peace and abundance. The
Communists advocate killings and destruction. Wherever they go
homes are destroyed, people are killed and misery and suffering
reign everywhere along their path.
With of the two scenes do you prefer?

Source: U.S., JUSPAO, leaflet number 4384.

security had failed them. However, Allied psychological
operations were introduced immediately, including medical
care and civil organization for relief and recovery.
Reportedly, the people's attitude soon shifted -- they
realized that the Viet Cong were the perpetrators of the
terror, and that the government, although initially
overwhelmed by the insurgent forces, was trying to
fulfill its security and public welfare
responsibilities. The attack was not given national
publicity.[21]

Another aspect of the anti-Communist campaign was
the Phung Hoang ("Phoenix") Program. One of the most
controversial U.S. efforts, its goal was to eliminate the
Viet Cong's underground political and administrative
infrastructure. Formed in July 1968 by amalgamating
various regional and departmental intelligence practices,
the project was not publicly acknowledged until October
1969. By pooling information from various sources, it
first attempted to identify members of the Communist
underground and then to liquidate them. American
advisors under CORDS assisted the South Vietnamese in all
phases of the campaign leading to elimination of the
suspects.[22]

JUSPAO's participation consisted of appealing for
information about members of the underground and
publicizing the identity of persons wanted by the
authorities (Fig 6.17). As put by one leaflet: "In
order to help the authorities prevent all terrorist
activites and sabotage of the Communists, the Phoenix
Committee of Cai Be District earnestly appeals to the
people to supply information and pictures of the
underground communist cadre and the communist soldiers so
that the authorities can capture them in time. . . .
Your names will be kept secret."

Various techniques were used to carry out the
task. "Wanted posters" were put up (with photographs
whenever possible), and leaflets were airdropped in
Communist areas to inform members of the underground by
name that they had been identified and should defect
immediately. Other practices included publicizing
rewards for information of the Viet Cong underground (up
to 10,000 piasters, or $85), explaining the drive to
school children in the hope that they would tell their
parents, and preparing a "Ten-Most-Wanted" list in one
province. Blacklists were also posted on village
bulletin boards with an "X" crossed over the names of
those eliminated to show the campaign's progress and the
steady depletion of the insurgent ranks. It reportedly
was an effective rally inducement.

The Phung Hoang Program was undoubtedly successful
in damaging the Front's underground. Nonetheless, it
worked against the creation of a favorable government
image because of the excesses and corruption that plagued

Figure 6.17
Phung Hoang Program

4168

THAM GIA CHIẾN DỊCH
"PHỤNG HOÀNG" LÀ GÓP PHẦN
BẢO VỆ AN NINH THÔN XÓM.

PARTICIPATION IN THE "PHUNG HOANG" CAMPAIGN IS
TO BUILD SECURITY FOR OUR HAMLETS

The Phung Hoang Campaign is aimed at neutralizing all the Viet
Cong infrastructures so that people can get rid of Viet Cong
terrorism and oppression. Therefore, people are encouraged to
participate in this campaign, thus contributing to the building of
peace and prosperity for themselves and their families. Inform all
Viet Cong activities to the National Police or other local security
agencies. Your names will be kept secret.

Source: U.S., JUSPAO, leaflet number 4168.

the campaign. Several writers and news reporters have documented a number of abuses. Professor Samuel Popkin reported that the National Police, to fill quotas, often arrested peasants on trivial offenses. He noted that corrupt policemen and others had great leeway for extortion. Newsman Harry Trimborn cited examples of Viet Cong suspects being thrown into prisons with little opportunity to defend themselves against the charges levied. Reporter Robert Shaplen added that the innocent often were apprehended while some Communists were buying their freedom from corrupt officials. And reporter Robert Kaiser cited similar practices -- he viewed the campaign as potentially dangerous because it could be used to eliminate Thieu's political opposition. Finally, Wayne Cooper, based on his personal experiences as an American Phung Hoang advisor until 1972, supported news reports that alleged the policy was alienating the people. He found bribery, intimidation, and influence rampant:

> In the field, we saw ineptitude and knew the program wasn't succeeding. But we failed to notice that Phung Hoang was becoming something else -- a means for repressive political control over the South Vietnamese. VCI [Viet Cong Infrastructure] . . . cadres would be captured again and again, only to be released. But the 'subversive' nationalist who expressed fatigue with the war, scorn for Thieu and Ky, and enthusiasm for a coalition government, was by definition a threat to public security. He might easily find himself on Conson Island, his arrest being explained to advisors by ascribing him a VCI title.[23]

In addition to its direct anti-Communist themes, JUSPAO indirectly attempted to damage the Liberation Front's image by depicting Saigon's magnanimity in welcoming former Viet Cong back to the "just cause" through the Chieu Hoi amnesty summons. They emphasized the program's success and its benefits to the public and the nation (Fig 6.18). Government promises and the treatment accorded ralliers in "welcoming them home" were also outlined. "The Chieu Hoi policy is not a political trick. . . ," the Southern populace was informed. "The Chieu Hoi policy is a policy of indulgence and generosity for the benefit of those persons who have gone the wrong way and who desire to return to the country and the people." These explanations often were linked with reward overtures for anyone convincing an insurgent to defect. As one handbill put it, "Be a Good Citizen, Help a Hoi Chanh to Rally to Your Government!"
Bounties were also offered for information about

Figure 6.18
Chieu Hoi Benefits the Nation

HỒI CHÁNH VIÊN CÓ CÔNG
ĐƯỢC TƯỞNG THƯỞNG
XỨNG ĐÁNG

Ngày 11-4-1970, ông Tổng
trưởng Chiêu-hồi Hồ-Văn-Châm
đã trao số tiền thưởng 1.348.000đ
cho hồi chánh viên Nguyễn-Văn-
Xăng tại Hậu-Nghĩa vì anh đã có
công, ba lần hướng dẫn hành
quân tịch thâu các loại vũ khí
của Cộng sản.   3778

The Chieu Hoi Program appeals to friends on the other side to
come back in the spirit of "National Reconciliation" and also
provides worthy rewards to meritorious returnees. The Government of
Vietnam encourages accomplishment of good services upon rallying to
the national cause and provides additional assistance for the
returnees to start their new life.

This is, of course, not the main reason that motivated
Communist cadre and soldiers to abandon their ranks and come back to
the national cause. But it does help returnees with additional
means to support their families and make a definite break from the
Communist cause.

Source: U.S., JUSPAO, leaflet number 3778.

Viet Cong movements and the location of their weapon and
food caches, as well as for assisting downed U.S. airmen
to return to Allied control. Such propaganda usually
promised the informer that his identity would remain
secret. The persuasive appeals contained both anti-
Communist and pro-government statements to provide a
moral rationale for supplying the information desired
(Fig 6.19). One poster, for example, appealed to the
populace to "Serve Your Country:" "If you help stop Viet
Cong crimes, rewards ranging from 50,000 to 1,000,000
piasters are reserved for you. . . . Inform the police
of Viet Cong terrorists and saboteurs, their weapons,
ammunition, and explosive caches or their transport
facilities. . . . STOP VIET CONG CRIMES AND HELP RESTORE
SECURITY AND HAPPINESS."
    These reward offers were often combined with
propaganda that attempted to ease popular concern over
local economic problems. Pleas for reports about
Communist movements and the location of their secreted
supplies were linked with the need to keep roads and
waterways open so people could take their goods to
market. The blame for skyrocketing prices was laid to
the Viet Cong's "economic warfare," while the government
was portrayed as taking meaningful actions to increase
the supply of commodities despite the construction caused
by the Liberation Front (Figs 6.20, 6.21). Such messages
were intended to show the farmer that it was in his self-
interest to inform on the insurgents and to support
Saigon's efforts.
    Sometimes these reward offers brought surprising
results. For example, two children, who had heard aerial
broadcasts advertising the program, startled American
soldiers by walking into their camp dragging a pair of
mortar rounds. In another case, a loudspeaker team
informed a group of peasants about the arms prizes and
moments later, the people began bringing them grenades
and mines, two and three at a time. Seeking to satisfy
their curiosity, the G.I.s followed the villagers and
found them digging just outside the hamlet, pulling
explosives out by the handful. Over five hundred items
were netted in this fashion.[24]

IMAGE OF THE UNITED STATES

    The third major psychological goal of the
Pacification and Rural Development Program was to create
a favorable U.S. image and to counter charges that the
Americans intended to colonize South Vietnam. This
campaign indirectly reinforced the pro-Saigon and anti-
Communist appeals, for it portrayed foreign presence as
necessary to assist the South Vietnamese in their fight
against a common enemy -- international Communism.
Supporting themes explained that the U.S. was determined

Figure 6.19
Rewards for Information

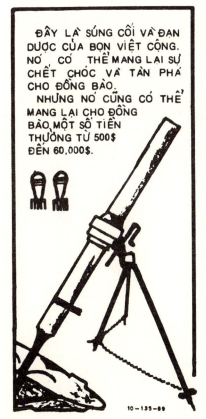

ĐÂY LÀ SÚNG CỐI VÀ ĐẠN DƯỢC CỦA BỌN VIỆT CỘNG. NÓ CÓ THỂ MANG LẠI SỰ CHẾT CHÓC VÀ TÀN PHÁ CHO ĐỒNG BÀO.
NHỮNG NÓ CŨNG CÓ THỂ MANG LẠI CHO ĐỒNG BÀO MỘT SỐ TIỀN THƯỞNG TỪ 500$ ĐẾN 60,000$.

10-135-69

THIS IS A COMMUNIST MORTAR AND MORTAR AMMUNITION. IT WILL KILL PEOPLE AND BE USED FOR SABOTAGE. BUT IT CAN ALSO BRING YOU A REWARD FROM 500 TO 60,000 PIASTERS.

Attention people,

We know the Viet Cong are hiding mortars in your hamlets. When the Viet Cong use these mortars, Allied Forces will shoot back to destroy them.

You can rid your hamlets of the Viet Cong. Give the Allied Forces information on the Viet Cong mortars and ammunition. You will be rewarded with from 500 to 60,000 piasters.

Take this leaflet to any Allied soldier and he will take you to an officer. You will be rewarded for your information. Your name will be kept secret.

Source: U.S., MACV, 10th Psychological Operations Battalion, PSYOP Catalog, leaflet number 10-135-69.

194

Figure 6.20
Viet Cong Disrupt the Economy

QUỐC-LỘ 4 LÀ LỘ CỦA NHÂN-DÂN, ĐỒNG BÀO
HÃY GIÚP CHÁNH PHỦ SỬA SANG VÀ GÌN GIỮ
AN-NINH TRÊN QUỐC-LỘ NẦY

ĐỒNG BÀO HÃY MẬT BÁO VỚI CHÁNH-QUYỀN, QUÂN-ĐỘI QUỐC-GIA HAY ĐỒNG-MINH, MỌI ÂM MƯU
CỦA VIỆT-CỘNG TOAN PHÁ HOẠI QUỐC-LỘ 4.
LÀM NHƯ VẬY, NGOÀI VIỆC ĐƯỢC TƯỞNG THƯỞNG XỨNG ĐÁNG, ĐỒNG BÀO CÒN BẢO VỆ TÀI-SẢN
QUỐC-GIA, SINH MẠNG CỦA THƯỜNG DÂN VÔ TỘI VÀ QUYỀN-LỢI CỦA CHÍNH GIA ĐÌNH MÌNH.

TO THE PEOPLE LIVING ALONG ROUTE #4

If the traffic on Route 4 is stopped, your goods, pigs, chickens, oxen, ducks, vegetables, fruits and rice cannot be brought to the markets by My Tho, Saigon or other cities. This situation of suspended traffic will injure your family's economic welfare.

If the traffic problems on Route 4 are solved, the people who live along Route 4 and the Western Zone will live in plenty.

Route 4 is the people's road. Help the Government of Vietnam to repair, protect, and secure this road. Secretly report to the Government of Vietnam or Allied Forces any Viet Cong plots to destroy Route 4. Besides receiving a reward for such information, you will also protect the nation's property, the lives of innocent people and the rights of your family.

Source: U.S., MACV, 10th Psychological Operations Battalion, PSYOP Catalog, leaflet number 10-001-69.

Figure 6.21
Government Brings Economic Prosperity

ACTIVITIES OF THE PEOPLE IN FREE AREA

SINH HOẠT CỦA NHÂN DÂN VÙNG TỰ DO

Chiếc xe bán đồ giải khát lưu động này là một phương tiện kiếm tiền rất hữu hiệu. Trong khi chồng đi làm, vợ ở nhà bán đồ giải khát, mức sống của gia đình ngày càng được nâng cao và con cái được ăn học đầy đủ.

This mobile cart selling refreshment drink is a means to earn money effectively. While husband goes to work, the wife sell soft drink; therefore the standard of living of the family improve gradually and their children are able to go to school.

Bread has become a popular breakfast meal of the people living in Free Area. Selling bread is also a popular business of the people. For only a small capital, you can get a fair benefit.

Bánh mì đã trở thành một món ăn sáng rất thông dụng của đồng bào sống trong vùng tự do. Bán bánh mì cũng là một nghề thông dụng của nhân dân. Chỉ cần một số vốn rất nhỏ nhưng số lãi lại khá lớn. 3009

Source: U.S., JUSPAO, leaflet number 3009.

to stay as long as necessary to help the Republic resist
outside aggression and subversion, that its presence was
assisting the government in furthering social and
economic development, that it was a rich nation and
therefore did not need the territory nor resources of
South Vietnam, and that its armed forces would leave when
the Communist threat no longer existed (Fig 6.22).
However, such claims of altruistic intentions may not
have been fully believed by population. A 1968 MACV
query to its field propagandists outlined the major
problem: "Ideas are being solicited on how to sell the
fact that the US has no colonial interest in South
Vietnam. . . . After 500 years of having various
countries try to control their resources, the people of
South Vietnam simply cannot visualize a nation that has
no interest in colonialism."[25]

Thus one JUSPAO poster, supposedly produced by the
Saigon government, explained why it had invited the
Americans to "our" country:

WHY HAVE AMERICANS COME TO VIETNAM?

Americans have come to Vietnam because they are
determined to help defeat Communist aggression.
Like us, they know that if this aggression is
not stopped it will spread like a deadly
disease and infect other parts of the world.
Like many of our soldiers they share a grave
responsibility. But Americans have come to
Vietnam to do more than help fight the war.
They have come to help us rebuild our homes and
our lives. Like us, Americans know tht the
ravages of war must be erased, so that a free
people can live in a prosperous land.

These psychological operations were buttressed by
the U.S. armed forces through a variety of propaganda-of-
deed activities, called "civic action." Most attention
was given to people who had been caught in the path of
military activities, and the victimized were helped to
rebuild destroyed or damaged houses and public works.
Typical projects included digging community wells,
grading and repairing roads, fixing bridges, supplying
books for schools, teaching English, and providing
materials for local construction (Fig 6.23).

A special form of civic action -- the Medical Civil
Assistance Program (MEDCAP) -- was carried out by U.S.
military physicians, dentists, nurses, and medical
corpsmen. Medics normally provided health care services
for people near their home bases, but some also were
flown to remote areas. Typically, when a MEDCAP team
visited a village, local first-aid workers and mid-wives
assisted in treating disease and wounds and in providing

Figure 6.22
American-South Vietnamese Friendship

Bốn sĩ quan Việt Mỹ cùng nghiên cứu tỷ mỹ vào một bản đồ để xác định những vị trí ẩn náu của Cộng Sản đã nói lên tình chiến đấu keo sơn của những con người đứng chung trong một trận tuyến và cùng chiến đấu cho một lý tưởng : TỰ DO-DÂN CHỦ.

2787

CÙNG CHUNG LÝ TƯỞNG

Khi đã chiến đấu cho một lý tưởng chung là chống lại Cộng Sản xâm lược thì nếp sống hàng ngày của hai dân tộc Việt Mỹ không còn cách biệt.

Bữa cơm thân mật, dẫn đi giữa hai sĩ quan Việt Mỹ đã nói lên tình nghĩa thắm thiết để cùng bảo vệ mảnh đất Tự Do của Việt Nam Cộng Hoà.

These four Vietnamese and American officers are studying carefully a map to pinpoint the Communist hideouts. This manifests the close fighting spirit of men who are standing on the same front line and are fighting together for the same ideology: FREEDOM AND DEMOCRACY.

When struggling for the common ideology which is to fight against Communist aggressors, the way of living of two people, Vietnamese and American, is no longer a big difference.

The simple meal of these two Vietnamese and American officers reflects the intimate friendship between them, who pledged to protect this land of Freedom of the Republic of Vietnam.

Source: U.S., JUSPAO, leaflet number 2787.

Figure 6.23
U.S. Civic Action Program

The 11th Armored Cavalry has arrived in Vietnam. They have mighty tanks that will seek out and destroy the Viet Cong. When not fighting the Viet Cong bandits who rebel against their own people, the U.S. 11th Armored Cavalry will be helping to build schools, treat the sick and injured and distribute food to the people of Vietnam.

But they can only help you, if you help them. When you see the American soldiers wearing the Big Black Horse on their shoulder, remember, we are your friends.

Source: U.S., MACV, 246th Psychological Operations Company, Leaflet Catalogue, leaflet number 110.

pre-natal instructions, innoculations, and dental
services.[26]

These good deeds were strengthened by propaganda-of-
word as JUSPAO leaflets, magazines, newspapers, soap, and
toothpaste were handed out during the MEDCAP visits.
Sometimes films were shown, and local VIS cadres made
loudspeaker broadcast appeals in support of various
government programs (Fig 6.24). JUSPAO also devised a
special "medicine envelope" for distribution by the
medics. It had spaces for writing instructions for the
use of medicine, a South Vietnamese flag, an appropriate
propaganda slogan, and a photograph or sketch of a
healthy family.

Credit for the medical treatment was given to the
Republic government -- a ground loudspeaker tape
explains:

"ATTENTION CITIZENS . . . ATTENTION CITIZENS . . .

We are members of the United States Forces
MEDCAP team. We are here at the request of the
Government of the Republic of Vietnam to help
you. . . . Your Government wants to help you
and your family to good health. The Viet Cong
wants to see you ill and helpless. The
soldiers you see in the area are here to
protect the team so that it can help you. You
can help by telling the soldiers where the Viet
Cong hide themselves, their weapons and their
food."

The effectiveness of the civic action programs is
difficult to judge. However, one Viet Cong document
commented that, "The enemy behaved kindly to the people
to win their heart. They carried the people's children
in their arms, washed and changed their clothes. . . .
Those who were wounded were given medical assistance. . .
. Our cadre's wives seemed to be unhappy because their
husbands worked for us. . . . The Vietnamese people did
not understand the enemy's scheme. . . . They
unintentionally propagandized that the Americans are
kind."[27]

Nonetheless, problems plagued the civic action
activities. Projects sometimes had to be abandoned
before completion when they were interrupted by combat
requirements, schools were constructed when no teachers
were available, and wells were dug in areas haunted by
"ghosts of ancestors," precluding their use. Important,
too, Americans often failed to involve the populace in
these projects. In other cases, soap, candy, gum, coins,
clothing, and similar items were handed out in the spirit
of charity, but these acts sometimes caused friction
because those most in need were often overlooked. Even

Figure 6.24
Medical Civil Assistance Program

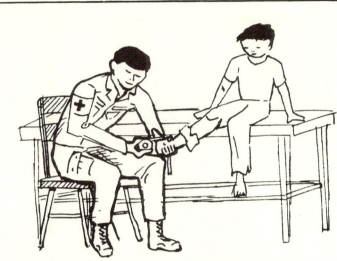

Sự giúp đỡ y tế là một trong những công tác Lữ Đoàn 173 Nhẩy.
Dū đã thực hiện cũng với chánh phủ VN để giúp đỡ dân chúng
Hẩy ủng hộ chánh phủ và Đồng Minh.

"SUPPORT THE GOVERNMENT OF VIETNAM AND IT'S ALLIES!"

At the request of and in cooperation with your government, the medical teams of the 173rd Airborne Brigade are assisting the government authorities in providing medical care for the people of South Vietnam. The well-trained personnel, modern equipment and abundant medicines of these teams are constantly at the disposal of the Vietnamese people. In one two-week period alone, from 22 May to 4 June 1966, 5,186 people were treated by doctors, dentists and medics of the 173rd Airborne Brigade. This medical assistance is only one of the many ways in which the sky-soldiers of the 173rd Airborne Brigade cooperate with your government authorities in building a better life for the people of South Vietnam. . . .

Source: U.S., MACV, 246th Psychological Operations Company, Leaflet Catalogue, leaflet number 286.

American friendliness toward children was resented by
some because they felt that giving gifts created a habit
of begging, degrading their parents and causing them to
lose face.

Among the negative aspects of having more than half
a million troops present in Vietnam at one time was the
so-called "ugly American" syndrome. The vast majority
conducted themselves with sufficient deportment to
reflect credit on the United States and its armed
forces. Most were periodically indoctrinated concerning
proper treatment of the people, their customs, elementary
Vietnamese phrases, and the behavior expected of them.
Apparently the Marine Corps did this best. Its chaplains
conducted a continuing community-understanding program
which, from all indications, was among the most
successful in Vietnam.

Despite such efforts, misconduct by some troops
(drunkenness, women-chasing, theft, and so on),
disrespect toward Vietnamese, and shooting domestic
animals were counterproductive. Among the most
nettlesome and widespread troop behavior problems was
their driving habits. Convoys often sped through
villages and hamlets, threatening lives of people and
livestock. Many persons were killed or injured -- a fact
which the Viet Cong were quick to exploit. Such
incidents as signs in public squares designating separate
toilets for Americans, and "U.S. soldiers urinating from
a truck into the path of a following sedan full of
Vietnamese" also cancelled out positive propaganda
efforts.[28]

It is obviously difficult to estimate the impact of
such misdeeds when compared with the good behavior of
most American troops and the effects of propaganda
designed to create a favorable U.S. image. A good guess
would be that the good will generated by the vast
majority of servicemen, reinforced by psychological
operations and civic action activities, outweighed the
negative influence of a few "ugly Americans."

Finally, JUSPAO and MACV put out a lot of propaganda
on behalf of other Allied nations with troops in
Vietnam. Some of this might be termed "double
surrogate," for they popularized New Zealand, South
Korea, Thailand, Australia, and the Philippines, while
purporting to have been produced by the Vietnamese
government (Fig 6.25). For example, one poster entitled
"New Zealand Is Another Brother In Our Fight Against
Communist Aggression" told the public: "These veterans,
who have fought against Communists in Malaysia, Korea and
Borneo, are now fighting at our side against the
Communist directed forces of North Vietnam. Because of
their past experience with Communist wars of aggression,
the New Zealanders recognized the grave danger facing the
people of South Vietnam and volunteered their help."

Figure 6.25
Australian-South Vietnamese Friendship

Chúng tôi những quân nhân thuộc lực
lượng Đặc Nhiệm Úc. Đơn vị chúng tôi hiện
đang hoạt động với Quân Lực Việt Nam Cộng
Hòa và các đơn vị Đồng Minh trong vùng này
để tiêu diệt Việt Cộng và các căn cứ của
chúng. . . . Trong khi đơn vị chúng tôi tiêu
trừ Việt Cộng thì các đơn vị khác lo kiến
thiết để giúp đỡ các bạn.

Chúng tôi tới đây là những người bạn. Chúng tôi là một phần
của lực lượng Đồng Minh tới Việt Nam để giúp đỡ các bạn chiến
thắng bọn Cộng Sản xâm lăng xứ sở của các bạn.
Chúng tôi mong ước các bạn được sống một cuộc sống tự do
không bị bọn Việt Cộng khủng bố. Xin các bạn hãy giúp đỡ chúng
tôi biết những tin tức về Việt Cộng.

We are members of the Australian Task Force. Our unit is
operating with Vietnamese and other units to destroy the Viet Cong
and their bases. While most of our units are busy defeating the
Viet Cong, others are working on projects to help you.

We come as friends. We are part of the Allied Forces in
Vietnam helping you achieve the inevitable victory over the
Communist aggression in your country. We want you to be able to
lead a life of happiness free from Viet Cong terror. Help us by
providing any information about the Viet Cong.

Source: U.S., MACV, 246th Psychological Operations Company, Leaflet
Catalogue, leaflet number 352.

EFFECTIVENESS

The central question surrounding the U.S. image-building psychological operations is how the Vietnamese people compared the government's case (albeit American) with that of the Viet Cong. Propaganda words undoubtedly would have fallen on deaf ears unless the content was based on reality and related to the people's experience. As theoretically explained by Jacques Ellul in his sociological analysis of propaganda:

> Propaganda of the word and propaganda of the deed are complementary. Talk must correspond to something visible; the visible, active element must be explained by talk. Oral or written propaganda, which plays on opinions or sentiments, must be reinforced by propaganda of action, which produces new attitudes and thus joins the individual firmly to a certain movement. Here again, you cannot have one without the other.[29]

Put into the context of Vietnam by Arnsten and Leites: "After many years of often glaring disparity between the government's words and its actions (or inactions), many in South Vietnam have probably learned to discount GVN assertions and promises."[30] Clearly, there were both hits and misses.

On the positive side, the Pacification and Rural Development Program was somewhat successful through 1972, demonstrating through its actions the government's concern for the people. It provided them with better security, administration at village and hamlet levels, community facilities (e.g., schools, roads, bridges, markets, wells, toilets), medical care and public health service, economic improvement through grants and credits for agricultural machinery and livestock, and instruction on farming methods, animal husbandry, and fishing techniques. Intensification of the effort to revive the economy after 1968 brought widespread introduction of the new IR-5/8 "miracle rice;" importation and distribution of fertilizer greatly enhanced agricultural production; key roads and waterways were re-opened and repaired, providing the farmer a means of getting his crop to markets; rural taxes were cancelled; various economic and resource control restrictions were abolished; and water pumps and tractors were introduced in large numbers. The capstone of the effort took place between 1970 and 1973 be redistribution of land and the virtual liquidation of tenant farming.

On the political scene, the Republic's attempt to revive local administration responsive to both the population and to the central authorities (i.e., a two-

way conduit communicating the people's needs to Saigon
and government policies to the populace) scored some
successes. Village councils and hamlet chiefs were
elected (albeit from an approved slate) and local leaders
were trained concerning their rights and duties. In
addition, villages were given local taxing powers and
allowed to spend revenues as their councils desired;
self-improvement was encouraged; and security forces,
police, and Rural Development cadres were placed under
control of the village chiefs. The People's Self-Defense
Force, ostensibly a military entity, represented an
opportunity to engage the populace in the political
struggle against the Viet Cong.

Elections involved the people more closely with
Saigon, and re-kindled some interest in managing public
affairs through local government. In spite of election
irregularities, village and hamlet balloting in 1969
showed an increase in the number of candidates running
for office, and voter participation was at the highest
level ever. By 1969, some 2,048 out of 2,151 villages
had elected local administrations. Although the people's
response to the electoral process cannot necessarily be
interpreted as a demonstration of support for the Saigon
government, former CORDs chief Ambassador R. W. Komer
places this development into the proper perspective:

> Some of the local elections were in name only,
> but given the sheer looseness and inefficiency
> of the GVN at all levels few would contend that
> local elections were mostly rigged. While
> difficult at yet to quantify, the GVN's
> continuing efforts to restore local autonomy at
> the grass roots level have apparently
> stimulated greater interest in local
> government.[31]

Against the positive factors enhancing the
government's image, one must try to balance the negative
elements -- the widespread corruption and inefficiency
that long characterized the Republic and the excesses
conducted under the guise of the Phung Hoang Program.
Similarly, confiscations of property and livestock
without remuneration by the Army, tribute payments
exacted from peasants for passage on rural roads, and
rough treatment of civilians meted out by soldiers were
inconsistent with attempts to depict Saigon positively.
A 1969 U.S. National Security Council study found that,
"The Republic of Vietnam armed forces as presently
constituted will only continue to widen the gap which
exists between the government and the rural populace." A
1973 report dealing with the reconstruction and
resettlement programs indicated that little improvement
in troop behavior or in elimination of corruption had

been made: "The lower echelons of the military and civil service are rife with corruption. It is difficult to say whether or not there is an increase. It has always been there. . . . This, along with a reported increase of troops' misbehavior toward the civilian population, does not assist in improving the reconstruction-resettlement situation."[32]

Actions to eliminate the Communist underground also were damaging to the effort to build a benevolent image of the Republic. The Phung Hoang drive undoubtedly was partially successful in rooting out and eliminating underground members of the Liberation Front, but the corruption, the heavy-handed treatment of civilians, the torture and imprisoning of innocent persons, and the use of the campaign to disguise political suppression of non-Communist criticism of the Thieu government doubtlessly destroyed much of the good will created by its pacification efforts.

On balance, how did the Vietnamese people judge Saigon's argument? How effective was its (U.S.) psychological operations? In the judgment of one American propagandist,

> Fundamentally, pacification was a success.
> . . . We did beat the National Liberation
> Front at its own game, and the cadres we
> trained to go out to the hamlets and influence
> people are now melting into the population.
> With the new mobility and communications we
> brought here, the Vietnamese people now are
> much more sophisticated and much less
> susceptible to enemy propaganda techniques.[33]

And a North Vietnamese general reportedly acknowledged, "We must admit that the enemy was partially successful in his pacification scheme in the Delta. . . . Communist political and military activities in the Mekong River Delta decreased, and the people's confidence concerning the revolution became weaker."[34]

But what about the Vietnamese people themselves? A host of factors worked against American efforts to create the pro-Saigon, anti-Communist, and pro-U.S. images. A tradition of loyalty and patriotism to a central government that could serve as a base upon which to build a modern nationalism did not exist in the Vietnamese culture. The Communists enjoyed a natural degree of popular sympathy because of their role in ridding the country of French rule. Most Southern peasants probably could not understand how their personal position would deteriorate under the Communists, and the stigma of "foreign invader" and "colonialism" used by the Viet Cong to discredit the United States was tough to counter.

Most important was the traditional Confucian

attitude which cautioned neutrality when caught between opposing forces -- a position of harmony with the present environment. The vast majority of people simply abstained from the war and withheld their support from both sides. Few abandoned this middle-of-the-road between Saigon and the National Liberation Front by openly committing themselves, for while the level of violence remained high, whoever temporarily held the "power of the gun" ruled in the countryside.

The net effect of these varied influences was that most people neither cared enough about the Republic nor received sufficient reason to depart from their neutral position and to commit themselves to the anti-Communist struggle. Taking the center road of pragmatism ensured they would be able to align themselves with the eventual winner. A major paradox of the Vietnam War was that this very denial of popular support for the government of the Republic of Vietnam was, in the end, a primary cause for its downfall. As an old saying cautioned the Vietnamese: "Chew when you eat, and think when you talk," because "Your mouth should be watched as a jar of wine and your thoughts protected like a fortress."

NOTES

1. See Appendix D for a listing of JUSPAO policy guidances that outline the major campaigns, appeals, and themes used in the attempt to win "hearts and minds." These directives have been used extensively in putting together Chapter 6.

2. U.S., MACV, CORDS, Guide for Province and District Advisors (Draft) (Saigon: February 1, 1968), p. 2-1.

3. Quoted in Daniel Ellsberg, The Day Loc Tien Was Pacified, P-3793 (Santa Monica, Calif.: Rand Corporation, February 1968), p. 17.

4. Ibid., p. iii.

5. Robert W. Komer, Impact of Pacification on Insurgency in South Vietnam, P-4443 (Santa Monica, Calif.: Rand Corporation, August 1970), U.S., MACV, CORDS, The Vietnamese Village 1970: Handbook for Advisors (Saigon: May 2, 1970), and Republic of Vietnam, Ministry of Rural Development, RD Cadres Handbook, English edition (Saigon: 1970).

6. U.S., JUSPAO, "National Psychological Operations Plan," Policy Number 20, in Consolidation of JUSPAO Guidances, Vol. I, p. 128.

7. U.S., JUSPAO, "People's Self-Defense," Policy Number 66 (August 8, 1968).

8. U.S., JUSPAO, "Vietnamese Farmer's Day, March 26, 1971," PSYOP Circular, Number 40 (March 10, 1971), R. L. Prosterman, "Vietnam's Land Reform Begins to Pay," Wall Street Journal (February 5, 1971), p. 2, and

Victoria Brittain, "Vietnam: Freezing Land and Capturing Votes," The Times (London: March 26, 1973), p. 12.

9. Michael Arnsten and Nathan Leites, Land Reform and the Quality of Propaganda in Rural Vietnam, RM-5764-ARPA (Santa Monica, Calif.: Rand Corporation, April 1970), pp. 46, 85-87.

10. U.S., JUSPAO, "Village and Hamlet Elections," Policy Number 29, in Consolidation of JUSPAO Guidances, Vol. II, p. 38.

11. Douglas Pike, War, Peace, and the Viet Cong (Cambridge, Mass.: MIT Press, 1969), p. 71.

12. Craig R. Whitney, "Saigon Abolishes Hamlet Elections," International Herald Tribune (September 8, 1972), p. 4, Shaplen, Road From War, p. 151, and Joseph Buttinger, Vietnam: A Political History (New York: Praeger, 1968), pp. 479-80.

13. White, Nobody Wanted War, pp. 81-82.

14. Ithiel de Sola Pool, "The Paradox of Nonviolent War in Vietnam," Life (July 4, 1970), p. 2.

15. Buttinger, Vietnam, pp. 491-93, and White, Nobody Wanted War, pp. 54-55. See also "Civilian Casualties in South Vietnam," International Herald Tribune (January 25, 1973), p. 3, and U.S., Senate, Vietnam: Policy and Prospects, pp. 54, 125-26.

16. As reported by Phillip P. Katz, A Systematic Approach to PSYOP Information (Kensington, Md.: American Institute for Research, Center for Research in Social Systems, February 1970), p. 41.

17. U.S., MACV, Guide for Psychological Operations (Saigon: August 6, 1967), p. 15.

18. Quoted in U.S., JUSPAO, "Psyops Aspects of Defoliation," Policy Number 31, in Consolidation of JUSPAO Guidances, Vol. II, pp. 47-51.

19. Hugh Mulligan, No Place to Die (New York: William Morrow & Company, 1967), p. 271.

20. Arnsten and Leites, Land Reform, p. 5.

21. U.S., MACV, PSYOP/POLWAR Newsletter, Vol. 5, No. 6 (June 1970), pp. 3-4.

22. U.S. MACV, CORDS, Phung Hoang Advisor Handbook (Saigon: November 20, 1970) and Military Operations--Phung Hoang Operations, MACV Directive 525-36 (Saigon: November 5, 1971). See also U.S., Senate, Vietnam: Policy and Prospects, pp. 56-57.

23. Wayne L. Cooper, "Operation Phoenix: A Vietnam Fiasco Seen From Within," Washington Post (June 18, 1972), p. B4, Samuel L. Popkin, "Pacification: Politics and the Village," Asian Survey, Vol. X, No. 8 (August 1970), p. 667, Harry Trimborn, "Saigon Spurs Drive on Underground Network," Los Angeles Times (October 4, 1969), Shaplen, Road From War, pp. 429-30, and Robert G. Kaiser, Jr., "U.S. Aides in Vietnam Scorn Phoenix Project," Washington Post (February 17, 1970).

24. U.S., MACV, PSYOP/POLWAR Newsletter, Vol. 4,

No. 1 (January 1969).

25. U.S., MACV, PSYOP/POLWAR Newsletter, Vol. 3, No. 4 (March 1968).

26. U.S., MACV, Military Civic Action, MACV Directive 515-2 (Saigon: April 30, 1966).

27. Quoted in U.S., U.S. Mission, Vietnam, press release (Saigon: August 25, 1967). The Viet Cong document is dated October 27, 1966.

28. Latimer, U.S. Psychological Operations, p. 38.

29. Jacques Ellul, Propaganda: The Formation of Men's Attitudes, Trans. by Konrad Kellen and Jean Lerner (New York: Alfred A. Knopf, 1971), p. 15.

30. Arnsten and Leites, Land Reform, p. 5.

31. Komer, Impact of Pacification, pp. 2-15, and James R. Bullington and James D. Rosenthal, "The South Vietnamese Countryside: Non-Communist Political Perceptions," Asian Survey, Vol. X, No. 8 (August 1970), pp. 652-54.

32. Quoted in Jacques Leslie, "Reports Show Saigon's Army Still Alienating Civilians," International Herald Tribune (May 29, 1973), p. 5.

33. Quoted in Browne, "U.S. Trims Psychological Warfare," p. 3.

34. Quoted in Vietnam Council on Foreign Relations, "Rationale Behind a New Theme: SELF-RELIANCE," Vietnam Magazine, Vol. 4, No. 8 (Saigon: 1971), p. 7.

Part 3
The Question
of Effectiveness

7
An Appraisal:
Problems and Perspectives

> Psychological effectiveness cannot be isolated
> because the sources of actions shaping the
> morale of the Vietnamese are the intertwined
> developments in the political, military,
> economic and psychological domains. Political
> stability, military victory, economic progress
> are the primary substance with which
> psychological action must work to be effective.
>
> --JUSPAO[1]

    With the ignominious collapse of the Republic in May
1975, it became obvious that the United States had failed
to achieve its two major national objectives: "to
prevent communist domination of South Vietnam" and "to
create a viable and increasingly democratic society."
Because the military and political-economic actions were
unsuccessful in stopping Hanoi's drive and rallying
active popular support for Saigon, psychological
operations, as supplements to these actions, could not
win the "hearts and minds" battle. But this observation
says little about the usefulness of the propaganda
program. How effective was it as a tool of foreign
policy? How well did it augment the military and
political-economic activities? How cogent were the
persuasive appeals? Were they credible? What were the
strengths and weaknesses of the campaign?
    To assess adequately the propaganda as an instrument
to achieve American goals in Vietnam, it is necessary to
trace national policy all the way through the final
messages employed. One useful approach, in simplified
terms, views communication as a process in which a source
"encodes" an idea into written or oral form and transmits
it via some channel (e.g., leaflet, radio broadcast) to a
receiver, who mentally interprets or "decodes" the
message. For communication to occur, the words used to
express a thought must have the same meaning for both the

sender and the receiver. When this stimulus-response procedure is transposed to an insurgent environment, the communication process undergoes a curious metamorphosis.

The representation shown in Figure 7.1, for example, incorporates the social relationship of the three Vietnamese target audiences: the leadership, military, and general population in the North; the enemy in the South, including the Viet Cong and Hanoi's soldiers and their civilian supporters; and, for lack of a better term, the "non-enemy" Southerners, including the political elite, armed forces, and the friendly, neutral, and hostile (but not necessarily followers of the Viet Cong) persons.[2]

One of the most salient features of this scheme is the single source (JUSPAO) and the JUSPAO and MACV elements engaged in preparing or "encoding" propaganda messages. A mutation is entered by including three separate communication-lines, each representing the transmission belt to one of the major target groups. The communication process is no longer only a single straight line from sender to receiver. The crisscrossed arrows between messages in the communication-lines and the "decoding" function of other appendages indicate interception of propaganda transmissions by "eavesdropping" audiences, similar to "cross-talk" in radio and telephone when interference between channels occurs.

This "cross-talk" was inherent to the environment in Vietnam, for the Viet Cong and general population were commingled and closely associated. Thus, once an appeal was delivered by some form of broadcast, airdrop, or posted on a tree, it could be received by both intended and chance audiences. And because the insurgent ranks were drawn from the populace, messages also could be discussed and spread between the Viet Cong and the public through relatives, friends, village neighbors, or casual acquaintances. In addition, Hanoi's troops were bombarded by propaganda in the North and along the Ho Chi Minh Trail before reaching South Vietnam where they received both enemy- and non-enemy-directed appeals.

This "cross-talk" potential, therefore, created a vital need for consistency of all communications, regardless of their intended audiences. Inconsistencies in messages for difference target groups surely would have been noticed and discussed, raising questions about the originator's credibility. Zorthian recognized this and offers the following axiom: ". . . there cannot exist a gap between the substance of messages to . . . different audiences. A different content may be delivered to different audiences but a contradictory one may not. Both the ancient and modern means of communication and the effort of the other side will serve to provide extensive circulation of differences."[3]

Figure 7.1
Psychological Operations in Vietnam:
The Communication Process

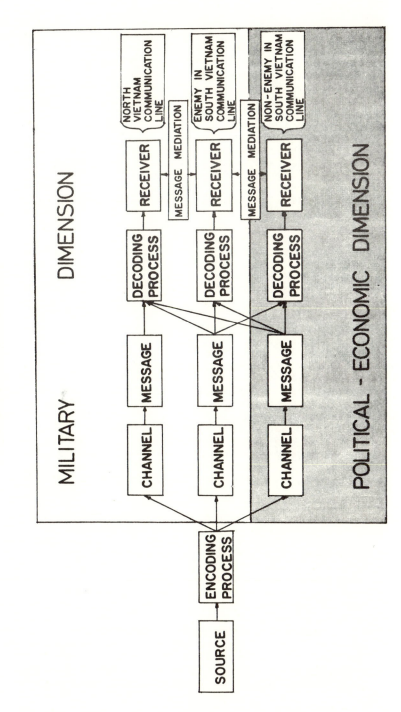

In a word, the possibility of "cross-talk" meant that chance audiences were as important as intended ones. It follows that a sole source of all U.S. propaganda was essential to ensure the credibility and consistency of messages supplementing the military and political-economic activities. As Zorthian explains, ". . . there can be no separate or uncoordinated approach to the military, political or economic aspects. . . . Communication is of one piece - and disregard of the principle leads to disaster in effectiveness for inevitably, the different parts end up at cross purposes. Particularly this is true for military and civilian aspects."[4]

JUSPAO, as the single agency responsible for U.S. psychological operations, played a crucial role. Its task was to transform national policy into appropriate messages for hostile, friendly, and neutral persons. That was not an easy job. How well it organized and planned could spell the difference between success and disaster. Wrong decisions, mistakes in judgment, and seemingly small errors at the origin would tend to snowball as their effects reverberated through the communication process. Incongruities in its propaganda could have vitally affected the <u>credibility</u>, <u>consistency</u>, and <u>specificity</u> needed for a cogent propaganda program: strict adherence to truth could have helped assure credibility; centralized direction and control could have guaranteed a consistent campaign; and decentralized preparation of messages could have resulted in potentially effective themes tailored especially for local target groups. In addition, trained and experienced psychological warriors could have ensured that propaganda appeals were in accord with Vietnamese culture, and adequate feedback on message effectiveness could have prevented them from "flying blind." In all these areas -- credibility, consistency, specificity, expertise, feedback -- the U.S. record was mixed.

CREDIBILITY

Traditionally, propaganda has been called "white," "gray," or "black," depending on the attribution given the communication source. "White" propaganda is open and the originator is not concealed in any way; "gray" propaganda is covert and the sender conceals his identity; and "black" propaganda is covert and the communications are said to come from a source other than the true one.

The U.S. psychological operations in Vietnam, however, cannot be neatly placed into any one of these categories. Although an overt campaign, it was not completely "white;" the Republic was purported to be the originator of most communications. But because it was an

overt effort, the psychological operations cannot be
described as either "gray" or "black." Instead, a new
category, "light-gray" propaganda, is used here to
characterize those American messages that claimed or
implied that Saigon was the source. These unorthodox
communications emerged because JUSPAO, frustrated in its
attempts to work through the Ministry of Information,
increasingly substituted for the Republic, preparing
propaganda appeals on behalf of that government and
delivering them directly to the Communist insurgents, the
North Vietnamese, and its own citizens. Zorthian
explains this makeshift effort: "In theory we tried to
work through the Vietnamese government when the
communication with the Vietnamese population was in
behalf of the government while we tried to communicate
directly with the Vietnamese population when the
communication was in behalf of the American government.
Unfortunately, the distinctions were not always clear or
observed when they were. In fact . . . one of our errors
in Vietnam was our tendency to substitute ourselves for
the Vietnamese in their own communications with their
people both because of their shortcomings and our own
impatience and confidence in our abilities."[5]
     There is little doubt that JUSPAO served as a
surrogate Republic ministry of information. Some ninety-
three percent of 1,249 sampled American communications
for South Vietnamese target audiences were "light-gray,"
one percent claimed to have originated from Thai, Korean,
Australian, New Zealander or Philippine sources, and only
six percent clearly acknowledged the U.S. as the
sender. Similarly, almost all communications for
Northern audiences during the 1965-1968 "Frantic Goat
North" campaign were "light-gray" (only a single leaflet
out of the fifty examined admitted American origin); a
notable shift occurred in mid-1972 during the "Field Goal
Operation" when the U.S. was given credit in thirty-nine
of the fifty leaflets considered; and almost two-thirds
of the sample of fifty scattered among the Ho Chi Minh
Trail said Saigon was the originator, while twenty-eight
percent contended that the Vientiane government (Laos)
was the sender. Examples of the "white" and "light-gray"
communications are depicted in Figures 7.2 through 7.5.
Note the key phrases: Figure 7.2 gives clear attribution
to the U.S., Figure 7.3 starts with an introduction "Dear
Countrymen" to the South Vietnamese (similar salutations
were used in leaflets for Northern audiences), Figure 7.4
begins "We Koreans," and Figure 7.5 shows a leaflet
alleged to have come from the Royal Laotian government.
     By purporting to have been produced and disseminated
by South Vietnamese and Laotian authorities, these
"light-gray" psychological operations violated one of the
basic and most important rules of propaganda -- strict
adherence to the truth. This "white lie" concerning the

Figure 7.2
"White" Propaganda

Chính-Phủ Hoa- Kỳ sẽ thưởng cho đồng-bào một triệu ba trăm bảy mươi lăm ngàn
đồng bạc (1.375.000$) nếu đồng-bào cung-cấp tin-tức để giúp cách đưa một quân-
nhân Hoa-Kỳ đang ở trong tình trạng nguy-hiểm trở về được bình-yên vô-sự.

4370 V

The United States Government will pay you 1,375,000 piasters
($5,000) for assisting a U.S. serviceman to return safely.

Source: U.S., JUSPAO, leaflet number 4370-V.

Figure 7.3
"Light-Gray" Propaganda: South Vietnam

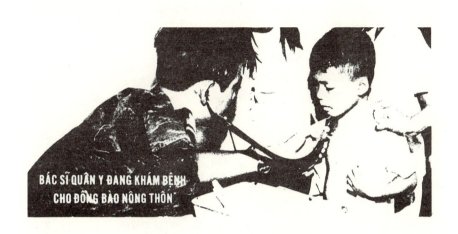

Dear Countrymen:

Besides their mission to destroy the enemy and defend the nation, Government of Vietnam forces are concerned about fighting several other enemies which are dangerous, they are: disease, illiteracy, and poverty.

In the field of fighting against disease, the Government of Vietnam has been making efforts to provide medicines and treatment facilities so that our entire population may enjoy good health and a longer life.

GVN Forces are wishing you a Happy New Year.

Source: U.S., JUSPAO, leaflet number 2933.

Figure 7.4
"Light-Gray" Propaganda: South Korea

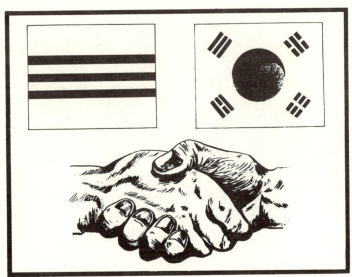

8-068 (3)

Dear Citizens!
We, Koreans, are the same Asians as you. We preserve the similar traditions and customs as you. Now, we are suffering from the same enemy, the Communist. However, our two countries are fighting on the same front line against the Communist conspiracy. We are not only combat soldiers at your side, but also we can be your true friends. We respect the aged people, protect weak females, and love children. Let us be good friends and be united for the realization of a peaceful and prosperous society.

Source: U.S., JUSPAO, leaflet number SP-1985.

source made it essential that all traces of foreignness
be eliminated from "light-gray" messages so recipients
would not be able to determine their alien origin. This
was important, furthermore, because people tend to give
greater credence to what their own government has to say
over foreign ones. In countries such as Vietnam, with a
long history of foreign colonization and domination, this
was especially so.

Communist propaganda often exposed the true source
of the "light-gray" communications. For instance, one of
the Viet Cong's most important themes depicted the United
States as a "foreign invader" and "colonizer," replacing
the French as the imperialist ruler of South Vietnam.
One Communist document told its cadres: "American
imperialism and America's lackeys are very dangerous and
wicked. But in the face of the intense political and
armed struggle of the people and of the armed forces led
by the Party, it is certain tht they will be repelled and
decisively defeated." Another claimed that, "the peoples
of the world, including American people, are strongly
protesting against the war of aggression and are fully
supporting us."[6] The effects of these and similar
charges were further strengthened whenever the true origin
of "light-gray" propaganda was revealed. Indeed, by
1965, "Americans became the prime political and military
target rather than the Government of Vietnam."[7]

The need to eliminate foreignness in "light-gray"
communications was crucial, and "how" it was said became
as important, if not paramount, as "what" was said
because JUSPAO and MACV were trying to cover a lie.
False attribution, although seemingly a harmless "white
lie," could have undermined the credibility of the
"hearts and minds" campaign if exposed, especially with
an adversary fanning the flames of indignation.

It is clear that Americans were not altogether
successful in masking their "white lie." As newsman
Malcolm Browne described the problem in 1972, ". . . over
the years senior American officials here felt
increasingly uneasy that the agency JUSPAO had become
'a surrogate Vietnamese ministry for information.' It
was argued that too much American assistance discouraged
the normal development of Vietnamese propaganda, that
Vietnamese pamphlets and posters prepared and printed by
Americans were too slick and professional and that
everything had an unpalatable American flavor."[8] A
simple error illustrates the point. In late 1967, JUSPAO
got around to checking on the quality of some of the
messages it had produced over the previous two-and-a-half
years, and discovered, to its horror, that the Vietnamese
often were able to spot their foreign origin. The clue
was in the document control number printed on each
message!

The origin of this index procedure went back to 1964
when USIS first began preparing propaganda for the Saigon

government. At that time someone decided to label these communications "Special Projects," and so the letters "SP" were encoded as a prefix to the document control number -- see Figure 7.6. JUSPAO continued the practice through 1967 when its qualitative check revealed that the two letters together had no meaning in the Vietnamese language; thus, the recipients were able to identify the source as foreign. Not surprisingly JUSPAO immediately dropped the "SP" prefix.

In the North, U.S. credibility probably failed to hold up because the Lao Dong Party clearly and vociferously denounced the "light-gray" propaganda. Radio Hanoi, for instance, ridiculed the United States for addressing "Northern Compatriots" in some leaflets. The broadcast, supposedly a dialogue between North Vietnamese gathering circulars to turn over to the authorities, presented this scene:

> One woman said: "I do not care to read them. Whatever the aggressors say, is dull, deceitful. . . ." A girl with big, bright eyes stood up. Trying to refrain from laughing she said: "It is so funny, my dear aunt!" She continued bitterly: "Affectionately to the Northern Compatriots! Is it not funny that the most barbarous and cruelest invaders in the world pretend to be affectionate to our compatriots?" An old woman said: "You are right, but there is more to this than the funny part . . . the boys tell me that the Americans are using psychological warfare."[9]

The precise effect of "light-gray" psychological operations on the over-all credibility of the "hearts and minds" campaign is not entirely clear. Nevertheless, it is apparent that this "white lie" had the potential of undermining American hopes for effective communications. While most former JUSPAO officers agree that a better procedure (working through the South Vietnamese rather than for them) was necessary, such an arrangement was virtually impossible until the Saigon government had been stabilized internally in 1967. By then the propaganda effort had its own momentum and a change in procedure was largely ignored, leaving JUSPAO with its unsolved credibility problem.

CONSISTENCY AND SPECIFICITY

The remaining two imperatives for JUSPAO, as the sole source of psychological operations, were consistency and specificity. They, too, posed serious problems. In any international political communications effort, success is determined largely by how well the

Figure 7.6
"SP" Prefix Shows Foreign Origin

TẠI SAO GIA ĐÌNH ÔNG TRẦN VĂN VI TƯƠI SÁNG?

SP-1548

___

Source: U.S., JUSPAO, leaflet number SP-1548.

communicator combines the national policies he is
supporting with the characteristics of the audience from
which he desires a response. These are the boundaries
with which he must work. Ideally, this policy-audience
relationship should be contracted in step-wise fashion so
that broad national ends, expressed in universal terms,
are carefully honed into persuasive themes for
distinctive target groups.

As both the goals and intended audiences are defined
in increasingly specific terms, a number of important
steps are necessary to ensure that the resulting messages
adequately reflect the policies they are designed to
support. Figure 7.7 below, for example, illustrates the
required narrowing of policies and audiences -- from
broad to specific -- in the context of Vietnam. The
major foreign policy aims of preventing Communist
domination and the creation of a viable democratic
society were focused on a universal target group -- the
Vietnamese people. Becoming specific (a) the propaganda
objectives outlined in the "National Psychological
Operations Plan for Vietnam" should have supported the
foreign policy goals in terms of general audiences (e.g.,
Communist armed forces, people of North and South
Vietnam); (b) the campaigns of persuasion outlined by
JUSPAO for field propagandists should have supported the
aims of the Plan in terms of particular audiences (e.g.,
Viet Cong, North Vietnamese soldiers, rural and urban
populations, minority groups, refugees); and (c) the
message themes should have been drawn from the guidelines
offered by JUSPAO and tailored for specific audiences
(e.g., selected villages, refugee groups, Viet Cong and
North Vietnamese units). The obvious question is whether
there was consistency and yet specificity among these
three.

The first, the U.S. "National Psychological
Operations Plan for Vietnam," was the blueprint which
served as a conceptual bridge between national objectives
and the JUSPAO policy directives which were prepared to
direct and control the field propagandists (see Appendix
B). The Plan transformed the foreign policy goals into
five psychological objectives and twelve persuasive aims
intended for the general audiences -- each designed
either to help create a strong anti-Communist nationalism
among the South Vietnamese or to undermine Viet Cong and
Northern morale.

Propaganda Goals	Target Audiences
1. To impress upon the Vietnamese people that free Vietnam will inevitably win its struggle against aggression and subversion, and that they would be best advised to support, wherever possible actively, the ultimate victor.	Non-enemy in South Vietnam

Figure 7.7
Synthetic Model of Objectives and Target Audiences

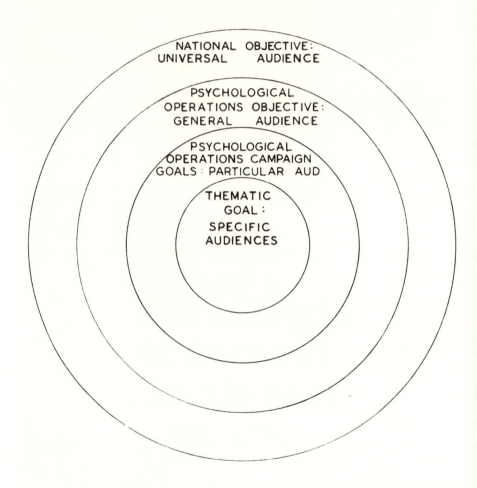

As in any targeting, whether archery, shooting, darts or
psychological operations, the closer you strike to the center of the
target the more points you score or better reward you will receive.
That is, in psychological operations greater effect of
communications will result the closer a message theme is identified
with explicit characteristics, problems, and receptivities of a
specific audience.

2. Conversely, to impress upon the
Viet Cong that their leaders cannot
expect to impose their will upon a
government and a people whose
struggle for peace, security and
independence is supported by the
might of the United States and
other Free World nations.

Viet Cong and
supporters in
South Vietnam

3. To create hope that the social
revolution proceeding in Free
Vietnam will produce a dynamic
nation responsive to the will and
aspirations of the people, and
capable of finding Vietnamese
solutions to Vietnamese problems;
and to commit ever-growing numbers
of the Vietnamese people to
active, personal, emotional
identification with the Republic's
quest for peace, humanity, social
justice and a vital national identity.

Viet Cong and
supporters, and
non-enemy in
South Vietnam

4. Conversely, to make the people
aware of the truth that the
communist leaders of North Vietnam
and the Viet Cong offer nothing
wherever tried, and are, in fact,
merely the instrumentalities of an
international conspiracy and of Red
Chinese imperialism; and to inspire
the people with contempt for the Viet
Cong who expose the nation to death,
destruction, misery and oppression,
and who oppose the creation of a truly
Vietnamese social order and the
preservation of Vietnamese values and
traditions.

North Vietnamese,
Viet Cong and
supporters, and
non-enemy in
South Vietnam

5. To convince all Vietnamese
people that the United States and
other Free World Nations are in
Vietnam to assist the Vietnamese
people in defeating the aggression
and to assist in building an improved
economy; and that the FWMAF [Free
World Military Assistance Forces]
will withdraw once the aggression is
defeated.

North Vietnamese,
Viet Cong and
supporters, and
non-enemy in
South Vietnam

Part IV expressed the need for adequate
coordination:

It is . . . essential that the Ministry of
Information and Open Arms, the Chief of the
General Political Warfare Department, the U.S.
Minister for Information (Director, JUSPAO) and
the Commanding General, USMACV, each in his
individual capacity and operating through his
normal organizational channels, serve as the
agency responsible for the execution of this
plan. <u>It is essential furthermore, that Action
Plans be closely coordinated.</u>[10] [emphasis
added]

This program of action was prepared to guide
psychological operations which supplemented the military
and political-economic actions taken to achieve <u>American</u>
foreign policy ends. It was not written in consultation
with the South Vietnamese to assist in attaining their
national goals. When the U.S. presented its scheme as a
<u>fait accompli</u>, Saigon adamantly refused to endorse it
throughout the war. M. Dean Havron and Herbert Vreeland
of Human Sciences Research analyzed the American design
and suggested that its Western orientation may have been
an underlying reason for the government's unwillingness
to subscribe to it. Use of the term "fledgling" to
describe the Republic of Vietnam, they pointed out, could
have been considered as condescending by Vietnamese and
could have caused resentment on the part of a culturally
proud people, whose history "antedates Columbus'
discovery of America." They noted, too, that the phrase,
"natural but naturally imperfect process of historical
change" reflected an Occidental concept of evolutionary
government which has little similarity to Oriental
political philosophy or experience. Finally, Havron and
Vreeland found the Plan entirely future-oriented,
offering each person the option of whether to support
Saigon or the Viet Cong; this decision, they believed,
probably was not accepted by the Vietnamese whose
Confucian socialization suggested that an important
choice such as this should be made by authority figures
rather than by an individual acting singularly.[11]
Although many former JUSPAO officers are at a loss
to explain Saigon's refusal to endorse the Plan, Havron
and Vreeland have likely come close to the mark.
Whatever the reason, failure to achieve a common
statement of propaganda purpose and operational procedure
hampered Allied coordination through the war. Although
the blueprint shows an excellent policy-audience
synthesis and compatibility with the U.S. aims in
Vietnam, lack of cooperation between the two allies was
regrettable and undoubtedly damaged the over-all
propaganda campaign.
JUSPAO policy directives were the second element
determining consistency and specificity. These

instructions were the heart of U.S. persuasive efforts
(see the sample in Appendix C). Outlining specific
campaigns in terms of particular target audiences, they
served as a bridge between the National Psychological
Operations Plan and the specific message themes. These
prescriptions were binding on all American agencies, and
they were JUSPAO's primary control mechanism over the
propaganda activities undertaken by the military and
CORDS psychological warriors. They were also designed to
allow field propagandists sufficient flexibility to tailor
message themes according to the current receptivities of
specific audiences. As Professor Morris Janowitz
explains, such policy instructions should foster both
centralized control and decentralized execution: "The
directive must seek to encourage the operator to make
full use of the resources at his command that are
consistent with policy objectives. Extreme diversity of
expression is required if the heavy hand of monotony in
output is to be avoided. The propaganda directive should
seek to encourage flexibility of expression in output
while stressing adherence to an over-all line."[12]

A review of eight-seven JUSPAO policy guidances
reveals each fully consistent with the persuasive
objectives outlined by the National Psychological
Operations Plan. This finding clearly shows that
American propagandists had prepared their directives with
the U.S. foreign policy goals foremost in mind.
Nevertheless, many appear to have had limited usefulness
for field personnel, especially during the early years of
the war. Until April 1968 contemplated target audiences
for the various campaigns were not clearly identified.
Rather, communication programs were broadly described
under the rubrics of "problem," "discussion," and
"guidance," leaving specific themes and target audiences
to be worked out by MACV and CORDS psychological
warriors. In reality, little guidance was given
concerning exactly what should have been done and what
should have been emphasized to which persons.

In 1967 the Department of Defense-sponsored ARPA
Committee on Psychological Operations criticized the
style and format of the JUSPAO prescriptions. The
Committee asserted that they met the needs of
propagandists more sophisticated than those in the
field: "It appears that the guidances are not widely
read by military PSYOP personnel; correctly or not, field
operators regard them of dubious value."[13] Perhaps as a
result of this criticism, JUSPAO changed the format and
orientation of its policy directives in 1968 to a more
direct and readable style. Generally, the revised
instructions were organized under the headings of
"purpose," "situation," "psychological objectives,"
"target audiences," "guidance," "discussion" or
"background." Some also specified the themes and media

to be used.

This revision formed an ideal policy-audience synthesis at the intermediate level: (a) directives for propaganda campaigns in both the military and political-economic aspects of the war were compatible with each other and with the persuasive objectives outlined by the National Psychological Operations Plan; and (b) they identified particular target audiences, especially after 1967, for use by MACV and CORDS propagandists in translating these guidelines into persuasive themes for specific audiences. However, to encourage psychological warriors to use their imagination and initiative in tailoring themes for local groups is one thing; to have them do an adequate job is another. This aspect -- personnel at the working level -- will be discussed later.

The third element determining consistency and specificity were the message appeals themselves. As microcosms of U.S. national policies, these communications should have been aimed at specific audiences to take full advantage of their current mental vulnerabilities and situation, and they should have been compatible with JUSPAO directives. A qualitative comparison of 1,249 messages supplementing the military and political-economic activities of the war with the guidance offered by the policy directives revealed that over ninety-six percent of those for the South Vietnamese were consonant with each other and with the JUSPAO prescriptions. Nearly all those for Northern target audiences were found to be compatible.

Four contradictory JUSPAO leaflets were produced in 1965 -- each was concerned with Viet Cong assassinations of government officials. These themes were contrary to a directive in force at the time specifying that Communist atrocities and terrorism were appropriate subjects for exploitation only when deaths resulted from indiscriminate targeting. Another leaflet was excessively gory in reporting the results of terrorism.

Military-produced messages considered inconsistent included those using the ace of spades as an omen of death, bikini-clad girls for sex appeals, photographs showing macabre death scenes, and excessive rhetoric. These latter communications were judged counterproductive because of their potential for arousing anger in the enemy ranks, e.g., allegations that the Viet Cong "plunder and murder" and such name calling as "Barbarous Robbers," "Cowards and Thieves," "Gang of Thieves," "VC Bandits," "Bandits from Hanoi" (Fig 7.8).

A single inappropriate leaflet was present in the sample of fifty for North Vietnam delivered during the 1965-1968 "Frantic Goat North" campaign. It described the good life of the South Vietnamese people, claiming that almost everyone was affluent and supported the

Figure 7.8
Name Calling

Live with pride instead of slinking through the jungle afraid
of airplanes and tanks. Stop eating poorly and being sick. Stop
living in fear of death. Rally now to the Government of Vietnam and
her allies. You are always welcome.

Source: U.S., MACV, 246th Psychological Operations Company, Leaflet
Catalogue, leaflet number 328.

Republic. This theme was probably received with a large grain -- if not a block -- of salt by the Northern recipients. All circulars in the samples of fifty for the 1972-1973 "Field Goal Operation" and Ho Chi Minh Trail campaigns were compatible with American foreign policy aims and with each other.

Several additional leaflets also present in the samples may best be termed as questionable. Although they cannot be judged conclusively as contradictory, they appear to at least raise the question of their potential effectiveness -- examples are discussed below and pertinent illustrations are provided.

Severe threats present in some messages may have aroused counterproductive feelings of ire and resistance among the enemy ranks (Fig 7.9).

Others depicted the Viet Cong as slaves to their Communist masters; these were likely to have stimulated anger and resentment (Fig 7.10).

Some leaflets, portraying Viet Cong recruiting techniques carried out at gunpoint, probably lacked credibility among non-enemy target audiences. The Communists used various pressure practices in their conscription efforts, but they normally stopped short of physical coercion and kidnapping (Fig 7.11).

And a few circulars depicted the Viet Cong wearing helmets with a red star, although they did not wear such headgear (Fig 7.12).

Most such MACV-produced messages judged discordant, and those considered to be questionable, were present in a single U.S. Army leaflet catalogue published in 1966. On the whole, it is clear that the armed forces generally followed the JUSPAO directives very closely in preparing communications for both enemy and non-enemy target groups. Specialist Janice Hopper also found from her 1967 analysis of about 800 leaflets prepared by the military that "there is considerable evidence of impact of JUSPAO policy guidances in substantive content of leaflets in the sample under consideration."[14] Indeed, given complexity of the insurgent environment and the long chains of coordination between the military and pacification aspects of the propaganda campaign, there was a surprising extent of consistency. This overwhelming compliance appears to be a plus for possible effectiveness. But there remained the problem of specificity, vital to a successful psychological operations campaign.

In an attempt to determine how well American communications were tailored to the specific

Figure 7.9
Severe Threats

Viet Cong Beware! There is nowhere to run, nowhere to hide!
The tanks and armored vehicles of the Blackhorse Regiment will find
and destroy you! It is too late to fight. Beware Viet Cong, we are
everywhere! Rally now under the Chieu Hoi Program, it is your only
hope to live!

Source: U.S., MACV, 246th Psychological Operations Company, Leaflet
Catalogue, leaflet number 111.

Figure 7.10
Communist Slaves

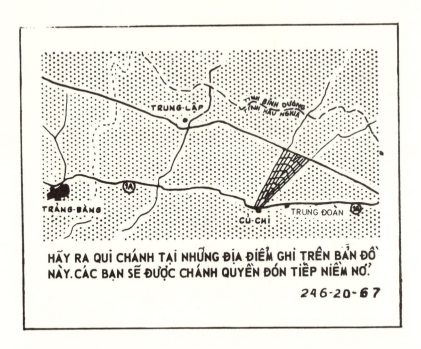

HÃY RA QUI CHÁNH TẠI NHỮNG ĐỊA ĐIỂM GHI TRÊN BẢN ĐỒ
NÀY. CÁC BẠN SẼ ĐƯỢC CHÁNH QUYỀN ĐÓN TIẾP NIỀM NỞ.
246-20-67

The government knows the Viet Cong steal your fellow countrymen to be slaves for the Communist puppets of the North. The Government knows the hardships you endure as a Viet Cong. You will be forgiven. Go to any of the four places shown on the map of this leaflet and the Government of Vietnam authorities will welcome you. Rally now and put your mind at rest with the government Chieu Hoi Program.

Source: U.S., MACV, 246th Psychological Operations Company, Leaflet Catalogue, leaflet number 20.

Figure 7.11
Recruitment at Gunpoint

VIỆT CỘNG ĐANG THẢM BẠI VÀ CHÚNG ĐANG TUYỆT VỌNG DÙNG BẠO LỰC VÀ HĂM DỌA ĐỂ CƯỞNG
ÉP CON EM 14 VÀ 15 TUỔI CỦA ĐỒNG BÀO ĐI LÍNH CHO CHÚNG. ĐỒNG BÀO ĐÙNG ĐỂ CHÚNG LÀM
NHƯ VẬY VÌ CON EM HÃY CÒN NHỎ DẠI VÀ RẤT ĐÁNG MẾN.

The Viet Cong are losing and are separately drafting by threat and by force your dear 14 and 15 year old children. Do not allow this. Your children are too young and too precious to you.

Insure that your children will be with you in your old age by sending them to Government controlled territory where they may be safe and find a job until the Viet Cong are defeated. If your sons are 18 or older send them to join the Army of the Republic of Vietnam where they can fight for freedom from Viet Cong and receive good pay, housing and security.

Source: U.S., MACV, 246th Psychological Operations Company, Leaflet Catalogue, leaflet number 115-1-R.

Figure 7.12
Red Star on Helmets

HÌNH VẼ MỘT KHẨU ĐẠI BAC Ở ĐANG XA VỚI MỘT QUẢ ĐẠN
ĐANG BAY TỚI LÀM MỘT NHÓM VIỆT-CÔNG TAN LOẠN CHẠY TRỐN

     Viet Cong Beware! See our giant cannon that can reach out a
great distance to destroy you. Your cause is hopeless and can only
result in your death. You Cannot Win. Your only alternative is to
rally to the government cause. If you persist in defying the
government, you will die. Tell your comrades from the North to go
home. Your time is running out. Rally or Die.

Source: U.S., MACV, 246th Psychological Operations Company, Leaflet
Catalogue, leaflet number 82.

circumstances of the various target groups, sampled
messages were categorized according to the general,
particular or specific audiences they addressed. The
results of this analysis are shown in Table 7.1 and
examples are illustrated in Figures 7.13 through 7.15.

Table 7.1
Target Audience Specificity

| | S. Vietnam (N-1,247) | North Vietnam | | Ho Chi Minh Trail (N-50) |
		"Frantic Goat North" (N-50)	"Field Goal Operation" (N-50)	
General Audience	51%	94%	78%	10%
Particular Audience	37	6	18	90
Specific Audience	12	0	4	0

These findings are particularly significant because
they show that only twelve percent of American
communications were aimed at specific target audiences in
South Vietnam and, except for very few, none in the
Northern and "Trail" campaigns. While national-level
efforts, with broad, relatively timeless messages on
subjects such as recruitment, public health and safety,
and nationalism clearly were useful in the South, fifty-
one percent of the total campaign embracing such topics
does appear excessive; the same can be said about the
large percentages that addressed general audiences in the
North. Along the Ho Chi Minh Trail, most leaflets were
addressed to Hanoi's soldiers (i.e., a particular
audience), accounting for a seeming disparity in the
statistics.
    In brief, it is apparent that MACV and CORDS
propagandists achieved a significant degree of
consistency by simply reproducing broad themes expressed
in terms of general and particular audiences suggested by
JUSPAO. It is equally obvious that there was little
inclination to transform policy guidance into themes for
local target groups. Thus there was mutual support
between the two dimensions of the conflict -- the
military and political-economic -- but it was achieved at
the expense of more effective specifically targeted
propaganda messages. In terms of contracting broad
national policies for a universal audience to message
themes for specific sub-audiences, U.S. psychological
operations did well in forming increasingly narrow
policy-audience syntheses in the intermediate steps

Figure 7.13
General Target Audience

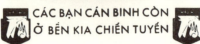

CÁC BẠN CÁN BINH CÒN
Ở BÊN KIA CHIẾN TUYẾN

Ngày nay, công cuộc chống
Cộng cứu nước là nhiệm vụ của
toàn dân, không phân biệt già, trẻ,
gái, trai. Vậy nên mọi hành động
xâm lăng phá hoại của các bạn
đều bị ngăn chặn và nhứt định
các bạn sẽ thảm bại.

Con đường tốt nhất cứu các
bạn thoát khỏi gông cùm của
Cộng sản là trở về với «Tiếng gọi
tình thương dân tộc», đề rút
ngắn đau thương cho đất nước,
và xây dựng cho các bạn một
đời sống Tự do, thanh bình.   3781

Communist cadre and soldiers on the other side:
Today, fighting Communists to save the country is the
responsibility of the people -- without distinction of age or sex.
Therefore, sabotage and aggressive attempts from your side will be
thwarted and you surely will be defeated.
The best way to rescue yourself from the chains and fetters of
the Communists is to come back in response to the "call of love and
compassion," to shorten suffering for the country and start your new
life in freedom and peace. . . .

Source: U.S., JUSPAO, leaflet number 3781.

Figure 7.14
Particular Target Audience

CÙNG CÁC BẠN CÁN-BINH CHÍNH-QUY BẮC-VIỆT : KHI CÁC BẠN VỀ QUY-HÀNG :

1. Bạn sẽ được bảo-đảm tính-mạng.

2. Bạn sẽ được bảo-đảm ăn-uống và thuốc-men đầy-đủ.

3. Các bạn sẽ được trở về với gia-đình nếu các bạn muốn khi hòa-bình lập lại.

4372

NORTH VIETNAMESE ARMY SOLDIERS:

The youth of North Vietnam are needed by their families and loved ones; the young men of North Vietnam are needed to build a prosperous society. Many young people in the North know this and have honorably chosen to avoid the draft, and their friends and neighbors are helping them.

You have been unlucky -- you have been conscripted and sent South by the Party to wage war and to bring destruction to the South Vietnamese society. There is still an honorable way out for you to participate in the task of building a better Vietnam.

-- You can report to Government of Vietnam forces when the opportunity comes, or, you can put yourself in a situation where you will be captured. . . .

Source: U.S., JUSPAO, leaflet number 4372.

Figure 7.15
Specific Target Audience

CÙNG CÁC CÁN BINH TRUNG ĐOÀN 273 BẮC VIỆT XÂM NHẬP!

Chúng tôi được biết trong đơn vị các bạn có trên 125 đồng đội ngã bịnh vì sốt rét.

Các bạn biết không? Sốt rét là một bệnh khó trị và nguy hiểm đến tánh mạng.

Qua lịch sử nhân loại, nó là mối lo của con người vì là một thứ bịnh nguy hiểm, làm kiệt quệ sức lực con người để rồi cuối cùng phải chịu chết.

CC-120-70

TO MEMBERS OF THE 273rd NORTH VIETNAMESE ARMY REGIMENT:
We can notice that your unit has over 126 comrades coming down with malaria. Do you know that malaria is a dangerous and devastating disease? It is hard to cure and can incapacitate you. . . .
The Government of Vietnam has excellent medical facilities which offer the best treatment to the people. If you catch malaria or any other type of fever you should immediately get a blood test and proper treatment. . . . You must either rally to the Government of Vietnam and take advantage of the Chieu Hoi Program or surrender to be a prisoner of war. In both cases the Government of Vietnam will take care of you. You will be entitled to hospital treatments. . . .

Source: U.S., MACV, 10th Psychological Operations Battalion, PSYOP Catalog, leaflet number CC-120-70.

leading to message development. But, at the critical
stage of this process, the Americans fumbled their
opportunity to communicate effectively with the
Vietnamese by failing to tailor a substantial portion of
their appeals to specific target groups. Some of the
reasons for this unfortunate development may be found in
competency of U.S. personnel and in their procedures for
securing communications feedback.

PSYCHOLOGICAL WARRIORS

There is little doubt that skilled specialists in
propaganda, psychology, sociology, and in the Vietnamese
language, history, and culture could have done much to
ensure effectiveness in the psychological operations
campaign. "Publicists who have written on the subject of
psychological warfare are," Daugherty writes, "in general
agreement that adequate personnel is an important key to
success or failure of any propaganda effort. Past
experience appears to suggest that money and elaborate
schemes or organization are not adequate substitutes for
competent personnel."[15]
The problem in Vietnam certainly was not one of
understaffing -- at any one time, close to 2,000
Americans and several hundred U.S.-paid Vietnamese took
part in the communications program. Normally, JUSPAO had
a combined group of 132 American civilians (130 from
USIA), 118 servicemen, and about 400 Vietnamese. In
addition, nearly a thousand Army psychological warriors,
fifty CORDS advisors, about a hundred political warfare
advisors, and several hundred soldiers, sailors, marines,
and airmen were involved in the communications campaign
throughout the country.[16]
This mixture of military and civilian officers
staffing JUSPAO was a major organizational innovation,
adapted to the dual nature of the Vietnam War. It
allowed JUSPAO to start off on the right foot by
enhancing the consistency of propaganda supplementing
both the military and pacification programs. And, as
Zorthian indicates, in this integration people were
assigned jobs on the basis of skill rather than their
agency of origin. Moreover, "it did take into account
the reality that there is not and therefore cannot be a
sharp line between political and military aspects of an
insurgency situation and that programs and efforts in
either area must be determined as complementary parts of
a whole and conducted with due regard for both."[17]
The key problem seemed to be that of competence.
While JUSPAO was fortunate in having skilled USIA
personnel available to work with experienced military
officers, it had a dearth of people holding advanced
academic degrees in the behavioral sciences. None, for
instance, had a background in psychology. This one

shortcoming alone raises serious questions about JUSPAO's communications; it appears logical that if a propagandist aims at exploiting psychological receptivities of foreign groups as a means of persuasion, then psychologists should be available to contribute to the development of persuasive appeals. As Terence Qualter explains, a propagandist "must first of all be a skilled psychologist with a deep understanding of the complexities of the human mind and its motivations."[18] Linebarger admits that "good propaganda can be conducted by persons with no knowledge of formal psychology," but, he adds,

> . . . the psychologist can bring to the attention of the soldier those elements of the human mind which are usually kept out of sight. He can show how to convert lust into resentment, individual resourcefulness into mass cowardice, friction into distrust, prejudice into fury . . . the psychologist can set up techniques for finding out how the enemy really does feel. Some of the worst blunders of history have arisen from miscalculations of the enemy state of mind . . . the psychologist can help the military psychological warfare operator by helping him maintain his sense of mission and of proportion . . . the psychologist can prescribe media. . . . He can coordinate the timing of propaganda with military, economic or political situations.[19]

The presence of trained and experienced specialists at JUSPAO may have helped make up for this absence of psychologists. Nonetheless, it is logical to assume that the quality of U.S. psychological operations might have been improved still more if JUSPAO's propagandists had worked closely with competent behavioral scientists.

Another personnel problem was an insufficient number of bilingual Americans. In 1970, for instance, only six of 132 civilians at JUSPAO could speak Vietnamese at a functional level, although several had an acceptable capability in French. The number of fluent military officers of the 118 assigned was not available. Undoubtedly, this scarcity of linguists impeded coordination with the Saigon government and created a reliance on interpreters in day-to-day operations, leaving room for errors and misunderstandings in the formulation of campaigns, appeals, and themes.

At face value, this working relationship could have been the best of two worlds -- American direction and propaganda expertise combined with indigenous employees. It could have reduced the elements of foreignness in the communications and resulted in messages compatible with local cultural

predispositions. However, it begs the question of
whether the U.S. employer, oriented toward direct
approach, action, and self-determination, might have
unwittingly forced or persuaded its native employees,
oriented toward indirect approaches, harmony, and
decision by authority, to agree with American notions of
good propaganda. After all, disagreement with the boss
could have disrupted harmony -- better "to bend in the
wind like the bamboo" and agree may have been the
Vietnamese attitude. As Ellen Hammer observes,
"communication with foreigners in Vietnam, as in other
countries influenced by Chinese culture, is made even
more difficult by the existence of certain rules of
courtesy which preclude telling a stranger what he might
not like to hear and out of the kindness of his heart,
the Vietnamese often adapts his answers to what he
believes to be in the desires of his interlocutor."[20]
     In the field, the weaknesses in personnel competence
and language capability which existed at the top were
magnified. Few, if any, of the psychological operations
officers assigned to MACV's propaganda battalions or to
CORDS had received graduate training in psychology or the
social sciences, and culture-history specialists and bi-
linguists were in short supply throughout the war.
Moreover, most military propagandists had little
experience and lacked training in psychological
operations. In 1967, for instance, the U.S. Army had
only forty-one trained psychological warfare
"specialists" compared with 346 officers actually filling
such jobs.
     Subsequently, MACV was somewhat successful in
upgrading the expertise of its personnel, requiring
officers to attend the Army's 12-week psychological
operations course at Fort Bragg before taking up duties
in Vietnam. But the curriculum dealt only with the
theoretical principles of propaganda, rudiments of
psychology, and dissemination techniques; it was not
oriented toward the Vietnamese environment nor was
language instruction provided. Late in the war most MACV
propagandists did attend a short language course before
reporting, which at least gave them a rudimentary
ability. Although these actions did enhance competence
in the armed forces, it is doubtful that they were
sufficient to reach the levels required for effective
psychological operations. Not surprisingly, the "hearts
and minds" battle suffered accordingly.
     On the other hand, CORDS propaganda supporting the
pacification program appears to have been better off --
some thirty to thirty-five percent of the Assistant
Province Advisors for Psychological Operations were
fluent in Vietnamese. Indeed, the cream of the available
crop of linguists was siphoned off by CORDS; the highly
qualified graduates of the 42-week Vietnamese language-

area study course conducted by the Department of State's
Foreign Service Institute were assigned to pacification
and rural development activities.

In addition to the problems created by having
insufficient numbers of bi-lingual, experienced, and
competent propagandists, especially in the military,
there was what was known in Vietnam as the "revolving
door" syndrome. This referred to the fact that tours of
duty for the armed forces were one year long. By the
time an inexperienced and partially trained neophyte
psychological warrior had gained sufficient expertise to
begin contributing to the communications campaign in a
meaningful way, his tour was completed and he returned to
the U.S. -- his replacement arrived and the cycle began
again. The "revolving door" had a significant, though
lesser, impact on JUSPAO and CORDS as well; tours of duty
for civilians were from eighteen to twenty-four months,
but they were often absent from their jobs for two 30-day
home leaves and periodic long weekends at "safe havens"
in Manila, Bangkok, and Hong Kong.[21]

In the end, this practice of shuffling people in and
out of the "hearts and minds" struggle wrought havoc. It
means that many of the some 2,000 Americans involved in
the communications efforts at any one time were
constantly undergoing on-the-job training. Mistakes
inevitably were made -- not once, but twice or three
times -- as the "revolving door" continued to buffet the
program, keeping it in a perpetual state of flux.

These weaknesses -- too few psychological warriors
adept in the Vietnamese language, culture, and history,
and a dearth of psychologists and social scientists -- do
not necessarily mean that the campaign of persuasion
failed to achieve its enunciated goals. JUSPAO's use of
Vietnamese to help prepare "light-gray" propaganda gave
some hope that these materials would reflect indigenous
cultural predispositions. Weaknesses in psychological
warfare skills among MACV's staff may have been at least
partially offset by reliance on the centralized direction
of JUSPAO, with its greater concentration of expertise
and experience. However, it is doubtful that these
arrangements sufficiently minimized the personnel
deficiencies and so the question of effectiveness remains
open. By undertaking "light-gray" psychological
operations without sufficient numbers of competent
specialists, the Americans were simply courting failure.

COMMUNICATION FEEDBACK

Adequate feedback is vital to the source of the
communication process because it provides the stimulus
for "course correction." These signals from the target
audiences and the messages themselves prevent the
propagandist from "flying blind." It can tell him

whether his appeals are impairing the campaign's
credibility, reflecting foreign origin, conforming to the
cultural biases of the target group, and, most important,
getting the desired response. It allows qualitative
adjustment and fine tuning in subsequent propaganda.

The JUSPAO and MACV staffs received such accountings
from the messages by pre-testing and post-testing them on
panels of Vietnamese. More determination of effect came
from intelligence channels, in-depth interviews with
defectors and prisoners, public opinion surveys, and
field reports by CORDS advisors.

The pre-testing and post-testing of communications
were extremely important as feedback because of the
inadequate knowledge of Vietnamese culture and language
by the personnel and the propaganda to keep the
recipients from discovering its true origin. But until
early 1967 little quality control was conducted by JUSPAO
and virtually none in the field. As one former JUSPAO
officer put it: "When I arrived in Vietnam in 1966,
everybody and his brother were preparing psychological
operations messages and no one was pre-testing."
Subsequently, according to Latimer, every product was
pre-tested by eight-member juries of Vietnamese and
sometimes refugees, defectors, and prisoners: "After
1966 very few 'bad' products were put out or in existence
very long without being picked up by quality control at
some level."[22] However, Hopper contends from her
investigation that problems continued:

> The Vietnamese argue that the leaflets are
> written in literary Vietnamese, rather than the
> peasant's vocabulary. . . . Utilization of
> literary language has a potential for the
> negative communication to the peasant audience
> of a reinforcement of traditional beliefs that
> the Saigon government has no real concern with
> rural man and the hinterlands. On the other
> hand, the traditional figures of speech and
> folk tales couched in the language of the
> countryside are conducive to communication of a
> favorable view of GVN perception and
> interest.[23]

Despite such continuing questions of effectiveness,
which could have been at least partially answered by
feedback, evaluation panels were not formed by MACV in
Saigon until 1969. In the field, leaflet pre-testing
instructions reached MACV and CORDS propagandists in mid-
1969, and JUSPAO finally issued a policy directive
outlining procedures for testing propaganda in 1971 --
almost six years into the conflict.[24]

Translation was another problem for feedback.
During the early years of the war, it was usual for

Americans to prepare the persuasive appeals and for Vietnamese employees to translate them. By 1968 the hazards of such procedures were recognized. JUSPAO noted: "Quite often it is found that the person translating gave a verbatim translation and left a foreign imprint on the leaflet." MACV put it more succinctly: "If PSYOP leaflets do not originate in Vietnamese they retain an 'American smell.'"[25] Moreover, because of the absence of panels for testing communications content in the field, the "American smell" in translated propaganda probably went undetected and effectiveness suffered.

Unfortunately, ideal "course correction" procedures were never fully achieved, in which all communications were pre-tested by indigenous groups prior to delivery. Although substantial and effective practices did exist at JUSPAO after 1967, the lack of adequate testing in the field reflected yet another weakness in MACV psychological operations. However, the potentially harmful impact of this deficiency was probably lessened to some degree because of the reliance by MACV and CORDS on national-level materials produced by JUSPAO.

Another major means of securing communications accounting was through intelligence channels. Timely information about Vietnamese target groups could have gone a long way toward mitigating the weaknesses in training and experience which plagued the propaganda campaign. "Psychological warfare depends on intelligence for all aspects of its operation," Daugherty summarizes. "Without up-to-date knowledge of one's own capability and a sympathetic and realistic awareness of a psychological warfare target people's hopes, aspirations, and political, sociological, and cultural backgrounds, a psychological effort is almost certain to fail. The more one knows of the target people to whom he addresses a propaganda appeal the more certainly he will leave his imprint on their attitudes and opinions, and through these influence their behavior patterns."[26]

However, intelligence for psychological operations in Vietnam was given a low priority; most information collection effort understandably was focused on the needs of combat commanders. Only twenty-five persons were assigned to propaganda intelligence in 1967, none of them in the field. So, little timely data on the mental vulnerabilities of target audiences were received through these formal channels. In fact, a Department of Defense research team found that most intelligence specialists in 1967 were not knowledgeable about JUSPAO's requirements. Normally, information relevant to psychological operations resulted as mere by-products of intelligence produced for other needs. The investigators concluded:

It was found that psychological operations intelligence is conducted at a low level of effectiveness in Vietnam. Problems related to the collection of intelligence information, dissemination of intelligence information, information storage and retrieval, personnel assignment and utilization, magnitude of the analytical effort, misdirection of the analytical effort, and lack of influence on the analytical effort upon media output and psychological operations have remained unsolved, to the detriment of the effort.[27]

Since intelligence support was dismal in all aspects, JUSPAO and MACV, in a desperate effort to avoid "flying blind," formed their own ad hoc interrogation teams at defector and prisoner-of-war camps. These efforts, combined with review of translated captured documents, were successful in securing some current information on various groups. But lack of intelligence at all levels in Vietnam hindered good quality propaganda.

A third means of obtaining feedback from target audiences, especially enemy groups, was a host of reports prepared by the Rand Corporation and other research firms under contact to the U.S. Government. Thousands of Viet Cong and North Vietnamese prisoners and defectors were interviewed in-depth by trained specialists to determine the underpinnings of their dedication to the Communist cause, the state of their morale, and their reasons for defecting or surrendering. A series of Rand studies on the motivation and morale of Communist soldiers was prepared between 1965 and 1969. These summaries provided a great deal of information about the mental vulnerabilities shared by numerous Viet Cong and Northern soldiers, and they helped fill the gap left by the intelligence deficiencies. Moreover, they provided much of the basis for the American approach, campaigns, appeals and themes in the Chieu Hoi and surrender programs.

A major drawback to their usefulness was the lag between the time when the interviews were conducted and the time that the final report reached the JUSPAO and MACV psychological warrior. The summaries still were useful in identifying general and relatively stable enemy receptivities which helped guide the national-level propaganda campaigns.

A fourth area of communication feedback, somewhat useful in the political-economic dimension of the war, was JUSPAO-sponsored public opinion surveys and weekly attitude reports prepared by CORDS psychological operations advisors.

The public opinion surveys were conducted under

contract by a Vietnamese affiliate of the International
Gallup Polls. Although they provided some useful
insight, most were focused on accessible urban
populations in Republic-controlled areas, and many
persons refused to respond. The surveys were conducted
in shotgun fashion, with dissimilar questions posed to
differing groups at different locations; thus valid
analyses of public opinion trends were not possible. On
the whole, the questioning provided very perishable
information on current attitudes of people in particular
localities. Latimer properly qualified their usefulness
in his summary that, ". . . it can be argued with some
persuasion that when interpreted cautiously without too
much reliance on single questions, wariness in some
areas, the reports were acceptably reliable in spite of
the difficulties."[28]

On the other hand, weekly attitude reports prepared
by CORDS psychological operations advisors were quite
useful to JUSPAO and MACV propaganda staff -- topics
normally included the image of the United States, and
confidence in the Saigon government and Army. The CORDS
specialists normally sounded out local opinions through
their personal contacts with the Vietnamese and other
Americans in the province. In addition, their native
staff members solicited opinions from the local populace,
and inputs were sought from the Vietnamese Information
Service.

These accounts, consolidated and summarized at
various levels, played a major role in keeping American
policy-makers in both Saigon and Washington apprised of
rural attitudes. Frequently, when popular discontent was
noted, high-level inquiries were sent to military
commanders to find out the root causes for the
dissatisfaction. Such queries often served to rectify
some frictions persisting between Vietnamese and
Americans, and they also helped to encourage restraint in
future combat operations. Unscientific as they were,
these reports provided a substantial amount of useful
data. In Latimer's view, they were "a reasonably
accurate portrayal of Vietnamese attitudes."[29]

In summary, communication feedback was seriously
lacking. The record of quality control through testing
propaganda by indigenous panels was spotty; intelligence
support was inadequate (although its effects were
lessened by JUSPAO and MACV ad hoc liaison practices and
the Rand reports); and surveys of non-enemy public
opinion were unavoidably slanted with several important
questions left unanswered. The impact of these
weaknesses, combined with less-than-fully competent
American propagandists (especially at the critical area
in the field agencies), further diluted the over-all
cogency of the campaign to persuade.

EFFECTIVENESS

Examination of the communication source thus shows
mixed results. Creation of JUSPAO as a single,
centralized USIA agency, managing all U.S. psychological
operations, undoubtedly improved consistency of the
propaganda in supplementing military and political-
economic initiatives. In addition, an excellent policy-
audience synthesis was formed at the higher levels;
JUSPAO's program of action and policy directives were
compatible and did adequately supplement national foreign
policy goals. An ideal organizational structure was
created in which JUSPAO maintained centralized control
while encouraging imaginative adaptation of its guidance
by psychological warriors in the field. Finally, all but
a few propaganda messages were consistent with JUSPAO
policy directives.

Incongruities also were nonetheless present.
JUSPAO's "white lie" of producing communications on
behalf of the Republic (and, on a lesser scale, the Royal
Laotian government) made it vital that all elements of
foreignness be eliminated in "light-gray" psychological
operations. Paradoxically, the American weaknessess --
insufficient numbers of behavioral scientists and
Vietnamese language, history, and culture specialists --
had a positive effect in that they forced Americans to
rely heavily on their native employees. As a result of
this collaboration, most communications probably were in
general accord with indigenous predispositions and
largely devoid of foreignness. On the other hand, it is
arguable whether this reliance on local talent provided
sufficient inspiration for high-quality psychological
operations. Such creativity should be expected from the
combined efforts of skilled psychologists and trained
propagandists having thorough knowledge and appreciation
of the target people's language and culture -- but
neither the Americans nor their Vietnamese subordinates
had an adequate blend of both desired attributes. Some
atrophy in the campaign of persuasion inevitably
resulted.

Field propagandists, poorly trained, lacking
expertise in Vietnamese without benefit of indigenous
employees, and short on insight into current mental
receptivities of enemy and non-enemy target groups (due
to inadequate feedback), did the best they could -- they
reproduced broad themes that were suggested by JUSPAO for
nationwide audiences. This led to centralization of the
psychological operations campaign by default. JUSPAO
added fuel to the fire by dumping great quantities of
standardized national-level persuasive materials on the
field agencies for distribution. In view of their
handicaps, it is little wonder that MACV and CORDS
propagandists made little effort to transform JUSPAO

guidance into themes for specific target audiences; if they had attempted to do so on a larger scale, they undoubtedly would have developed both ineffective and counterproductive appeals. These weaknesses paradoxically also had a positive influence -- they forced personnel in the field to rely on nationally-produced materials, bringing greater consistency to the over-all psychological operations program. But the resulting overemphasis on messages for general and particular target groups ended in a communications effort more resembling a huge advertising campaign than a persuasive endeavor designed to win "hearts and minds." There is little doubt that effectiveness was reduced.

These deficiencies at the communication source and its encoding agencies prompted a comment by a French expatriate who had spent many years in Vietnam. As loosely quoted by a former CORDS advisor, he said, "you Americans have done everything wrong that was possible to do wrong in your propaganda. But it has been successful in spite of your failings because of the huge volume and your total control of the media." Indeed, whether by fate or design, U.S. psychological operations scored some impressive successes despite the difficulties persisting at the origin.

NOTES

1. U.S., JUSPAO, General Briefing Book (Saigon: July 13, 1965).

2. Wilbur Schramm, ed., "How Communication Works," The Process and Effects of Mass Communication (Urbana, Ill.: University of Illinois Press, 1955), pp. 3-26, David K. Berlo, The Process of Communication (New York: Holt, Rinehart and Winston, 1960), pp. 30-32, Ole R. Holsti, Content Analysis for the Social Sciences and Humanities, (Reading, Mass.: Addison-Wesley Publishing Company, 1969), p. 25, and Wilbur Schramm, "Nature of Communication Between Humans," in The Process and Effects of Mass Communication, ed. by Wilbur Schramm and Donald F. Roberts, rev. ed. (Chicago: University of Illinois Press, 1971), pp. 7-8.

3. Zorthian, "Psychological Operations," p. 8.

4. Ibid., p. 10.

5. Barry Zorthian, personal letter to the author, July 10, 1972.

6. Quoted in U.S., Department of the Army, Communist Insurgent Warfare, pp. 313, 305.

7. William A. Nighswonger, Rural Pacification in Vietnam, (New York: Praeger, 1966), p. 22.

8. Browne, "U.S. Trims Psychological Warfare," p. 3.

9. "The Block No. 66 in Badinh Ward Pushes Forward the Maintenance of Security and Order," Thu Do (Hanoi:

January 29, 1966).
    10. U.S., JUSPAO, "National Psychological
Operations Plan," Policy Number 20, in Consolidation of
JUSPAO Guidances, Vol. I.
    11. M. Dean Havron and Herbert Vreeland, Some Uses
of Values Information (McLean, Va.: Human Sciences
Research, 1967), pp. 6-8.
    12. Morris Janowitz, "Written Directives," in
Psychological Warfare Casebook, ed. by William E.
Daugherty, p. 314.
    13. ARPA-Supported Committee, Clark, chairman, pp.
36-37.
    14. Janice H. Hopper, "Leaflet Operations,
Vietnam: An Analysis," in ARPA-Supported Committee,
Clark, chairman, p. D-6.
    15. Daugherty, ed., Psychological Warfare Casebook,
p. 156.
    16. U.S., Senate, Vietnam: Policy and Prospects,
p. 695.
    17. Zorthian, "Psychological Operations," p. 19.
    18. Terence H. Qualter, Propaganda and
Psychological Warfare (New York: Random House, 1962), p.
71.
    19. Linebarger, Psychological Warfare, pp. 25-27.
    20. Ellen Hammer, Vietnam Yesterday and Today (New
York: Holt, Rinehart and Winston, 1966), p. 30.
    21. Bairdain and Bairdain, Psychological Operations
Studies, p. 52, ARPA-Supported Committee, Clark,
chairman, p. 149, U.S., Department of the Army,
Psychological Operations Units in Vietnam, pp. II-14 to
II-15, and Latimer, U.S. Psychological Operations, pp.
28-29, 44.
    22. Latimer, U.S. Psychological Operations, p. 46.
    23. Hopper, "Leaflet Operations, Vietnam," in ARPA-
Supported Committee, Clark, chairman, p. D-10.
    24. U.S., JUSPAO, "Testing Psyop Material in Viet-
Nam," Psyop Circular, Number 9 (Saigon: January 14,
1969) and Testing of PSYOP Materials in Viet-Nam, Policy
Number 104 (Saigon: February 18, 1971).
    25. U.S., JUSPAO, "Supplement 1 to JUSPAO Field
Memorandum Number 42" (April 12, 1968), in Consolidation
of Field Memoranda, Vol. III, p. 21, and U.S., MACV,
PSYOP Newsletter, Vol. 3, No. 2 (February 1968), pp. 2-3.
    26. Daugherty, ed., Psychological Warfare Casebook
p. 425.
    27. William Stockton, Jr. and James W. Holiman,
"Psychological Operations Intelligence in Vietnam," in
ARPA-Supported Committee, Clark, chairman, p. F-1.
    28. Latimer, U.S. Psychological Operations, p. 20.
    29. Ibid., p. 42.

8
Some Lessons Learned

> The psychological operations program is the
> least understood, the most difficult to
> explain, and surely the hardest to measure of
> any of our efforts in Vietnam.
> -- U.S., Report on the War in Vietnam[1]

The interjection of U.S. psychological operations
into the Vietnamese war of ideas was ill fated from the
start. When used simultaneously as a means of achieving
American foreign policy goals and as a substitute
communications tool for the Republic of Vietnam in
creating a potent nationalism among its countrymen, the
objectives set for the propaganda instrument were
untenable. From the beginning, American leaders
misjudged the dedication and tenacity of the Communists
to continue the revolution and bring about reunification;
they underestimated the Lao Dong Party's extensive
support among the Northern populace and its ability to
maintain the justness of the "national salvation"
struggle in their eyes; and they failed to recognize the
South Vietnamese people's strong passivity and reluctance
to support any central government, especially while the
Viet Cong were present in much of the countryside. Nor
could the U.S. overcome the "foreign invader" stigma
attached to it by the other side, and the persuasive
power of mass media communications was insufficient. In
the end, Americans could not win "hearts and minds" for
Saigon, and the latter's actions often gave the populace
little reason to fully support the anti-Communist
struggle.
    The Americans working in JUSPAO and MACV had a
rather clear view of their own success and failure in the
effort "to prevent communist domination of South Vietnam"
and "to create a viable and increasingly democratic
society." Trying to instill nationalism by integration
of the three major appeals of pro-Saigon, anti-Communist,
and pro-U.S. images among the South Vietnamese while

251

attempting to undermine the Communist brand of
nationalism in the North had taught them a lot about
psychological operations waged by a surrogate information
agency.

On the military side of the war, the morale of the
Viet Cong and Northern troops remained relatively high
throughout the conflict, despite enormous manpower and
equipment lossess. Their "revolutionary zeal" left them
undaunted by the overwhelming firepower arrayed against
them. Nevertheless, more than 200,000 lower-echelon
enemy soldiers and civilian cadres did defect during the
nine-year period from 1963 through 1973, and thousands
more surrendered. War-related effects may have been
ultimately responsible for motivating those who gave up
the fight; thus U.S. propaganda cannot claim a great
victory. On the other hand, the campaign was not
entirely unsuccessful, since it did convey an alternative
course of action to the 200,000-plus hoi chanh. In
addition, there is no way of knowing how many more might
have rallied or surrendered had they had the opportunity
to do so; nor is it clear how many enemy troops may have
held back in battle, malingered, or questioned their
leader's policies as the result of the psychological
operations.

In the North, it seems doubtful that the
communications were believed by many persons, especially
in light of the extensive political indoctrination and
counterpropaganda conducted by the ruling Lao Dong
Party. It does seem logical, however, to assume that the
leaflets and radio broadcasts created at least some
difficulties for Hanoi, as reflected by the vehemence of
the anti-United States campaigns waged by that regime.
But the extent of influence enjoyed by the American
appeals in increasing the people's war-weariness and
apathy remains unclear. There is also no way of
calculating the impact that the propaganda may have had
in pre-conditioning the limited numbers of Northern
soldiers who accepted the Chieu Hoi and surrender offers
once they were in the South. As a result of these many
uncertainties, the effectiveness of the psychological
operations against the North largely remains open to
question.

On the political-economic side of the war, American
attempts to win the people's "hearts and minds" failed to
persuade a majority of the largely passive and ambivalent
public to side openly with the Republic. However, the
mere fact that the government (and the U.S. on its
behalf) considered them important enough to try to win
their support may have motivated some latent backing.
While the communications may not have been fully
believed, they at least conveyed the notion (albeit
vague) that Saigon considered the peasants important in
its struggle against Hanoi and that it held some regard

for their welfare. Such an expression of concern for the rural population was unique in Vietnamese political history. Additionally, psychological operations supporting the Pacification and Rural Development Program surely had some success in increasing the number of persons who knew of and to some degree believed in the beneficial aspects of the nation-building efforts. While the majority of Vietnamese were not ready to stand in the trenches with the Republic to fight against Hanoi's forces, they should at least have been aware that the government was interested in them and that it had taken some actions to improve their lives and livelihood.

The major problem, of course, both on the military and political-economic side of the war was that no outsider could hope to substitute effectively for the native government in appeals to its own people. Nevertheless, as has been shown, the United States as early as 1965 abandoned traditional prescriptions for psychological operations and evolved into a surrogate Vietnamese ministry of information. It seems clear that if the obverse situation had occurred -- if the U.S. had worked through, rather than on behalf of, the Republic of Vietnam -- many of the incongruities present in the "white lie" communications could have been eliminated: U.S.-sponsored but government-developed propaganda could have been more in accord with cultural values and predispositions, largely free from elements of foreignness, conducted by means of more personalized and credible communication channels with a resulting de-emphasis on the printed and broadcast word, and oriented more toward specific target audiences. Additionally, South Vietnamese propagandists could have received more training and experience if JUSPAO, MACV, and CORDS had truly been advisors, rather than a huge production agency.

The modest results achieved, combined with the inferior persuasive power of most "light-gray" message appeals, clearly suggests that any attempt by one government to substitute for another in communicating with its own people is probably destined to fail. Thus, the most significant lesson to be learned from the propaganda campaign is one of a reinforcement, by negative example, of the previously held American doctrine that an assisting power must work through the host government in psychological operations. A nation clearly should not try to conduct such an unorthodox communications effort as that attempted by the U.S. in Vietnam.

American propaganda doctrine took another wrong road in 1965 when it blurred the distinction between national-level and lower-echelon psychological operations. According to traditional propaganda theory, upper-level efforts support the broad aspects of propaganda strategy

and address messages to the country-wide audience, but
the "key to success" is where communications can exploit
current psychological vulnerabilities of local sub-
audiences with specifically tailored appeals.
Nonetheless, U.S. operations primarily emphasized broad
appeals to general target groups instead of carefully
honed themes to specific target groups. Also by negative
example, the Vietnam experience reinforces the need in
counterinsurgency efforts to stress lower-level
psychological operations and to supplement them with
complementary national-level communications.

   A key factor in this de-emphasis of locally-oriented
propaganda was the competence of psychological warriors
assigned in the field. Similar difficulties had been
encountered in both World Wars and in Korea. Trained and
experienced USIA communications specialists and military
officers assigned to JUSPAO provided a competent,
centralized propaganda directorate. But at the lower-
level -- critical in the communication process --
expertise was lacking. The weakest link in the
psychological operations campaign existed precisely where
proficiency was required most to transform broad national
guidelines into hard-hitting appeals relevant to specific
target groups. No number of highly trained staff
officers at the top could make up for weaknesses in the
field agencies.

   These deficiencies in MACV and, to a lesser degree,
in CORDS indicates a dire need for peacetime
psychological operations training and experience in the
armed forces. Such an extensive instruction program,
however, certainly would not be tenable because of its
cost. But, as demonstrated in World War II, the United
States has a national reserve of ready-made propagandists
among its newsmen, advertising specialists, mass media
technicians, linguists, historians, political scientists,
psychologists, sociologists, and others whose skills are
readily transferable to wartime psychological
operations. Organizing and training these persons in the
National Guard and reserve forces would be one way of
establishing a reservoir of skilled military
propagandists for lower-level operations.

   Beyond the inadequate performance by MACV propaganda
battalions, there also was dismal intelligence support.
In fact, the Vietnam experience suggests that there is an
urgent need to take another look at procedures for
gathering information about the psychological
vulnerabilities of likely target audiences. The problem
is that of competition with combat commanders for the
time and effort of intelligence specialists. Since it is
doubtful that normal channels would give the required
attention to psychological operations, the ad hoc
arrangements by JUSPAO and MACV in assignment of liaison
officers to intelligence activities appears worthy of

repeating in the future on a formalized basis.

In a word, it is indisputable that the propaganda campaign failed to meet its stated goals of generating support for U.S. foreign policies. But, this is not to say that it was a useless effort. The alternative to JUSPAO's surrogate role would have been not to conduct "light-gray" psychological operations at all, or carry out a communications program through the Vietnamese on a radically reduced scale. Had either of these options been taken, many of the limited successes achieved by JUSPAO probably would have been missed. Although the initial U.S. substitution for the Republic was regrettable, it was the best choice among several poor alternatives at the time; it was, after all, the result of many compromises between the ideal and the reality of conditions existing in Vietnam. However, it must also be admitted that once the Saigon government had been internally stabilized in late 1967, JUSPAO should have turned its "light-gray" operations over to the Ministry of Information.

Given all these circumstances surrounding U.S. participation in the Vietnamese war of ideas and the lofty goals set for the psychological operations campaign, JUSPAO's limited accomplishments were probably just about all that was possible. Indeed, as Barry Zorthian aptly concluded in 1971: "We meant well and understood the needs better [than in past wars] but our achievements were generally quite modest."[2]

A "WAR OF NATIONAL LIBERATION"

Marxist-Leninist doctrine concerning "Wars of National Liberation" provided the basic blueprint for final reunification of Vietnam. Accordingly, nationalism was promoted among the population as a way of awakening latent patriotism and building popular support for the "National Salvation" struggle -- first against the French and then against the Americans. Communist theorists decry charges that nationalism is used as a tactic to achieve power and that its use as a device to motivate people's support is a betrayal of their just aspirations. Professing to approach nationalism from a historical point of view, they consider its use as a necessary step toward "social progress," a transition to socialism. In this way, they are able to embrace "Wars of National Liberation" without violating long-term goals of proletarian internationalism, the feelings of brotherhood between workers of different countries. The people's natural love of homeland is supported by the Communists only as far as it serves the cause of winning "national freedom and victory over imperialism." As Lenin candidly explained, "the bourgeois nationalism of every oppressed nation has a general democratic content

which is directed <u>against</u> oppression, and it is this
content that we support <u>unconditionally</u>."[3] Once
"independence" is achieved under nationalist banners and
slogans, Marxist-Leninist political and social values
then are imposed and "socialist construction" begins.

The Communists are also adept at manipulating events
to portray "Wars of National Liberation" as "just wars,"
or in their terms "defensive patriotic struggles against
imperialist aggression." Thus, Hanoi was able to claim
that it held the "just cause" in the people's fight for
independence. In a 1945 address to "Southern
Compatriots," for instance, Ho Chi Minh proclaimed the
justness of the "revolution" against the French:
"Victory will definitely be ours because we have the
united force of our entire people. We are sure to win
the battle because our struggle is a just one."[4]

It is not surprising, therefore, that this line of
reasoning was followed by labeling the United States as a
new "imperialist aggressor" or by appealing to the
people's love of Vietnam by calling the United States a
new "foreign invader." But the battle was long and
arduous before Ho's 1945 prophecy was fulfilled.
Nonetheless, he was ultimately proven correct; it was
popular support and acquiescence that resolved the
Saigon-Hanoi conflict in favor of the North. With the
"War of National Liberation" won in 1975, the popular
love of Vietnam that was so instrumental in driving the
"foreign invaders" from the country became old-fashioned
as Communist values were imposed on the hapless patriots
under the banner of "socialist construction."

When considering the aftermath of the Vietnam War,
one is struck by the bitter irony of a startling
historical parallel. Two centuries ago a handful of
somewhat backward American farmers fought for
independence and successfully brought a superpower of
their day to its knees through unconventional, protracted
warfare. From 1965 to 1975 a group of somewhat backward
Vietnamese farmers, also fighting for what they believed
would be independence, successfully brought a superpower
of their day to its knees through unconventional,
protracted conflict. While chary of carrying this
parallel too far, one should note that in both cases the
odds for success against nations so powerful appeared
miniscule. Nonetheless, armed psychologically with both
patriotism and a vision of the future, the weak prevailed
over the mighty -- a common denominator in both
revolutions was love of country and an uncompromising
desire to achieve freedom from foreign rule.

As put by one British commentator, "well, the
Americans finally have had their colonial war." At first
glance this remark does not appear especially erudite;
"colonialism" was never an American goal. What he meant,
however, was that the United States had fought against

the passions of a Vietnamese nationalism, and, like so many colonial countries of the past, it eventually tired of the struggle and gave in to nationalist demands.

Indeed, "there are," as Napoleon observed, "but two powers in the world, the sword and the mind. In the long run the sword is always beaten by the mind." So it was in Vietnam.

NOTES

1. U.S., Report on the War in Vietnam, as of June 30, 1968 (Washington, D.C.: Government Printing Office, 1968), p. 237.
2. Zorthian, "Psychological Operations," p. 6.
3. Quoted in U.S.S.R., Fundamentals of Marxism-Leninism, 2nd rev. ed. (Moscow: Foreign Languages Publishing House, 1963), p. 401.
4. Ho Chi Minh, On Revolution, p. 148.

Appendixes

Appendix A

10 August 1966

MEMORANDUM OF AGREEMENT ON DIRECTION AND SUPERVISION OF
U.S. PSYCHOLOGICAL OPERATIONS IN VIETNAM

1. The United States Government has established the
Joint U.S. Public Affairs Office (JUSPAO) as the U.S.
Mission organization for coordination and direction of
all U.S. psychological operations in Vietnam, including
psychological operations advice and assistance to the
Government of Vietnam. The Minister Counselor for Public
Affairs, U.S. Embassy, Saigon, has been designated as
Director, JUSPAO. He functions under the overall
authority of the Ambassador.

2. The responsibility for development of psyops policy
and for substantive supervision and coordination of all
psychological operations in Vietnam is delegated to the
Director, JUSPAO. This responsibility is applicable to
all U.S. Mission Agencies in Vietnam. The Director,
JUSPAO, through his planning office develops
psychological operations directives applicable, with
Mission Council concurrence when appropriate, to all U.S.
Mission Agencies in Vietnam.

3. JUSPAO serves a three-fold function of providing
advice and assistance to the Ministry of Information and
Chieu Hoi (Vietnamese Information Service), conducting
psychological operations in support of U.S. objectives
and of providing substantive (technical) supervision,
direction and support of all Mission elements involved in
psychological operations. Within this framework, the
primary task of the JUSPAO field organization is support
of Revolutionary Development

4. The responsibility for coordination of regional/
provincial psychological operations rests with the JUSPAO

regional provincial representatives who serve as principal psychological operations advisors to the corps commanders and provincial chiefs for civil matters and provide advice on psyops policy and substantive supervision, direction and support to all U.S. efforts in the field of psychological operations.

5. The Mission Psychological Operations Committee chaired by Director, JUSPAO, consists of representatives of the Mission Agencies convened as necessary to review substantive psychological operations questions and coordinate the management of Mission participation in a support of psychological operations programs. All Mission Agencies are represented on the Mission Psychological Operations Committee, with ACofS, J-3 representing COMUSMACV.

6. Inter-agency support of approved psychological campaigns will be coordinated through the U.S. Mission Council, the Mission Psychological Operations Committee, or by other duly appointed representatives of the agencies concerned.

7. COMUSMACV conducts psychological operations in support of US/FWMAF/RVNAF military operations and in other areas as agreed to by COMUSMACV and Director, JUSPAO, within the context of JUSPAO guidance and directives. COMUSMACV provides advice and assistance to RVNAF psychological warfare activities, to include corps commanders and sector and sub-sector commanders for military matters.

8. This agreement replaces Joint MACV/JUSPAO message dated 18 May 1965, Subject: Direction and Supervision of U.S. Psychological Operations in Vietnam.

(signed)	(signed)
General William C. Westmoreland	Barry Zorthian
COMUSMACV	Director JUSPAO, Vietnam

Appendix B

JUSPAO GUIDANCE
NUMBER 20
12 September 1966

Reissue of
NATIONAL PSYCHOLOGICAL OPERATIONS PLAN
FOR VIETNAM

This plan is the basis for U.S. and
FWMAF psychological actions. It is
reissued because of a large turnover
of personnel engaged in Psychological
Operations. Its approval by the GVN
to provide a combined plan is under
consideration.

APPROVED BY:
DIRECTOR JUSPAO
September 12, 1966

JUSPAO PLANNING OFFICE
SAIGON, VIETNAM

<u>INDEX</u>

NATIONAL PSYCHOLOGICAL OPERATIONS PLAN
FOR VIETNAM

PART I

INTRODUCTION

Psychological Operations cannot live up to their
full potential unless committed to the offensive. Only
on the offensive can propaganda choose its own
battleground: saturating the atmosphere with its own
arguments, it need not contend with those of the enemy
and in doing so take a chance on reinforcing their
impact.
To achieve maximum momentum, a psychological
offensive must be total and concentrated; all
psychological activities must be synchronized and meshed
into a single, driving effort. It thus depends for
effectiveness on central direction, clear and simple
channels of command, flawless coordination, sharp focus
and severe limitation to the smallest possible number of
the simplest possible themes -- themes that can be
disseminated and repeated by the least skilled operator
and the least sophisticated communicator. A
psychological offensive in Vietnam, therefore, requires
the integration of all Vietnamese and U.S. capabilities,
both civilian and military.
While a maximum of technical capabilities is
desirable, it is not essential. Clear and simple
approaches to elemental emotions and reasoning, endlessly
repeated, can spread like wildfire if made to key
communicators, individuals or groups. The means by which
elemental emotions or basic reasoning can be affected
rarely change. They are restricted to ordinary, natural,
human, obvious words. Attempts to devise original or
sophisticated solutions may doom the effort.

PART II

ESSENTIAL ELEMENTS

The opportunity for taking the psychological
offensive in Vietnam is promising. The essential
elements for success are given:
1. Prime Minister Ky's emphasis on the
revolutionary nature of his administration lends itself
to the suggestion that the Republic of Vietnam and its
government are turning into a magnetic hope and are on
the way to finding Vietnamese solutions to Vietnamese
problems -- solutions which will satisfy the legitimate
aspirations of the Vietnamese people and which are more
attractive and alien communist blandishments. It is

265

necessary to convince the insurgent elements in Vietnam that:

      a. The Government of the Republic of Vietnam is the rightful and just government and represents the National just cause.

      b. Under this government, the people of the Republic will increasingly enjoy prosperity and, once the aggression is defeated, will enjoy peace.

    2. The American military build-up and U.S policy as promulgated by President Johnson -- "as much as it takes for as long as it takes" -- projects power and determination sufficient to allow for the indispensable claim that Free Vietnam will inevitably win, that there is advantage to siding with the stronger battalions of the Republic and the United States.

    3. There are, finally, continuing indications that the Viet Cong keep alienating the population by actions which they can no longer avoid taking. Communist doctrine according to which the success of revolutionary warfare depends upon the VOLUNTARY support of the people thus lends itself to persuading the hard core of the revolution has not caught fire: and the conscripts on which the Viet Cong cadres must increasingly rely, find it increasingly difficult to stand up under and against firepower of U.S. and Vietnamese aircraft and artillery. Rarely has an enemy been as vulnerable psychologically as are the Viet Cong today.

PART III

OBJECTIVES

    A psychological offensive in Vietnam must aim at the achievement of the following objectives:

    1. To impress upon the Vietnamese people that Free Vietnam will inevitably win its struggle against aggression and subversion, and that they would be best advised to support, wherever possible actively, the ultimate victor.

    2. Conversely, to impress upon the Viet Cong that their leaders cannot expect to impose their will upon a government and a people whose struggle for peace, security and independence is supported by the might of the United States and other Free World nations.

    3. To create hope that the social revolution proceeding in Free Vietnam will produce a dynamic nation responsive to the will and aspirations of the people, and capable of finding Vietnamese solutions to Vietnamese problems; and to commit ever-growing numbers of the Vietnamese people to active, personal, emotional identification with the Republic's quest for peace, humanity, social justice and a vital national identity.

    4. Conversely, to make the people aware of the

truth that the communist leaders of North Vietnam and the Viet Cong offer nothing but alien schemes which are oppressive and reactionary, have failed wherever tried, and are, in fact, merely the instrumentalities of an international conspiracy and of Red Chinese imperialism; and to inspire the people with contempt for the Viet Cong who expose the nation to death, destruction, misery and oppression, and who oppose the creation of a truly Vietnamese social order and the preservation of Vietnamese values and traditions.

5. To convince all Vietnamese people that the United States and other Free World Nations are in Vietnam to assist the Vietnamese people in defeating the aggression and to assist in building an improved economy; and that the FWMAF will withdraw once the aggression is defeated.

PART IV

TARGET AUDIENCES encompass four broad groups:

1. The foundation corps of those upon whom the accomplishment of national and psychological objectives depends, primarily opinion leaders on all levels who are capable of carrying the message to the people.

2. The majority public whose opposition or support will determine the outcome of the conflict: city dwellers and peasants, intelligentsia, students and youth, organized labor, refugees and women, religious, ethnic and regional groups, people subject to VC control but not committed to communism.

3. The enemy camp with Free Vietnam; the hard-core and soft-core Viet Cong; Viet Cong sympathizers; those who provide military, political or economic support to the Viet Cong; infiltrators from North Vietnam in Viet Cong units; and members of the North Vietnamese military forces in South Vietnam.

4. The decision-making cadres in Hanoi and the people of North Vietnam. And the infiltrators from North Vietnam, members of the North Vietnamese Army.

A systematic effort to define the tasks which ideally should be accomplished to achieve the basic psychological objectives with regard to each major target audience established 97 specific categories. As this number is far too great for realistic consideration with the framework of a national psychological offensive -- the success of which depends upon limitation to the smallest possible number of the simplest possible themes -- priority was assigned to those tasks which are either applicable to all or most audiences or which are so closely related to others as to permit amalgamation while retaining those which, though only applicable to specific audiences, appeared to be indispensable to achieving the objective of the offensive.

This process resulted in the definition of 12
Priority Tasks: six applicable to all target groups,
four to the Viet Cong and one each to minority groups and
to the people of North Vietnam.

PART V

PRIORITY TASKS

ALL AUDIENCES

1. Persuade them that the victory of Free Vietnam
is inevitable because its military capabilities supported
by the United States and many other nations doom
insurgency and aggression.
2. Persuade them that the fastest way to end the
war and achieve peace and security is to support Free
Vietnam and oppose the Viet Cong.
3. Convince them that the fledgling Republic of
Vietnam reflects the natural and naturally imperfect
process of historical change and development toward a
distinctly Vietnamese but modern revolutionary society,
offers to each Vietnamese opportunity to advance within
and to influence the course of the revolution, and thus
represents the only true and realistic hope for the
achievement of national and personal aspirations.
4. Make them fully aware that the Viet Cong leaders
are conscious instruments of a foreign power, Red China,
and that the rank-and-file members are mislead or
unwitting instruments of these leaders.
5. Convince them that the American presence in
Vietnam is a consequence of the external aggression
against Free Vietnam by a COMMON enemy, is decisive but
supplementary to Free Vietnam's effort, and that the
United States will withdraw its armed forces from Vietnam
when the threat to Vietnamese independence has been
overcome.
6. Convince them that there will be no compromise
with appeasement and "neutralism" which the enemy
systematically exploits as instruments for the
achievement of his own imperialist objectives.

THE VIET CONG

1. Make the Viet Cong fully conscious of the fact
that they have alienated the people and cannot avoid to
alienate them further; that they violate the principles
of revolutionary warfare by relying on terror as a
substitute for popular support; that communist doctrine
itself presages their defeat because it holds that the
success of revolutionary warfare depends on the voluntary
support of the people; and that they are, therefore,
conducting an isolated, futile struggle against the

massing and inexhaustible firepower of Free Vietnam, the United States and Free Vietnam's other supporters.

2. Make the Viet Cong fully aware of the fact that they are agents of a foreign power which threatens the peace for its own imperialist ends, is willing to fight to the last Vietnamese, and is, therefore, unwilling to permit negotiation of a genuine peace.

3. Convince the Viet Cong and their supporters that they are doomed to inevitable military defeat, and that each member faces death for a cause that cannot achieve either the national aspirations of the Vietnamese people or the personal aspiration of any Vietnamese individual.

4. Persuade the Viet Cong, particularly the soft core, to defect to Free Vietnam where they will be received with open arms and given the opportunity to reintegrate themselves into a truly revolutionary society.

MINORITIES

Persuade them that the government respects their identity, beliefs and traditions, will improve their situation together with that of all peoples and groups united in the Republic, and will assure equality -- permitting no religious, ethnic or regional group a position of partisan privilege.

NORTH VIETNAM

Make the people of North Vietnam aware that their leaders subject them to terrible dangers by continuing aggression against their brethren in the South. With respect to the North Vietnamese soldiers in the South, to persuade them of the futility of their efforts.

PART VI

INTEGRATION & COORDINATION

The key to conducting a psychological offensive is the integration of all available Psychological Warfare capabilities and their concentration on a single objective -- the offensive itself. None of the priority tasks which have been defined suggests departures from accepted lines; most have in fact been previously codified in Vietnamese and JUSPAO Directives. All an offensive requires is a saturation effort focusing on a severely limited number of potentially effective and simple approaches. However, such an effort can only be initiated and maintained if all Psychological Warfare capabilities which can be brought to bear -- Vietnamese as well as American, military as well as civilian -- are committed to carrying it out.

It is, therefore, essential that the Minister of
Information and Open Arms, the Chief of the General
Political Warfare Department, the U.S. Minister for
Information (Director, JUSPAO) and the Commanding
General, USMACV, each in his individual capacity and
operating through his normal organizational channels,
serve as the agency responsible for the execution of this
plan.

It is essential, furthermore, that Action Plans be
closely coordinated -- especially those concerned with
the themes required to carry out the eleven Priority
Tasks. These themes should be defined as lines of
thought rather than slogans in order to leave to
operators in the field maximum flexibility and room to
maneuver, within frameworks defined sharply enough to
guarantee focus and direction.

Appendix C:
Example of a JUSPAO
Policy Directive

PSYOP POLICY

Policy Number 68   23 August 1968

ENHANCEMENT OF RVNAF IMAGE

Approved by:
Director, JUSPAO

JUSPAO Planning Office
Saigon, Viet Nam

In accordance with U.S. Mission directives this is
Mission psychological policy and guidance and is to be
implemented as pertinent by all U.S. elements in Vietnam.

I. PURPOSE:

To increase public awareness of the operations and
steadily increasing effectiveness of the Republic of Viet
Nam Armed Forces (RVNAF).

II. SITUATION:

Recent GVN actions, including the promulgation of
the General Mobilization Law, have made clear the
determination of the leadership of the GVN to strengthen
the RVNAF in order to counter communist aggression more
effectively. RVNAF successes in recent military
operations have also demonstrated their ability to defend
their country against communist aggression. At the same
time, statements by US military and civilian leaders and
the efforts by the US to equip RVNAF units with modern
weaponry have underscored the intention of the US to make
it possible for the RVNAF to assume an even greater share
of the mutual responsibility for defense.

III. PSYOP OBJECTIVES: (by target audience)

1. South Vietnamese Population
a. To instill pride in the RVNAF for its
successes in military and civic action activities.
b. To increase public identification with
RVNAF units as composed of fellow countrymen working and
fighting for the same cause.
c. To create an atmosphere in which the

population will more readily cooperate with RVNAF units
in the task of eliminating VC infrastructure, and local
and main-force VC/NVA units.
    2. RVNAF Troops:
        a. To increase esprit de corps among troops.
        b. To increase RVNAF troops' sense of
identification with the South Vietnamese population whom
they defend and aid, and to foster a sense of
responsibility for the welfare of civilians in areas
where RVNAF units are quartered and operate.
    3. Third Country Audience:
        a. To increase awareness of the sacrifices,
dedication, and effectiveness of the men and women of
RVNAF in their long and continuing struggle against
communist aggression and for national self-determination.
        b. To generate respect for the RVNAF by
comparison with proportionate military force levels in
other countries.
        c. To enhance the RVNAF image by reporting
successful RVNAF tactical operations and the growing
preponderance in quantity and quality of the RVNAF over
the enemy.

IV. GUIDANCE:

    1. Advisors to RVNAF units and PSYOP personnel are
in good positions to become aware of RVNAF
accomplishments and should publicize them both in the
RVNAF and among the South Vietnamese population. These
two audiences are both crucial, for increased recognition
of RVNAF effectiveness will have beneficial results
within the armed forces as well as throughout the general
population. Reports from the field continue to suggest
that people in many parts of the country are often
unaware of successful operations by their armed forces
unless these operations are conducted in their own
immediate area.
    2. All support possible should be given to the
command information program of the RVNAF designed to
improve esprit de corps. Although this program is
assisted by MACV, PSYOP personnel may find it possible to
provide support with audiovisual materials, prepared
literature or ideas.
    3. GVN personnel, especially PSYOP personnel,
should be encouraged to devote increased attention in
public gatherings and ceremonies to recognition of the
role of the RVNAF in the growth and development of the
Republic since 1954. It should be emphasized and re-
emphasized that such recognition from Vietnamese leaders
will be much more effective in enhancing the RVNAF image
among South Vietnamese than similar recognition from
American individuals or units.
    4. PSYOP dealing with RVNAF, like all other topics,

must be solidly based on facts and achievements, rather than on generalities which may not fit all local situations. The credibility of claims of increased effectiveness on the part of RVNAF units may well prove greater with emphasis upon a number of smaller operations and civic action projects rather than on a massive campaign which is too general to strike home to the target audience.

V. **DISCUSSION:**

The Republic of Viet Nam Armed Forces are composed of the Army (ARVN -- which includes the Airborne and Rangers), Navy, Marines, Air Force, Regional Forces, Popular Forces, and paramilitary organizations such as the National Policy and Civilian Irregular Defense Groups. (A separate guidance on the National Police has already been issued: No. 52, January 1968). The total number serving in each of these units as of June 30, 1968, was as follows:

ARVN	360,000	National Police	77,000
Navy	17,000	CIDG	43,000
Marines	10,000	Total Paramilitary	
Air Forces	17,000	Forces:	120,000
Regional Forces	191,000		
Popular Forces	162,000		
Total Regular Forces	757,500	Total RVNAF:	887,500

As President Johnson noted in Honolulu, these armed forces as a percentage of the population are the proportionate equivalent of fifteen million American troops. It is estimated that by the end of 1968 the total number of men and women in RVNAF will be more than a million. These increases are in accordance with the General Mobilization Law passed by the National Assembly in June and promulgated by President Thieu. They also reflect an increased rate of voluntary enlistment among South Vietnamese youth since the Tet offensive.

Other recent events which affect the image and the capabilities of RVNAF forces include:

1. The generally excellent response by RVNAF units to the attacks at Tet and in subsequent months against major South Vietnamese population centers.

2. The equipping of RVNAF units as rapidly as possible with advanced weaponry and increased firepower, along with strengthened logistics and support capabilities. Paramilitary forces down to the hamlet level are also scheduled to be equipped with improved weapons.

3. The establishment of "People's Self-Defense" forces in major cities and villages. These units are being provided with weapons and training in defensive

tactics, and represent a new and significant dimension of RVNAF's ability to defend the population of South Viet Nam. (For additional data and PSYOP guidance, see JUSPAO Policy Guidance No. 66).

VI. OPERATIONAL SUPPORT:

General:
In all cases recipients should encourage GVN elements to undertake their own coverage and exploitation to support this guidance. What follows is largely a description of JUSPAO support but can also help serve as suggested operational guidelines for your GVN associates.

Press:
JUSPAO's reporter-photographer teams will be sent into areas in which RVNAF units are operating for weekly stories on these operations as well as RF/PF Regional Forces/Popular Forces activity. These stories and pictures will be distributed to Vietnam Press and to the Vietnamese- and Chinese-language dailies in Saigon. In addition, copies of the stories will be sent to members of the National Assembly and other prominent GVN/RVNAF officials.

Mopix:
JUSPAO's Information Division will arrange for periodic motion picture coverage of such RVNAF activities as training centers, the Vietnamese Air Forces in action, life at a remote outpost manned by RF/PF, Vietnamese Navy patrols on station, and ARVN forces engaged in combat operations. These films will be distributed throughout South Viet Nam as well as to THVN.

Radio:
The daily report on RVNAF activities over VOA will be continued, covering the varied aspects of RVNAF and joint RVNAF/FWMAF operations. This material is made available to VOA correspondents for use in their daily English-language feeds. JUSPAO's Radio Branch will continue to cover daily RVNAF briefings for exploitable items.

Television:
A special effort will be made to provide film clips and commentary on RVNAF military and civic action operations in support of the above PSYOP objectives in THVN.
Where local RVNAF operations merit coverage, local PSYOP personnel should contact JUSPAO with a brief

description of the proposed coverage and its potential
impact upon the provincial or regional audience
envisaged. Arrangements to cover such stories will be
made with the Press and Information Division of the
General Political Warfare Department of the RVNAF.

Appendix D:
JUSPAO Policy Guidances
(Directives)

Number	Date	Title
4	July 22, 1965	Propaganda Approaches to the Presence of Major PAVN Units in South Vietnam
6	July 2, 1965	Exploitation of Vietnamese Efforts and Successes
7	July 17, 1965	Exploitation of Communist Atrocities
9	August 5, 1965	Exploitation of VC Vulnerabilities
12	December 18, 1965	Exploitation of Divisiveness in the Ranks of the Viet Cong
13	December 27, 1965	Cambodian Minority Problem in the IV Corps Area
14	February 9, 1966	Inflation in Vietnam
16	July 9, 1966	The Chieu Hoi Inducement Program
17	July 28, 1966	Debriefing of Key Personnel Engaged in Psychological Operations in Vietnam
18	August 30, 1966	The Prospect of Interminable War as an Enemy Vulnerability
19	September 8, 1966	American Presence in Vietnam

20	September 12, 1966	Reissue of National Psychological Operations Plan for Vietnam
23	October 14, 1966	Exploitation of VC Vulnerabilities
25	November 7, 1966	Manila Conference
26	December 12, 1966	Psychological Problem Areas
27	January 25, 1967	Use of Interpreters
28	February 20, 1967	Psyops aspects of the Employment of Third Country Nationals in the RVN
29	March 1, 1967	Psyops Aspects of Village and Hamlet Elections in the RVN
30	May 5, 1967	The New ARVN Role in Winning the War
31	February 25, 1967	Psyops Aspects of Defoliation
32	March 1, 1967	Psyops Aspects of the Refugee Program
34	May 6, 1967	Psyops Aspects of the GVN Land Title and Land Tenure Program
35	May 7, 1967	The New Constitution of the Republic of Vietnam
36	May 10, 1967	The Use of Superstitions in Psychological Operations in Vietnam
37	June 14, 1967	National Identity Registration Program
38	April 19, 1967	The GVN National Reconciliation Policy (Doan Ket)
39	June 30, 1967	Viet Cong Cadre Vulnerabilities

40	June 28, 1967	The Vietnamese National Elections
41	July 3, 1967	Exploiting North-South Regionalism Among the Viet Cong
42	July 27, 1967	Further Exploitation of the Nguyen Van Be Case
43	August 17, 1967	1967 Chief Hoi Fall Campaign
44	September 20, 1967	JUSPAO Guidance for Conduct of 1968 Tet/Chieu Hoi/Dai Doan Ket
46	September 26, 1967	JUSPAO Guidance for Psyops Support in Building a Favorable Image of the Elected GVN
47	October 16, 1967	The Montagnards
48	November 5, 1967	Exploitation of NLF
49	December 6, 1967	Exploitation of VC Vulnerabilities
50	January 7, 1968	JUSPAO Guidance for PSYOP Support in Building a Favorable Image of the Elected GVN
51	December 28, 1967	Priorities in the PSYOP Effort
52	January 16, 1968	PSYOP Aspects of the Public Safety Program (National Police)
53	January 22, 1968	PSYOP Support of Pacification
54	January 23, 1968	PSYOP Aspects of the Refugee Program
56	February 6, 1968	Restoring Civil Confidence: Popular Rejection of Call for General Uprising

57	February 8, 1968	Chieu Hoi Campaign to Capitalize on Failure of Communist General Offensive
58	February 8, 1968	Re-Firming US Support for the GVN: Eliminating Viet Cong-inspired rumors of Coalition
59	February 20, 1968	The NVA Soldier in SVN as a PSYOP Target
60	February 23, 1968	The Use of Prisoners of War in PSYOP Output
62	April 19, 1968	PSYOP Program in Support of the President's Offer of Negotiations with North Vietnam
64	July 11, 1968	Use of Prisoners of War in PSYOP
65	August 7, 1968	"United Front" Tactics: The Viet Nam Alliance of National, Democratic and Peace Forces
66	August 8, 1968	"People's Self-Defense"
67	August 15, 1968	PSYOP Support for the National Identify Registration Program
68	August 23, 1968	Enhancement of RVNAF Image
69	October 4, 1968	Riot Control Operations in Populated Areas
70	October 29, 1968	Use of Sex Appeal on Propaganda Programs and Material
71	November 7, 1968	Bombing Halt
74	November 27, 1968	New Paris Talks
75	December 18, 1968	Chieu Hoi and Dai Doan Ket National Reconciliation Programs
76	December 18, 1968	Christmas Cease-Fire

78	February 14, 1969	Counter-Actions to Communist Terrorism
79	March 3, 1969	Current Enemy Offensive
80	April 8, 1969	PSYOP Support for 1969 Pacification and Development Plan
81	June 16, 1969	Support for the Freezing of Land Occupancy and Rent: Land Reform
82	June 27, 1969	"NLF/Provisional Revolutionary Government"
83	July 1, 1969	Troop Replacement
84	July 15, 1969	President Thieu's July 11, 1969 Speech
85	July 25, 1969	Distribution of Government-Owned Lands: Land Reform
86	September 5, 1969	The Death of Ho Chi Minh
88	November 4, 1969	President Nixon's November 3, 1969 Speech
90	March 23, 1970	Forthcoming Change of VC POW's to Hoi Chanh
92	May 2, 1970	President Nixon's Speech on the Cambodian Situation: April 30, 1970
94	August 22, 1970	Vietnamese Elections
95	August 29, 1970	Communist Propaganda and Activities on NVN Memorial Days
97	October 8, 1970	President Nixon's New Peace Proposal for Settlement of Indochina War: October 7, 1970
98	October 15, 1970	President Nixon's New Peace Proposal for Settlement of Indochina War: October 8, 1970

99	October 15, 1970	"Tet" 1971
100	November 6, 1970	The National Tax Survey Campaign
101	January 13, 1971	Building Confidence in the Vietnamese Economy
102	February 10, 1971	ARVN Operation in Laos
103	February 15, 1971	Counter-Actions to Communist Terrorism
104	February 18, 1971	Testing of PSYOP Materials in Viet-Nam
105	February 26, 1971	Troop Replacement
107	April 19, 1971	People's Self-Defense
108	April 22, 1971	Labor and the U.S Redeployment
109	April 27, 1971	1971 GVN Elections
110	May 14, 1971	Enhancement of RVNAF Image
111	July 30, 1971	U.S. Relationship with the People's Republic of China

Selected Bibliography

GOVERNMENT DOCUMENTS:

Republic of Vietnam. General Political Warfare
Department, Handbook for Company Level Political
Warfare Officers. Trans. by U.S., Military
Assistance Command, Vietnam, Saigon: n.d.
_____. Ministry of Chieu Hoi. APT Handbook. Rev.
ed. Saigon: 1970.
_____. Ministry of Chieu Hoi. The Policy of Greater
Unity of the People: Results of Chieu Hoi
Activities. Saigon: 1971.
_____. Ministry of Information. Vietnam 1967-1971:
Toward Peace and Prosperity. Saigon: 1971.
_____. Ministry of Rural Development. RD Cadres
Handbook. Saigon: 1970.
_____. Vietnamese Realities. Saigon: 1969.
U.S. Congress. Senate. Hearings Before the Committee
on Foreign Relations. Vietnam: Policy and
Prospects, 1970. 91st Cong., 2nd sess., 1970.
U.S. Joint Chiefs of Staff. Dictionary of Military and
Associated Terms. JCS Pubn. 1. Washington, D.C.:
Government Printing Office, September 3, 1974.
U.S. Department of State. Foreign Service Institute.
"The Viet Cong: Five Steps in Running a
Revolution," M-362-66. IOP/RF/Vietnam Unit.
Washington, D.C.: July 28, 1966. (mimeographed.)
_____. "U.S. Support of Pacification Effort in Viet-
Nam Reorganized," by Ambassador Ellsworth Bunker.
Department of State Bulletin. Vol. LVI, No. 1458,
June 5, 1967.
U.S. Department of the Air Force. Psychological
Operations and Civic Action in Special Air
Warfare: Psychological Operations Methods. Eglin
AFB, Fla.: Special Air Warfare Center, April 1968.
U.S. Department of the Army. Area Handbook for North
Vietnam. Pamphlet No. 550-57. Washington, D.C.:
Government Printing Office, June 1967.
_____. Area Handbook for South Vietnam. Pamphlet No.
550-55. Washington, D.C.: Government Printing
Office, April 1967.
_____. Employment of US Army Psychological Operations
Units in Vietnam. ACTIV Project No. ACG-47F (Final
Report). APO San Francisco 96384: June 7, 1969.
_____. Low Medium and High Altitude Leaflet
Dissemination Guide. APO San Francisco 96248: 7th
Psychological Operations Group, n.d.
_____. Psychological Operations--Techniques and
Procedures. Field Manual No. 33-5. Washington,
D.C.: Government Printing Office, October 20, 1966.
_____. Psychological Operations--U.S. Army
Doctrine. Field Manual No. 33-1. Washington,
D.C.: Government Printing Office, May 28, 1965.
_____. Psychological Operations--U.S. Army

Doctrine. Field Manual No. 33-1. Washington,
D.C.: Government Printing Office, February 4, 1971.
_____. Report of the Internal Defense/Development
Psychological Operations Instructor's Conference.
October 31-November 4, 1966. Fort Bragg, N.C.:
n.d.
_____. Stability Operations--Intelligence. Field
Manual No. 30-31. Washington, D.C.: Government
Printing Office, 1970.
_____. The Communist Insurgent Infrastructure in
South Vietnam: A Study of Organization and
Strategy. Written by Michael C. Conley. Pamphlet
No. 550-106. Washington, D.C.: Government Printing
Office, March 1967.
U.S. Military Assistance Command, Vietnam. Military
Civic Action. MACV Directive 515-2. Saigon: April
30, 1966.
_____. Military Intelligence: Procedures for
Handling and Utilization of Returnees (MACCORDS)
Chieu Hoi Program. MACV Directive 381-50.
Saigon: February 22, 1971.
_____. Military Operations: Luc Luong 66 Program
(Kit Carson Scout Program). MACV Directive 525-6.
Saigon: June 15, 1970.
_____. Military Operations--Phung Hoang Operations.
MACV Directive 525-36. Saigon: November 5, 1971.
_____. Military Operations--Political Warfare
(POLWAR). MACV Directive 525-32. Saigon: August
10, 1969.
_____. Organization and Functions--Organization and
Functions for Civil Operations and Revolutionary
Development Support. MACV Directive 10-12.
Saigon: May 28, 1968.
_____. Organization and Functions--Psychological
Operations. MACV Directive 10-1. Saigon: December
11, 1967.
_____. Guide for Psychological Operations. Saigon:
April 27, 1968.
_____. Guide for Psychological Operations. Saigon:
August 6, 1967.
_____. Psychological Operations Directorate
Newsletter. Vol. 1, Nos. 3 and 4. Saigon: 1966.
_____. PSYOP Newsletter. Vol. 2, Nos. 2-12.
Saigon: 1967.
_____. PSYOP Newsletter. Vol. 3, Nos. 1-12.
Saigon: 1968.
_____. PSYOP/POLWAR Newsletter. Vol. 4, Nos. 1-12.
Saigon: 1969.
_____. PSYOP/POLWAR Newsletter. Vol. 5, Nos. 1-10.
Saigon: 1970.
_____. PSYOP/POLWAR Newsletter. Vol. 6, Nos. 1-3,
5-8. Saigon: 1971.
_____. PSYOP/POLWAR Newsletter. Vol. 7, No. 1.

287

Saigon: 1972.
_____. Regional Force and Popular Force Handbook for
Advisors. Saigon: January 1, 1971.
U.S. Military Assistance Command, Vietnam. Civil
Operations and Rural Development Support. Chieu Hoi
Program. Rev. Saigon: February 1971.
_____. Chieu Hoi Operational Memorandum No. 32/68:
"Chieu Hoi Nationwide Rewards Campaign (1 November
1968-31 January 1969)". Saigon: October 31, 1968.
_____. Guide for Province and District Advisors
(Draft). Saigon: February 1, 1968.
_____. Phung Hoang Advisor Handbook. Saigon:
November 20, 1970.
_____. The Chieu Hoi Program: Questions and
Answers. Saigon: January 1, 1968.
_____. The Vietnamese Village 1970: Handbook for
Advisors. Saigon: May 2, 1970.
U.S. Military Assistance Command, Vietnam. 4th
Psychological Operations Group. Development of
Leaflets and Posters. Vol. II. Saigon: June 10,
1968.
_____. Guidelines for Production of Taped
Propaganda. Vol. I. Saigon: April 10, 1968.
_____. 7th Psychological Operations Battalion.
Leaflet Catalog. Danang, South Vietnam: July 1,
1969.
_____. 10th Psychological Operations Battalion.
PSYOP Catalog. Can Tho, South Vietnam: March 3,
1970.
_____. 246th Psychological Operations Company.
Leaflet Catalogue. Bien Hoa, South Vietnam:
December 20, 1966.
U.S. Report on the War in Vietnam (as of June 30,
1968). Washington, D.C.: Government Printing
Office, 1968.
U.S. U.S. Information Agency. The Vietnamese Peasant:
His Value System, R-138-65. Washington, D.C.:
October 1965.
_____. Vietnamese Communist Propaganda Offensive:
1965 (North Vietnam and the Viet Cong), R-62-66.
Washington, D.C.: March 1966.
_____. Viet Cong Haunted by Still Living "Dead
Hero". USIA Feature No. 67-SM-95. Washington,
D.C.: August 1967.
_____. Voice of America. "Voice of America Story
About Nguyen Van Be." Washington, D.C.: June
1967. (mimeographed.)
U.S. U.S. Mission, Vietnam. Joint U.S. Public Affairs
Office. Catalogue of Psyops Tapes. Saigon: n.d.
_____. "Connotations of Vietnamese Words and Phrases
Used Most Frequently in Appeals to Enemy
Audience." Saigon: June 3, 1970.
_____. Consolidation of JUSPAO Field Memoranda 1 Thru

__32.__ Vol. I. Saigon: June 17, 1967.
_____. Consolidation of JUSPAO Field Memoranda 33
Thru 41. Vol. II. Saigon: n.d.
_____. Consolidation of JUSPAO Field Memoranda 42
Thru 58. Vol. III. Saigon: n.d.
_____. Consolidation of JUSPAO Guidances 1 Thru 22.
Vol. I. Saigon: June 1, 1967.
_____. Consolidation of JUSPAO Guidances 47 Thru
__63.__ Vol. III. Saigon: May 20, 1968.
_____. Final Report on Ex-Hoi Chanh Survey. Research
Report. Saigon: March 19, 1967.
_____. General Briefing Book. Rev. ed. Saigon:
June 1968.
_____. General Briefing Book. Saigon: July 13,
1965.
_____. Highlight Analysis of Post-Election Survey.
Research Report. Saigon: February 10, 1968.
_____. National Catalog of Psyops Material.
Saigon: March 1969.
_____. National Rural Public Opinion - Highlights.
Saigon: January 1966.
_____. National Urban Public Opinion - Highlights.
Saigon: January 1966.
_____. Nationwide Hamlet Survey (An Interpretive
Analysis). Research Report. Saigon: January 23,
1968.
_____. "1967 Highlights--JUSPAO." Attached to
"JUSPAO Monthly Report for December 1967." Field
Message No. 33. Saigon: January 16, 1968.
_____. 1967 Tet/Chieu Hoi Campaign Plan. Saigon:
October 17, 1966.
_____. "Operations Memorandum: Newspaper Nhan Van
(NP-3) for Airdrop in North Vietnam." Saigon:
October 29, 1965.
_____. "Panel Evaluation of Voice of Freedom
Broadcasts." JUSPAO Memorandum. Saigon: September
9, 1970. (mimeographed.)
_____. "Professionalism of the Vietnamese Information
Service: Concept for Short and Long-Term Training
Programs," letter by Barry Zorthian, Director,
JUSPAO. Saigon: April 26, 1966.
_____. Psyops in Vietnam: Indications of
Effectiveness. Saigon: May 1967.
_____. Public Attitudes in Danang and Hue as
Expressed in Sample Survey Conducted in April
1969. Research Report. Saigon: May 21, 1969.
_____. Public Attitudes in Danang and Hue May-June
1970. Saigon: June 1970.
_____. Results of 60 Interviews with Recent NVA
Ralliers Conducted at National Chieu Hoi Center on
September 24, 1969. Research Report. Saigon:
October 9, 1969.
_____. Saigon Public Attitudes As Expressed in Sample

Survey Conducted May 3 through 10, 1970. Research
Report. Saigon: May 1970.
_____. Some Findings of the Survey of the Chieu Hoi
Tet Campaign - 1966. Saigon: December 1966.
_____. Some Preliminary Findings from the Tet
Returnee Survey. Research Report. Saigon:
February 15, 1966.
_____. Summary Report on the 1967 Returnee Survey.
Research Report. Saigon: May 12, 1967.
_____. "Testing of Psyop Material in Viet-Nam."
Psyop Circular, No. 9. Saigon: January 14, 1969.
_____. Unbound JUSPAO "Policy Directives" (see
listing in Appendix D).
_____. "Viet Cong Live 'Dead' Hero." Field Message
No. 144. Saigon: April 1, 1967.
_____. "Vietnamese Farmers Day, March 26, 1971."
Psyop Circular, No. 40. Saigon: March 10, 1971.
_____. Vietnamese Public Opinion 1970. Saigon: n.d.
_____. "Village And Hamlet Elections." Psyop
Circular, No. 22. Saigon: September 8, 1969.
U.S. U.S. Mission, Vietnam. "Memorandum of Agreement on
Direction and Supervision of U.S. Psychological
Operations in Vietnam." Saigon: August 10, 1966
(see Appendix A).
_____. Press Release. Saigon: August 25, 1967.
U.S.S.R. Fundamentals of Marxism-Leninism. 2nd rev.
ed. Moscow: Foreign Languages Publishing House,
1963.

BOOKS AND MONOGRAPHS

Arnsten, Michael and Leites, Nathan. Land Reform and the
Quality of Propaganda in Rural Vietnam. RM-5764-
ARPA. Santa Monica, Calif.: Rand Corporation, April
1970.
Bairdain, Ernest F. and Bairdain, Edith M. Final
Technical Report: Psychological Operations
Studies--Vietnam. Vol. I. McLean, Va.: Human
Sciences Research, Inc., May 25, 1971.
Berger, Carl. An Introduction to Wartime Leaflets.
Washington, D.C.: American University, Special
Operations Research Office, 1959.
Berlo, David K. The Process of Communication. New
York: Holt, Rinehart and Winston, Inc., 1960.
Bush, H.C. Pretesting Psyops Leaflets in Vietnam.
Honolulu: Pacific Technical Analysts, Inc., March
1969.
_____. The Effectiveness of U.S. Psyops Leaflets: A
Scale for Pretesting. Honolulu: Pacific Technical
Analysts, Inc., January 1969.
Buttinger, Joseph. Vietnam: A Political History. New
York: Frederick A. Praeger, Inc., 1968.
Daugherty, William E., ed. A Psychological Warfare

Casebook. Baltimore: Johns Hopkins Press, 1958.

Davison, W. Phillips. International Political Communication. New York: Frederick A. Praeger, Inc., 1965.

Ellsberg, Daniel, The Day Loc Tien Was Pacified. P-3793. Santa Monica, Calif.: Rand Corporation, February 1968.

Ellul, Jacques. Propaganda: The Formation of Men's Attitudes. Trans. by Konrad Kellen and Jean Lerner. New York: Alfred A. Knopf, Inc., 1971.

Hammer, Ellen. Vietnam Yesterday and Today. New York: Holt, Rinehart and Winston, Inc., 1966.

Havron, M. Dean and Vreeland, Herbert H. Some Uses of Values Information. McLean, Va.: Human Sciences Research, Inc., 1967.

Havron, M. Dean, Sternin, Martin, and Teare, Robert J. The Use of Cultural Data in Psychological Operations Programs in Vietnam. ARPA-TIO 72-4. Arlington, Va.: Department of Defense, Advanced Research Projects Agency, 1972.

Ho Chi Minh. On Revolution. Ed. and with an introduction by Bernard B. Fall. New York: Frederick A. Praeger, Inc., 1967.

Holsti, Ole R. Content Analysis for the Social Sciences and Humanities. Reading, Mass.: Addison-Wesley Publishing Company, Inc., 1969.

Holt, Robert T. and van de Velde, Robert W. Strategic Psychological Operations and American Foreign Policy. Chicago: University of Chicago Press, 1960.

Jenkins, Brian M. Why the North Vietnamese Keep Fighting. P-4395. Santa Monica, Calif.: Rand Corporation, August 1970.

Katz, Phillip P. A Systematic Approach to PSYOP Information. Kensington, Md.: American Institute for Research, Center for Research in Social Systems, February 1970.

Kellen, Konrad. A Profile of the PAVN Soldier in South Vietnam. RM-5013-1. Santa Monica, Calif.: Rand Corporation, March 1967.

_____. Conversations with Enemy Soldiers in late 1968/Early 1969: A Study of Motivation and Morale. RM-6131-1-ISA/ARPA. Santa Monica, Calif.: Rand Corporation, September 1970.

Komer, R. W. Impact of Pacification on Insurgency In South Vietnam. P-4443. Santa Monica, Calif: Rand Corporation, August 1970.

Latimer, Harry D. U.S. Psychological Operations in Vietnam. Providence, R.I.: Brown University, September 1973.

Linebarger, Paul M. A. Psychological Warfare. 2nd rev. ed. Washington, D.C.: Combat Forces Press, 1954.

McAlister, John T., Jr. and Mus, Paul. The Vietnamese

and Their Revolution. New York: Harper & Row, Publishers, Inc., 1970.

Mulligan, Hugh. No Place to Die. New York: William Morrow & Company, Inc., 1967.

Nighswonger, William A. Rural Pacification in Vietnam. New York: Frederick A. Praeger, Inc., 1966.

O'Ballance, Edgar. Malaya: The Communist Insurgent War, 1948-60. Hamden, Conn.: Archon Books, 1966.

Parsons, John S., Brown, Dale K., and Kingsbury, Nancy R., Americans and Vietnamese: A Comparison of Values in Two Cultures. ARPA-TIO 72-6. Arlington, Va.: Department of Defense, Advanced Research Projects Agency, 1972.

Pike, Douglas. War, Peace, and the Viet Cong. Cambridge Mass.: M.I.T. Press, 1969.

Pye, Lucian W., ed. Communication and Political Development. Princeton, N.J.: Princeton University Press, 1963.

Qualter, Terence H. Propaganda and Psychological Warfare. New York: Random House, Inc., 1962.

Report of the ARPA-Supported Committee on Psychological Operations, Vietnam, 1967. Kenneth E. Clark, chairman. McLean, Va.: Human Sciences Research, Inc., 1967.

Scaff, Alvin H. The Philippine Answer to Communism. Stanford, Calif.: Stanford University Press, 1955.

Schramm, Wilbur, ed. The Process and Effects of Mass Communication. Urbana, Ill.: University of Illinois Press, 1955.

_____. The Nature of Psychological Warfare. Technical Memorandum ORO-T-214. Chevy Chase, Md.: Johns Hopkins University, Operations Research Office, 1953.

Schramm, Wilbur and Roberts, Donald F., eds. The Process and Effects of Mass Communication. Rev. ed. Chicago: University of Illinois Press, 1971.

Shaplen, Robert. The Road From War: Vietnam 1965-1971. Rev. ed. New York: Harper & Row, Publishers, Inc., 1971.

Sheehan, Neil et al. The Pentagon Papers. New York: Bantam Books, Inc., 1971.

Simulmatics Corporations. Improving Effectiveness of the Chieu Hoi Program: Functional Aspects of the Chieu Hoi Program: Vol. III. New York: September 1967.

Slote, Walter H. Observations on Psychodynamic Structures in Vietnamese Personality, Summary and Implications. New York: Simulmatics Corp., April 1971.

Sternin, Martin, Teare, Robert J., and Nordlie, Peter G. A Study of Values, Communication Patterns and Demography Rural South Vietnam. ARPA-TIO 72-5. Arlington, Va.: Department of Defense, Advanced Research Projects Agency, 1972.

Steward, Joe F. The Story of Kit Carson Scouts.
    Saigon: U.S., Military Assistance Command, Vietnam,
    n.d.
White, Ralph K. Nobody Wanted War. Rev. ed. Garden
    City, N.Y.: Doubleday & Company, Inc., 1970.
Zorthian, Barry. "The Use of Psychological Operations in
    Combatting 'Wars of National Liberation.'" Paper
    presented at the National Strategy Information
    Center Conference, March 11-14, 1971.

NEWSPAPERS, PERIODICALS, AND RADIO BROADCASTS:

"A Big Cheat." Doc-Lap (Hanoi), April 1967.
"A Dirty Psychological Warfare Trick." Radio Hanoi in
    Vietnamese to South Vietnam, March 16, 1967.
"Americans Drop Forged Banknotes on N. Vietnam." The
    Times (London), October 10, 1972.
Brittain, Victoria. "Vietnam: Freezing Land and
    Capturing Votes." The Times (London), March 26,
    1973.
Browne, Malcolm W. "U.S. Trims Psychological Warfare
    Effort in Vietnam." New York Times, June 13, 1972.
Bullington, James R. and Rosenthal, James D. "The South
    Vietnamese Countryside: Non-Communist Political
    Perceptions." Asian Survey, Vol. X, No. 8 (August
    1970).
"Civilian Casualties in South Vietnam." International
    Herald Tribune, January 25, 1973.
Cooper, Wayne L. "Operation Phoenix: A Vietnam Fiasco
    Seen From Within." Washington Post, June 18, 1972.
Crossman, R.H.S., M.P. "Psychological Warfare." Journal
    of the Royal United Service Institution, Vol. 97,
    No. 587 (August 1952), Vol. 98, No. 591 (August
    1953), and Vol. 98, No. 592 (November 1953).
Deepe, Beverly. "U.S. Unit 'Persuades' Viet Cong to
    Defect." Christian Science Monitor, October 15,
    1968.
"Emulate Nguyen Van Be's Offensive Spirit." Quan Doi
    Nhan Dan (Hanoi), June 10, 1967.
Erlandson, Robert A. "Reds Offer $16,950 for 'Dead
    Hero.'" Baltimore Sun, July 21, 1967.
Gleason, Robert L. "Psychological Operations and Air
    Power: Its Hits and Misses." Air University
    Review, Vol. 22 (March-April 1971).
Hughes, Richard. "Saigon's Losing Propaganda War." San
    Francisco Chronicle, April 8, 1969.
Kaiser, Robert G., Jr. "U.S. Aides in Vietnam Scorn
    Phoenix Project." Washington Post, February 17,
    1970.
Leslie, Jacques. "Reports Show Saigon's Army Still
    Alienating Civilians." International Herald
    Tribune, May 29, 1973.
McArthur, George. "Hanoi's Army: Good Soldiers But

Human." Washington Post, April 23, 1972.
"Nguyen Van Be." Radio Hanoi International Service in
    English, March 21, 1967.
Pool, Ithiel de Sola. "The Paradox of Nonviolent War in
    Vietnam." Life, July 4, 1970.
Popkin, Samuel L. "Pacification: Politics and the
    Village." Asian Survey, Vol. X, No. 8 (August
    1970).
Prosterman, R. L. "Vietnam's Land Reform Begins to
    Pay." Wall Street Journal, February 5, 1971.
Reston, Richard. "U.S. Steps Up Its Propaganda Aimed at
    N. Vietnam's Morale." International Herald
    Tribune. August 3, 1972.
Riley, John W., Jr. and Cottrell, Leonard S., Jr.
    "Research for Psychological Warfare." Public
    Opinion Quarterly, Vol. 21, No. 1 (Spring 1957).
Smith, Terence. "The Mission of the B-52's." New York
    Times, April 6, 1969.
"South Viet Nam: Psywar." Time, October 29, 1965.

"South Viet Nam: The Tube Takes Hold." Time, November
    30, 1970.
Tran Van. Hoc Tap (Hanoi), September 1969.
"The Block No. 66 in Badinh Ward Pushes Forward the
    Maintenance of Security and Order." Thu Do (Hanoi),
    January 29, 1966.
"The Guerrilla's Mine." Nhan Dan (Hanoi), May 21, 1967.
"The Heart of the Matter." Newsweek, May 22, 1967.
"The Ho Chi Minh Trail: A Spidery, Constantly Shifting
    Route." New York Times, February 5, 1971.
"The War of Words." Wall Street Journal, December 5,
    1969.
Tomalin, Nicholas. "What They Leave Behind Them: The
    Aftermath of the American War in Vietnam." The
    Sunday Times Magazine, (London), January 21, 1973.
Trimborn, Harry. "Saigon Spurs Drive on Underground
    Network." Los Angeles Times, October 4, 1969.
"USAF Dropping 'Money' Leaflets on N. Vietnam."
    International Herald Tribune, September 20, 1972.
Veaudry, Wallace F. "A New Look at Psywar." Army, Vol.
    15, No. 1 (August 1964).
Vietnam Council on Foreign Relations. "Rationale Behind
    a New Theme: SELF-RELIANCE." Vietnam Magazine,
    Vol. 4, No. 8 (Saigon), 1971.
Whitney, Craig R. "Saigon Abolishes Hamlet Elections."
    International Herald Tribune, September 8, 1972.
Woodruff, John E. "Psychological Uses of Ho's Death
    Defined." Baltimore Sun, September 11, 1969.

Index

Accelerated Pacification
   Program, 157
Ace-of-Spades, as death
   omen, 48, 228
Allied nations, 30-31,
   201, 215
American Indian wars, 89
American Revolution, 13
Anti-Communist images,
   4-5, 155, 158, 183-92
Armed propaganda teams, 82
Arnsten, Michael, 167,
   183, 203
ARPA Committee on
   Psychological
   Operations, 85, 227
Australia, 31, 201, 215

B-52 bomber raids, 44
Bairdain, Ernest and
   Edith, 91-92
"Bandwagon" appeal, 56
Banners, as communication
   channel, 161, 167
Barrett, Edward W., 26
Be, Nguyen Van, 99, 139-46
Berger, Carl, 13, 73
Black propaganda, 214
Bookcovers, as
   communication channel,
   161
Bookmarkers, as
   communication channel,
   161
"Boomerang," results in
   U.S. psychological
   operations, ace-of-

spades as death omen,
   48, 228; affluence in
   South Vietnam, 228, 230;
   anti-Communist Tet
   leaflets on Saigon's
   soldiers, 82; bombing
   of North Vietnam, 9, 10,
   147; Communist
   terrorism, 228;
   excessive rhetoric, 228;
   grisly photographs, 48,
   228; over provision of
   hardware to Saigon, 35;
   sex appeal, 19-20, 228;
   use of facsimile North
   Vietnamese currency,
   117, 123
Brochures, as
   communication channel, 3
Browne, Malcolm 26, 220
Bumper stickers, as
   communication channel,
   3, 90
Bunker, Ellsworth, 30
Bureaucracy, U.S., 25-35
Buttinger, Joseph, 173,
   179

Cambodia, 3, 26, 117, 123
Cambodians, minority in
   South Vietnam, 176
Cartoons, as communication
   channel, 3, 99, 105,
   113, 141, 173, 176
Casualties, civilian, 179-
   81
Checkpoints, roadway, 164